FINDING OUR VOICE

FINDING OUR VOICE

A STORY OF LEADERSHIP IN CRISIS
AND THE AMERICAN SPIRIT ABROAD

ADAM CASTILLO

COPYRIGHT © 2026 ADAM CASTILLO

All rights reserved.

FINDING OUR VOICE

A Story of Leadership in Crisis and the American Spirit Abroad

FIRST EDITION

ISBN   978-1-5445-5164-7   *Hardcover*
         978-1-5445-5163-0   *Paperback*
         978-1-5445-5162-3   *Ebook*

For My People

CONTENTS

DISCLAIMER

Some names and identifying details in this memoir have been changed to protect individuals' privacy. While pseudonyms are used, the experiences and events described are true.

PROLOGUE

BUILT IN EXILE, TEMPERED BY
DARKNESS, CARRIED BY BELIEF

This is not a book of speeches. Not entirely.

Yes, the chapters that follow are speeches I gave as president of the American Chamber of Commerce in Myanmar, or AMCHAM Myanmar. Twelve of them to be exact, delivered in hotel ballrooms scattered across a city in a faraway land most people can't even find on a map. Some still call it Burma, but for those of us who stayed when others fled, for those of us who built, believed, and bled for our homes here, we call it what it is:

Myanmar.

Yet, these speeches weren't written for headlines. They weren't delivered in safety or celebrated by the powerful. They were forged in crisis, spoken into rooms filled with tension, fear, and uncertainty. Each one marked a moment in the journey when the ground beneath us shifted, and someone had to stand up and say: This is where we are, and this is where we go next.

Finding Our Voice is a collection of speech transcripts (and one testimonial from a Burmese refugee), yes; but it is *also* the story of what happened before, between, and after them. The darkness that inspired them, and the light that followed. It is about a community that found its voice through survival.

I didn't write this book in the safety of ivory towers, but within the chaos itself. The insights I share in these pages were forged in darkness, amid blackouts and bomb blasts, through economic collapse and tragedies wrought by both human cruelty and nature's wrath. This is not a history you'll find in books. It is a history I endured, and now write about, not as a historian, but as one who survived it.

AMCHAM MYANMAR: AN AMERICAN BUSINESS COMMUNITY IN EXILE

My story is bound up with the story of the American business community in Myanmar. In April 2023, I assumed the leadership of this community, formally known as the Presidency of AMCHAM Myanmar.

But what is AMCHAM?

An American Chamber of Commerce, or AMCHAM, is an independent, nonprofit, membership-driven organization operating around the world. Overseas, it represents the interests of American companies abroad, serving as an advocacy bridge between host-country governments and the US government. In practice, AMCHAMs give American commerce a public voice abroad, particularly in countries where American commercial interests may appear absent.

To become president of AMCHAM, you must first be elected to the Board of Governors.

Think of it like a traditional board of directors but replace "director" with "governor." The Board of Governors, like any nonprofit leadership body, is elected by the general membership at the Annual General Meeting. It is the Chamber's highest governing authority, responsible for shaping the mission, overseeing the paid staff of the Chamber, and safeguarding the long-term interests of its members.

And yet, it is entirely voluntary. No salary. No perks. Just the mantle of leadership, one that comes with expectations and challenges.

I was first elected to the Board in January 2020. I didn't run for attention or applause. I ran because I wanted to serve. While I was a founding member of AMCHAM Myanmar, I didn't volunteer for a board position when it was first created. I joined the Board later because I felt a responsibility to contribute to something larger. I had come to believe that American commerce is one of the most powerful instruments of American influence abroad. Beyond our military, and even beyond the strength of the dollar, our true soft power lies in our investments, our brands, and services that carry American values into the world.

Stepping into that role did not replace the patriotism that once drove my military service. It evolved it. This was a post-military expression of the same impulse, not serving my own company or chasing sales, but helping advance American commerce overseas, especially in places where it barely existed at all, like Myanmar. Within a year, I was elected vice president, a role I held for nearly two and a half years.

Those years were filled with crisis and unprecedented turmoil. First the pandemic of 2020 and then the coup d'état. On February 1, 2021, Myanmar's fragile democracy was snuffed out as the country's military seized power, referred to throughout this book by their official name, the Tatmadaw. Protests erupted, followed by violent crackdowns, and then war.

The United States responded as it usually does, with sanctions. Some were targeted. Many were sweeping. These measures, however noble in intent, turned the economy radioactive for investors and strangled humanitarian aid. Local communities bore the brunt of this international moral posturing. Jobs were lost. Communities of workers disappeared. Hope dimmed.

Yet, amidst all that, AMCHAM Myanmar remained. Not because it was safe (far from it) but because it was necessary. When every other institutional presence faded, we became the last flag standing.

But why is AMCHAM Myanmar so different from AMCHAMs in other countries?

Well, because AMCHAM Myanmar had to be more than just a chamber of commerce, a building, a logo, or even an organization in the traditional sense. AMCHAM Myanmar is a community: a living, breathing network of businesses, employees, and their families who chose to stay in Myanmar when the world walked away.

Now many in the business world treat a chamber of commerce board seat as a résumé booster; this is especially the case overseas in larger expatriate business communities like Singapore, Hong Kong, or Thailand. For any executive working at a large multinational corporation abroad, governorship on the Board is a badge of prestige. An unofficial knighthood in the international business community, especially in frontier markets like Myanmar.

Vanity was never my reason. I am my own boss, I have my own company, I've never even had a real job before (more on that later).

For me, it was never about titles or legacy. It was first and foremost about my own patriotism, my deep, abiding love for my country, the United States of America. I once served her in uniform. Out of uniform, I served her by championing her greatest soft power: American commerce, our investments, our products, our services, our standards.

But even that wasn't the only "why" for me in this story. Because what began as duty to a flag became devotion to a people in a country I never imagined would become my home. Yet over time, that's exactly what happened.

I built a company here. I built a life here, and around that company, I built a community, one that I came to love as my own. These people weren't just employees or colleagues. These were *my* people; and so, yes, this journey of mine has always been about belief.

Belief in America, belief in the power of commerce, and belief in a community I built alongside others.

A community that refused to look away when the world turned its back on us. I never wanted to be a chairman, a president, or a leader in name only. I wanted to build something real.

That belief did not stay personal for long. It took shape as AMCHAM Myanmar, a community that did not remain through crisis after crisis for profit (there was little of that left anyway). They stayed because their employees were here, their families were here, and their hope was here. When faced with collapse, we did what communities in crisis must do. We did not just resume activities. We created new ones. We adapted. We fought back against policies that sought to erase what remained of Myanmar's private sector, and held fast to a simple belief:

Economic opportunity is a human right. Jobs are dignity. Families, no matter where they live, deserve the chance to survive.

Many of the speeches you will read in this book were written in moments of exhaustion, late at night or during some of the most tragic moments in Myanmar's history. They were not polished oratory. They were declarations of belief. This story is more than a memoir of a chamber president giving speeches in a faraway land. Every speech in this book stands as a testament to a community that chose to believe in something greater than its circumstances. It is a story of leadership in crisis, and of a community that refused to die quietly in the darkness that engulfed Myanmar.

A MARINE'S EDUCATION IN LEADERSHIP

Before this tale of leadership in crisis can begin, I need to explain how I first arrived in what was once a golden land called Myanmar. That path began with my education in leadership, but I learned to lead in a world very different from most. I learned in the United States Marine Corps, where leadership is not a theory but a matter of life and death. In the Marines, we do not talk about "company culture" the way businesses do. We have something deeper. We have ethos.

Ethos is what you're willing to sacrifice to uphold, even if that means your own life. As a Marine, you sign up knowing the job guarantees hardship, not ease. You're issued the worst gear. Offered the fewest incentives. There are no big signing bonuses, or flashy Air Force desk jobs, just a silent promise that the price of entry is everything you have. That, and maybe a cool T-shirt.

So why would anyone volunteer to do this?

Because for a Marine, it's not about the benefits. It's about the title. That single word, Marine, earned not in ink, but through pain and rebirth.

Every Marine remembers their moment of rebirth. The moment they receive their Eagle, Globe, and Anchor, the emblem they will wear on their uniform. Before graduation, whether enlisted or commissioned, every Marine takes part in a private ceremony with their drill instructors. The emblem is pressed into your palm by the same men who spent months breaking you down, physically and mentally, so that you could be reborn a Devil Dog.

For many, this moment is more powerful than graduation itself, or for officers, even their commissioning ceremony or first salute. Marines openly cry here not out of sentimentality, but recognition. This is the moment they know they have made it. The moment they have earned the title of Marine. Graduation is rehearsed and choreographed like any other drill. This private and sacred ceremony comes after months of relentless training, often immediately following a brutal field exercise, when you are still soaked in sweat, often bloodied, and always physically exhausted.

I remember that moment more vividly than my commissioning as an officer on March 26, 2010, in Quantico, Virginia, which came only days later. More vividly even than the pinning of my lieutenant bars by my own parents.

Because in that moment, time stood still. There were no worries in the world I lived in. I was no longer a boy who had just graduated from college. I was a man. A Marine, bound to the Corps by blood, by code, and by sacrifice. I will carry that code of sacrifice in my soul for the rest of my life.

The first book handed to me at Quantico was a manual called *Leading Marines (FMFM 1-0)*. It isn't just a field manual; it's the ethical DNA of the Corps. Its pages instill a simple creed: Every Marine is a leader. In the Marine Corps, rank and authority exist, but leadership is expected across the chain of command, from the highest-ranked officer to the lowest-ranked enlisted Marine. In the Fog of War and moments of friction or chaos, any Marine, private or general, must step up and lead when nobody else will. We are taught from day one that leadership is the definition of every Marine on the battlefield, not a rank or title on some organization chart. And leadership, at its core, is sacrifice.

I will never forget a grizzled sergeant instructor pulling me aside at Officer Candidate School (OCS) in Quantico, Virginia in 2010:

"Candidate," he said, "You need to grow the f**k up, and that starts with setting the example, always. Never ask your Marines to do anything you wouldn't. Be the first one up, the last one to sleep. The last to eat. Sacrifice is what it takes to be an officer of Marines, to lead enlisted Marines like me. Leadership is sacrifice."

Leadership is sacrifice.

These words have seared themselves into my soul since I accepted them as gospel at that moment. Here was a senior-enlisted leader who had more combat deployments under his belt than I had jobs in my lifetime. Basically, telling me to set the example, show the work, prove to my Marines that I will sacrifice just as much, if not more than they will. If I want to lead, I must bear the heaviest burdens on my shoulders and mine alone; that's the sacrifice a leader makes.

Now, most Marine Corps officers do not get to choose their job.

Sure, you list your "preferences," but it is about as meaningful as choosing a seat on a budget airline. Your fate is decided by something called the quality spread, a sorting hat that assigns top, middle, and lower performers across whatever jobs the Corps needs filled. Supposedly strategic. Allegedly "fair."

However, if you land on the wrong end of it, which most young officers do, it feels like neither.

Picture Quantico, Virginia. The Basic School. A six-month course of humid misery that every new second lieutenant is required to pass. I was marching through that swamp convinced the Marine Corps was about to stamp my record with the glorious MOS code 0302, Infantry Officer. That was the dream.

Then came MOS assignment day, the Marine Corps version of the Hunger Games, except the odds were never in your favor. They call you in one by one to avoid public meltdowns. When my turn came, I stood at attention in my Company Commander's office. He glanced at his list.

"3002."

For a split second I thought he misread the MOS designation code. I blinked. "What's that, sir?"

"You're Supply, Castillo."

That was it. No buildup. No explanation. I'd been assigned the one job I hadn't ranked anywhere near my top choices. It felt like I had been misread. Like the Marine Corps sorting hat had placed me into the wrong life.

The infantry dream vanished in an instant, buried under requisition forms, asset logs, and useless acronyms like the SMU (which I refuse to explain). I barely knew what Supply Officers did, though, to be fair, most Battalion Commanders didn't either. I knew one thing: I was going to do anything to avoid being a Supply Officer.

And I did.

For nearly two years, I chased every collateral duty I could find. I became a martial arts (otherwise known as MCMAP) addict and instructor because getting punched in the face daily with an elbow was better than paperwork. I became qualified to set up ranges from the firing lines to the safety protocols. Shotgun, pistol, anything with gunpowder to keep me away from toner cartridges. One of the more unusual jobs I volunteered for was serving as Headquarters and Services Company Commander, a billet few wanted.

Under normal circumstances, no second lieutenant would ever command a company in a regular unit unless something had gone catastrophically wrong, such as a captain being killed or hospitalized. Headquarters and Services Company is a different kind of job altogether; one most Marine officers are not trained to handle. It oversees administrative functions, communications, and logistics including cooks, supply, maintenance, and medical elements staffed by Navy personnel. Many senior officers are not prepared to manage that breadth of responsibility, let alone a newly commissioned lieutenant. For me, however, the alternative was the supply warehouse of purgatory. While most second lieutenants offered the role would run for the hills, I accepted it immediately.

Why?

Because supply is the most thankless job in the Marine Corps: endless paperwork and scoldings from commanders who don't understand supply but hate signing the reports they're legally required to approve. Supply Officers deliver the harsh truth that warrior-officers avoid. Even in the Marines, being an officer is mostly administration, not being Chesty Puller on Guadalcanal. "Don't shoot the messenger" doesn't apply here, because in an operating unit they shoot the Supply Officer daily.

Ironically, the only time I embraced supply was in Afghanistan because it was the only way they would let me deploy. Even then, I wore multiple hats in Musa Qala, Helmand Province. I was the de facto camp commandant for my outpost. I was the "Convoy Kid," riding shotgun on every logistical movement in our area of operations. I was the acting motor transport officer because someone had to keep the vehicles moving after they were blown up by the Taliban. Most days were spent eight hours bouncing between outposts and patrol bases, followed by three more under a tent light, logging maintenance or supply requests.

One of my fellow lieutenants liked to joke during daily briefs, "Castillo hates supply, but somehow he is outside the wire more than the grunts, using his mythical 'wall-to-wall inventory' as an excuse to navigate our battlespace."

He wasn't wrong.

During my deployment to Helmand Province in 2012, "leadership is sacrifice" was embedded in daily life. Lives were not measured by rank or titles, but by the ethos of the Marine Corps. Setting the example. Leading from the front. Doing the hard work when no one else was watching. I successfully commanded more than thirty tactical convoys across territory frequently targeted by enemy ambushes, and every Marine under my command survived. That was my war.

And yet, everyone's war eventually ends.

When I returned in 2012, the drawdown of our forces was already underway. The Corps was shifting back to peacetime, and budgets were tightening. Most Marines could see the writing on the wall. I was fortunate to be slated for the reserves, and I stepped into that role willingly. I had checked the boxes I needed to check, and it was time to pivot toward what I wanted to do with my life. Make money. Start a family. Settle down in my beloved California.

At the time, I thought I was ahead of the curve. I had spent years planning for a dual career in the civilian world and the reserves. I believed I was prepared. I had a plan and a killer résumé to match. I stepped into the civilian world ready to fight for a future I believed I had earned.

That's when the real gut punch came.

THE LOST GENERATION OF MARINE CORPS OFFICERS

I left active-duty orders shortly after returning home to Riverside, California, from my 2012 deployment to Afghanistan. I transitioned to the Marine Corps Reserves but quickly realized that the reserves only works if you already have a stable civilian career. I did not. Without that foundation, I struggled, no longer able to rely on the structure and certainty the Marine Corps had once provided.

I wasn't alone.

I was part of a lost generation of Marine officers who had commissioned between 2009 and 2011, trained for a "Global War on Terror," bled for the flag, and then were quietly shown the door. Under then Commandant of the Marine Corps, General James Amos, the Corps was downsizing, hard.

"Manpower cuts were needed," they said. "Career designation boards were 'selective,'" they said. Yet, for many of my fellow officers who had commissioned alongside me, it was a sanitized purge. Only about 55 percent of lieutenants in my class or in classes around mine in 2010 were retained. The rest were handed rejection letters and polite suggestions to "consider the reserves." The official line from the administration and the Marine Corps was that only 20,000 Marines would be cut from active duty, but in reality, they massaged the true numbers by exiting many officers and enlisted Marines to the reserves. That didn't include the early 15-year retirement "buyouts" that were implemented.

"We were cutting into bone, not just fat," was a common statement expressed by Marines in the years after this purge.

Ironically, I had already planned to transition to the Marine Corps Reserves; it was built into my contract. The goal was clear: complete a combat deployment, hit the three-year mark to qualify for the GI Bill, and move on. I never saw the Marines as a full-time career once they made me a Supply Officer.

I had applied for hundreds of jobs. A couple dozen, maybe more. Interviews followed. Some went well, at least I thought they did. I'd meet the executive team, shake hands, maybe even get a wink and a nod. "You're exactly the kind of leader we need." And then...silence. Or worse, an email weeks later saying the role had been filled. No feedback. No follow-up. Just some HR troll and their away message.

I realized the harshest truth: I wasn't a serious candidate for these companies. I was a box on some compliance sheet that they needed to check to ensure they interviewed a qualified veteran.

This was the age of the great Barack Obama defense cuts, the infamous sequestration era. While the administration gutted the military and quietly let thousands of servicemen go, companies launched flashy campaigns like "Hire Heroes" to fill the vacuum of responsibility. Corporate America wanted to talk about hiring veterans, but they didn't want to hire leaders. Not really. Not in roles that mattered. We were a public relations slogan. A mascot they could parade around. Something they could put on their careers page or drop into an investor call.

"We support our troops."

Sure, as long as they were stocking shelves or supervising warehouses. Walmart pledged to hire 100,000 veterans, but they were not hiring Marine leaders for their boardrooms, or even for middle management. They were hiring us to push carts and manage aisles. Amazon wanted warriors who had managed millions of dollars in assets in Iraq and Afghanistan to sort boxes in windowless fulfillment centers.

They did not care about our operational planning, our crisis management skills, or the fact that we had led human beings in combat. We were warfighters, and now we were reduced to numbers meant to satisfy an HR metric on an Excel spreadsheet. We were called heroes, but once we came home, once we took off the uniform, we became just another box to check on someone's diversity dashboard. It was dehumanizing, not just for me, but for thousands of veterans who volunteered to serve during the Global War on Terror.

Just over a year earlier, I had worn the uniform of the United States Marine Corps, ready to give my life for my country. But when I came home, I found there was no place for me. A nation that thanked me for my service, then quietly shut every door in my face. A president I once believed in, so deeply that his words inspired me to serve, had become a symbol of betrayal. The institutions I once revered felt hollow.

This was a very dangerous time for me. A time when many veterans had turned to the bottle or to drugs, but I wasn't depressed. I was angry. I did not want an apology. I wanted a fight!

And here is the saddest part. I did not want applause or another "thank you for your service." I just wanted a chance!

America did not give me one.

And so, I left.

I left the Marine Corps. I left America. I chose to exile myself from the country I love, not to escape, but to find purpose again.

HOW I ENDED UP IN MYANMAR

So there I was, an unemployed veteran drifting in quiet indifference. Ashamed of being reduced to just another number collecting unemployment, perhaps one or two bad decisions away from sleeping in the street. I was not just struggling. I was drowning in my own anger, in my own darkness. I spent long hours alone, thinking in a room. Searching for the last moment I could remember feeling whole, before the Marine Corps, before the war, before everything inside me hardened. The answer came in one word:

Thailand.

During my fourth year of college, I studied abroad in Bangkok for an entire year. That year, before the uniform, was the last time I truly felt like a kid. I loved that city, and to this day I still consider it a second home. During that year abroad, I made lifelong friends, immersed myself in the culture, and found a sense of belonging I had not felt anywhere else.

Those friends stayed. They built lives and careers across Southeast Asia. When I reached out to one of them in my darkest moment, he reminded me of who I was before the Marines and asked me simply:

"Why are you even still in America?"

He believed I could thrive again, not just in Thailand, but anywhere in Southeast Asia. The region was full of energy and opportunity for people our age. Once the idea took hold, I moved quickly. I made my plan. It involved several moving parts, careful timing, and absolute confidence in my ability to persuade my Commanding Officer. I would leave the reserves and return to Thailand.

One day, during one of my required reservist duty weekends, I walked into my Commanding Officer's(CO) office, the first female CO I had ever served under, and told her the truth.

"Ma'am, this isn't working out for me. I have no idea what I'm going to do with my life. And I'm angry. Angry at the world. At everything. I'm not staying past my four-year mark, and I need to leave. I need to leave now."

To her credit, she did not try to talk me out of it or pull rank. I think she understood I was in a very bad place.

And so, we made a deal.

First, I would find a qualified replacement, which I had already done before I walked into that meeting. He was a fellow lieutenant I had trained with at supply school, a seasoned Supply Officer with four years of active-duty experience. He was one of many from our lost generation of Marine officers, men and women who were not retained during the great purge of military servicemembers. He stepped up gladly to volunteer. It was his chance to stay in the game.

Second, I promised I would return to America one last time to finish planning the Marine Corps Ball, which I had already begun at SeaWorld in San Diego. It ended up being a huge hit, even with protesters slamming signs against our car windows that read, "Empty the Tanks!"

And third, I had to show her I was not just running away. I was building a future. Within a month, I applied to and was accepted into a master's program at Norwich University, focusing on international relations and terrorism. I completed the GI Bill paperwork, secured my funding, and enrolled in the online program.

Within a week of that meeting with my commanding officer, I booked a one-way ticket to Bangkok. So, that is how I officially left the Marines. With a plan and the help of a leader who understood that sometimes the strongest thing you can do is start over.

I will never forget her compassion.

I was not searching for comfort. I was searching for purpose. I had a few thousand dollars in savings, a GI Bill housing stipend, and a laptop loaded with coursework. By the time I landed in Bangkok, I immediately hit the ground running. I reconnected with my old network, explored every option I could find, and even worked as a fitness instructor at a holiday boot camp for tourists. I was trying to gain a foothold anywhere.

That was when one of my old university friends introduced me to a group of Americans who had launched a string of business ventures in Myanmar. They had an idea they thought I could help with.

"Let's start a private security company in Yangon, Myanmar."

To most people in my life, it sounded insane. A security startup in Myanmar? A country that had been under authoritarian rule and was only just emerging from decades of isolation.

To me though, it sounded like exactly the kind of fight I needed.

I was offered a simple promise. If the company succeeded, I would earn partnership, and I could name my compensation. That was it. No contract. Just a handshake deal with a man I had met barely a month earlier.

I did not arrive in Myanmar with a five-year plan or investor backing. I showed up with three assets (or liabilities) in my name. A GI Bill housing stipend. An online graduate program I mostly used to keep the student loan sharks at bay, a deferment strategy that sort of worked, minus the interest ballooning my debt to over $138,000 by the time I began paying it off. And a couch.

Not my couch, but one in my soon-to-be business partner's apartment in Yangon. That couch became my first headquarters. My bed. My command post. My dining room table. I still have it to this day, not because it is comfortable, but because it reminds me of how far I have come. Also my cats have since destroyed it and still love to scratch it, so it stays.

And so, on January 4, 2014, after a month of traveling back and forth between Bangkok and Yangon, I made my decision. I packed up my condo in Bangkok and moved my entire life, one suitcase, to Yangon. There were no guarantees. No job title. No salary. Just the promise of a company I could build in my own image. Myanmar did not hand me anything, but it gave me what America could not at the time.

Myanmar gave me a chance.

If the Marine Corps had been the crucible that forged my ability as a leader, then Myanmar would become my proving ground.

BUILDING SOMETHING REAL: BEGIN WITH THE BASICS

In 2013, the year after Myanmar opened to the world, the rush was immediate. Investors, consultants, and corporations poured in, convinced this place would be the next frontier miracle. It felt like a modern-day gold rush. Everyone thought they would become multimillionaires overnight, especially Westerners. Growth was assumed, profit was promised.

And behind it all stood the all-knowing Barack Obama, yes, that Obama again, in his usual soaring cadence. He declared Myanmar a crowning triumph of twenty-first-century diplomacy. He opened the country to the world with speeches about reform, opportunity, and the promise of democracy.

Fool me once, they say. This made it twice.

Obama's words helped inspire me to join the Marine Corps. Now, here I was, halfway around the world, once again walking into a conflict zone he had framed as a frontier of hope. Maybe, deep down, it was one last attempt to believe in what he once sold us, that his America of Hope could still be a force for change in the world. That America could help shepherd this fragile nation toward democracy.

Yup, I fell for this chicanery again. Just like in Afghanistan.

Ironically, I had just come from Afghanistan, another war-torn country with decades of blood in the soil. Myanmar, however, was something else, murkier and more complex. A never-ending civil war masked by a thin ceasefire and generational inter-ethnic mistrust.

I arrived with one suitcase and a head full of ideals, and I quickly learned this country would never reward quick wins or speculation. The people who thought they could drop in, flip an investment, and fly out with their treasures did not even make it to 2020. The rest were wiped out by the pandemic. Their failure was not timing. It was a misunderstanding of what Myanmar actually needed. It did not need tourists. It needed commitment.

So from day one, my priority was not growth, profit, or headlines. I came to build something real. I quickly learned that the most valuable asset in Myanmar was not land or licenses. It was human capital.

Myanmar's development challenge has never been a lack of talent. It has always been a lack of opportunity. The people here know they have been dealt a bad hand, and instead of making excuses, they show up and work harder anyway. That was what hooked me. The honesty. The work ethic. The spirit of the people I came to call the workers of Myanmar. They did not want charity. Like me at the time, they just wanted a chance.

Back then, I had one vehicle, two local staff, and a modest house that doubled as both home and my would-be headquarters for the next seven years. I trained every guard myself. I wrote every standard operating procedure and training manual from scratch, often by laptop light when the power went out. I did every inspection, showing up at sites in the dead of night to make sure no security guard was sleeping on the job.

There was no margin for error. No room for complacency. No safety net.

We were lean, maybe too lean. Cash flow was life or death. We rarely had enough to feel comfortable about the next payroll, so I hustled. I worked alongside my team and took whatever paid quickly. Event security. Close protection (bodyguards), including one job for the Armenian Pope. Risk assessments for even high-stakes extortion response deep in ethnic armed group territory.

Every job did two things. It kept the lights on and it built the culture around the basics. Show up. Lead from the front. Be the first to sacrifice. That was when I finally had the freedom to live by a principle we talked about in Afghanistan but rarely had the power to put into practice.

A local problem needs a local solution. A Myanmar problem needs a Myanmar solution.

From then on, I stopped looking for résumés and started looking at character. I sought out young men and women no one else was betting on, overlooked, too young, underqualified on paper, but hungry and angry at the world for not giving them a chance. Sound familiar? I made them all a promise:

"Believe in me. Follow me. Trust me. Do what I say, and I'll make you a leader."

And they did. Many of the guards I trained in 2013 are now senior leaders. My general manager was an early hire. My head of finance, Zar, started as my assistant at twenty. They were not polished corporate recruits. They were believers. As the company took shape, I found myself guided by one of the first lessons the Marine Corps ever taught me:

"The basics. The basics. The basics. The basics will keep you alive."

Excellence begins with the basics. If you cannot perfect the small things, you have no business leading people toward larger goals. You can have all the vision and strategy in the world, but if you cannot execute the fundamentals, none of it matters. If I was going to build a company in my image, that is where it would start. Something as simple as wearing your uniform properly mattered. Not because it was cosmetic, but because it was cultural. It set the tone. Discipline. Strength. Sacrifice.

"Excellence begins with the basics" became our unofficial motto, our ethos, a pledge to push one another toward greatness. We plastered it on the walls of our training rooms. We made guards chant it during training until it was burned into muscle memory. That is how our culture was born.

This was the Marine Corps' leadership ethos translated into civilian life. Leadership rooted in the local community. Built from scratch in a place most people overlooked. To this day, I refuse to hire expatriates into my company's ranks. No foreigner was going to parachute in and fix Myanmar. We would develop our own leaders.

I did not hire guards. I hired, trained, and empowered leaders.

We weren't just a security firm; we were a leadership academy. The culture we built paid dividends almost immediately. The company grew quietly at first, then rapidly. We became trusted not just for what we offered, but for how we operated. We were viewed as more of a platoon than a company in those days, defined by discipline, relentless training, and uncompromising standards. By 2016, that success had carried us far enough that a European multinational acquired a majority stake in the company, bought out my business partners, and expanded the business beyond security into multiple service lines.

That moment marked my full transformation from an unemployed veteran into a successful entrepreneur, someone who had built a company from nothing in one of the most complex countries on earth. And yet, everything I had built was about to be tested. A gauntlet of crisis was approaching, one that would demand a new way of leading.

A leadership doctrine forged in fire.

THE THREE ACTS OF LEADERSHIP

If there was a moment when my leadership and my company were truly tested, it was the firestorm that began in 2020. First, the pandemic, and then the coup d'état, then the conflict that collapsed the economy almost overnight. Banks froze, the internet went black, and the streets turned into war zones. Diplomats and foreign executives fled by the hundreds on evacuation flights, but I did not. I could not. When the lights went out in Yangon, when even the embassies gave up, I made a choice that would define my path as a leader: I stayed.

That decision wasn't driven by strategy or some calculated business risk. It was instinct. It was ethos. It was the Marine in me, long out of uniform but still bound by a code: you stay with your people. In those early weeks of March 2021, whispers spread of a "crazy American Marine" darting, and sometimes blowing, through the barricaded streets of Yangon in a black Ford Ranger, helping people escape shuttered buildings, evacuating foreigners while the airport was closed to commercial flights. That Marine was me, but I don't share this for applause. I share it because this was the job I had signed up to do.

Since founding my company in 2013, I had trained my people for that moment, the moment when instinct overrides fear and protecting others is no longer about orders, but about responsibility. We were security professionals. This was the mission. That is the cost. That is the test. If you want to lead, you had better be the first to bleed, the first to lose sleep, the first to sacrifice. I learned that in the Marine Corps, and that lesson carried me through crisis after crisis.

Yet for many avid readers of military leadership memoirs, there is a quiet truth rarely acknowledged: much of what works in uniform does not automatically translate to the private sector. This is what the Marines did not teach me, and what I had to learn in Myanmar. You cannot lead a civilian business community the same way you lead Marines.

In the Marine Corps, leadership is reinforced by rank, orders, and discipline. Marines sign their lives away for duty and title. That is not how the private sector works. Most people do not sign up to follow a leader. They sign up for a job, to earn a living, to feed their families, and to pay rent. It took me years to build leadership within my company and instill a culture of strength and sacrifice among my people. I could do that because I had time, I had leverage, and I was offering something concrete in return: a future, a livelihood, and quite frankly, a paycheck. The Marine Corps ethos translated because it was paired with stability, and with a core staff that believed in me and stayed with me for over a decade.

A chamber of commerce is radically different, even from this private-sector example, especially one in collapse.

I didn't have the luxury of time, let alone years, to develop leaders across the community. More importantly, I had no leverage to compel anyone to do anything. I wasn't paying people. In fact, they were paying AMCHAM for their yearly membership dues and volunteering their time even if they chose to help. All I had was a message, and the strength to carry it.

As I prepared to take on the mantle of leadership at AMCHAM Myanmar in April 2023, I knew I was stepping into an institution that needed something fundamentally different. Not management. Not consensus. Something radical.

That was the birth of the Three Acts of Leadership.

The idea was simple and deliberate: if a message is the *only* way to lead, then that message must be built around speeches delivered at deliberate moments. Throughout my presidency, I orchestrated those opportunities. Every AMCHAM has a standardized calendar. Some events evolve, new ones are added, but these gatherings serve a constant purpose. They are public forums to inspire people and, more importantly, to move them to action.

Every speech I delivered was written with a doctrine in mind. They were not random remarks made along the way. They were checkpoints. Signals to the community that marked where we stood and declared where we were going next. Each one defined a phase, launched a campaign, or crystallized a shared sense of purpose. None of them were accidental. They were written deliberately. Because for leaders, milestones are not ceremonial. They are directional.

That is the true power of a good speech. It creates focus, coordination, and clarity. Over time, this doctrine became our community's compass, quietly guiding us through the storm.

Maybe it came from my brief flirtation with theater in my younger years, or maybe it's simply because leadership, like life, unfolds in scenes rather than straight lines. Either way, I came to see my leadership journey as a play in three acts. Thus, the Three Acts of Leadership.

Act One: *Do the Work.*

Act Two: *Survive the Crucible.*

Act Three: *Give Them Something to Believe In.*

The Three Acts of Leadership is a doctrine forged on the principle that leadership can evolve when the leader is capable and circumstances change, moving from execution to endurance to belief. Act One, *Do the Work*, is about earning the right to lead by setting the standard and showing, through action, what excellence looks like. Act Two, *Survive the Crucible*, is where leadership is tested under resistance and uncertainty; demanding resilience, adaptability, and the courage to hold the line when the ground gives way. Act Three, *Give Them Something to Believe In*, is when leadership becomes human. You let your people see your heart and believe in it. If you can do that, they'll follow you anywhere.

I hope the Three Acts of Leadership shows readers how I used this doctrine to give my people something solid in a world coming apart. Through the speeches, it becomes clear that there was structure beneath the chaos, even when it did not appear that way at the time. Yet it is important to note that not every leader will reach all three Acts. Some will master only one, others will endure two, and that is not failure. The full doctrine demands emotional depth and an oratorical capability that not every leader is built to carry.

This is a doctrine shaped not by theory, but by necessity. This is how I led my community through collapse and how others can too.

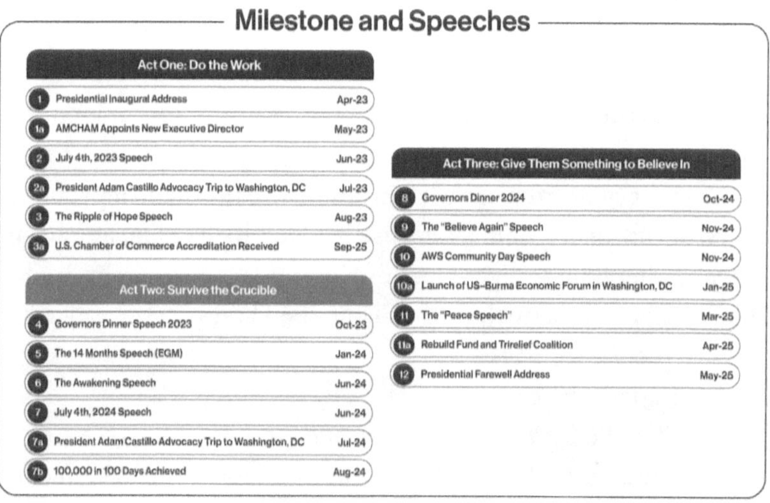

Leadership is not granted by title. It is earned, in silence, in fire, and through belief.

Yet belief alone does not make a leader, nor does action alone. Leadership in crisis demands something greater: the ability to turn both into something lasting. Success, real and durable success, never arrives by accident, especially in collapsing countries like Myanmar. Leadership in crisis is not survival for its own sake. It is not heroism or martyrdom. It is continuity with purpose. It is the discipline to build with intent even as the world is falling apart.

Some call that vision. To me, vision is not a picture in the mind. It is the destination on the other side of the fog. It is the end state you fight to see even when the path is obscured. Vision gives struggle its meaning, but vision alone is only half the equation. A vision without execution is a fantasy. Execution without a plan is chaos, and a leader without a plan?

Just another figure drifting in the storm.

From the day I took the Presidency of AMCHAM Myanmar, I led with a plan: the Three Acts of Leadership. Not as a slogan, not even publicly, but as a discipline. The board structure, the cadence of speeches, the campaigns we launched, even my most strategic trips to Washington, DC, none of it was reactive or random. Every move, every milestone, every statement was nested within this broader doctrine, one designed to create something that could outlive me.

Not for legacy, but for the survival of my people.

You do not stumble your way into belief. You build it: step by step, word by word, act by act; and every one of those steps must answer one question:

When your time as a leader ends, what do you leave behind that your people can still stand on?

Not a checklist of wins. Not a trophy case. A story of who we were, how we stood together, and what we were willing to fight for. For AMCHAM, that meant laying a foundation stronger than any one presidency. It meant constructing a compass of moral courage, not just for where to go, but for how to carry ourselves along the way.

Each speech was part of a larger structure, signals in a broader campaign, all guided by the same doctrine that defined my presidency. First, you do the work. Then, you survive the fire. Only then, when you have earned it, do you give them something to believe in. That belief is not the conclusion of leadership. It is its ignition.

If there is one thesis to this memoir, it is this:

The American business community did not survive because we had the best strategy, the deepest resources, or a savior swooping in at the last moment. AMCHAM Myanmar survived because its people believed, and from that belief, everything else followed.

My hope is that you, the reader, whether you're a CEO, a nonprofit organizer, a veteran looking for a job, or simply someone trying to guide your family through tough times, will find something in these pages to help light your way through your own darkness. Belief precedes strategy, and courage is often a whisper before it's a roar. If you can nurture belief in those around you and inspire them to find their voice even when fear is loud, then you can lead them anywhere, through any crisis. As I close this opening prologue, let me state plainly what leadership came to mean for me in Myanmar:

Leadership is not about the absence of fear; it is about finding your voice despite it.

I was afraid often. Afraid for my safety. Afraid for my people's future. Afraid for a country whose suffering defies description. Leadership meant showing up anyway. It meant raising your hand when others flinched. It meant stepping into the silence and saying to the world that "we will not go gentle into that good night."

Finding Our Voice is not a metaphor. It was the turning point in our story, and in mine. A battered community, long overlooked, chose to speak clearly, publicly, and without apology. When we found that voice, when we dared to use it, we rediscovered that we still mattered. The chapters ahead will show how that voice evolved, how it was tested, and how it grew stronger through broken boards, sanctions, sabotage, and despair, until it was no longer just the voice of a president.

It was the voice of a community.

This book is the legacy of that belief. It is a testament to what we carried together: that even in darkness, you can find your voice.

DO THE WORK

SHOW THEM THE WORK. SET THE STANDARD.

Accomplishments do not come from promises. They come from effort, from execution, from work that shows up every single day. Especially in a crisis, people do not need platitudes. They need purpose. They need a goal. Something visible. Something measurable. Something that, once achieved, says clearly: We are still alive, and we are still capable of greatness.

Every story has to start somewhere.

For me, it began with a question: what could we build, together, that would not only prove we still mattered, but show them I was the leader who could make it happen?

You will read about the importance of organized events in the next chapter, but let's be honest. Chamber of Commerce events are supposed to happen anyway. They are the baseline, not the benchmark.

The benchmark for leadership, real leadership, is accomplishments. Accomplishments do not come from promises. They come from effort, from execution, from work that shows up every single day. Especially in a crisis, people do not need platitudes. They need purpose. They need a goal. Something visible. Something measurable. Something that, once achieved, says clearly: We are still alive, and we are still capable of greatness. That is why I set the first goal deliberately. I chose a milestone no one had ever reached.

Accreditation.

AMCHAM Myanmar did not have accreditation when I became president of the Board, so I made it my first milestone. Accreditation from the US Chamber of Commerce sounds bureaucratic, but it meant everything.

So, I did the work and submitted the application, but I did not stop there. I timed our submission with my annual advocacy trip to Washington, DC, as part of the AMCHAM Asia-Pacific Doorknock Delegation. I walked the halls, met the people, and pushed our story into every room I entered. In every meeting, I repeated the same message: We are still here, and we matter.

One month later, we were accredited.

From the day I became president on April 27, 2023, to the moment we secured accreditation in August, it took four months. Four months after years of drift, avoidance, and outright incompetence, we proved what could be done when leadership simply does the work. Leadership is not waiting, deferring, asking for permission, or calling for a show of hands. It is setting a milestone and pulling the organization across the finish line when hesitation threatens to stall it.

That milestone worked only because alignment was intentional. The Board, the staff, and the membership moved together, and that did not happen by accident. One of the first changes I made as president was restructuring how the Board operated. There would be no more decisions in small circles and no more rubber-stamping behind closed doors. We locked in board meetings for the entire year, published agendas in advance, and made accreditation a top priority for every one of them.

And we discussed it together.

From the beginning, I made expectations clear. Serving as a governor on this Board was not about visibility at events. It was about presence in meetings, engagement in deliberations, and commitment to the work, no matter how long it took. The Board rose to that challenge and bought in, though not without resistance, which I will address later.

The same clarity extended to the membership. We scheduled our Fourth of July celebration, one of the largest events of the year, just days before my departure for Washington, DC. Standing before hundreds of members, I said it plainly: this was the milestone, and this was what we were working toward.

When I boarded that flight, I was not traveling alone. I was carrying the trust of a Board, a staff, and a membership that had committed themselves to something that once seemed unattainable.

That is what showing the work really means. It is not only doing the labor yourself, though that mattered too, with late nights, endless emails, and phone calls that never seemed to end. It is creating a culture where everyone understands the objective and believes the outcome is possible.

And this is the part that matters most. Hitting the first milestone did not mean the work was finished. It meant the standard had been set. Accreditation was not a finish line, it was a precedent. It signaled to everyone watching, inside and outside the Chamber, that this community no longer reacted to events. It acted.

For those planning their own Act One of leadership, this is the lesson. Putting in the work and making it visible begins in Act One, but it does not end there. Leaders set goals, pursue them with discipline, and then achieve them.

With that precedent established, I could move into the next act of my leadership journey.

A harder one. A darker one. The crucible.

A VOICE BEGINS

THE INAUGURAL ADDRESS

Title does not grant a voice. Do the
work. The voice follows.

*The Flag of American Commerce wasn't just a symbol.
It was my promise, but to deliver that promise, to make
those words live, I had to earn the right to speak to them.*

My decision to run for president of the Board came after a difficult realization. The change this community needed could not come from the sidelines. Not in a chamber drowning in crisis, blood, and apathy. The leadership our community required demanded full command. So when the previous president finally stepped down (with a year still left on his term) to the quiet relief of much of the business community, I stepped forward and threw my hat into the ring.

It was April 27, 2023, at the Pan Pacific Hotel in Yangon, Myanmar. The occasion was AMCHAM's Sixth Annual General Meeting, known simply as the AGM. It is a required formal business meeting held annually to present annual reports and outline the Chamber's plans for the year ahead. More importantly, it is where vacant seats on the Board of Governors are filled and where the Board elects its president.

There are eleven seats on the AMCHAM Myanmar Board of Governors. Five are officer positions: a president, two vice presidents, a treasurer, and a secretary. Election to an officer role requires one governor to nominate, another to second, and a majority vote of the Board. Six out of eleven.

When I was nominated for president, no one else stood. I ran unopposed. The Board placed its full confidence in me with eleven out of eleven votes. I accepted the presidency with gratitude and a clear understanding of the responsibility I was assuming.

Following the AGM and officer elections, a members' luncheon was scheduled to introduce the new Board and officers. This luncheon would also mark the incoming president's first address. The speech that would become *The Inaugural Address* had to be written before I was officially voted in as president. Yet in truth, I knew the outcome long before the vote. Too many members had urged me to take on the mantle. Their encouragement was not about ambition or ego. It was about survival. Not just the survival of the Chamber's operations, but the morale of a community under siege.

Our community was a sinking ship.

Yet, I still believed that American commerce, even in a place as isolated as Myanmar, could be a force for good. I believed our voice mattered. Yet, we had become a chamber in exile. Exiled from policy relevance. Cut off from international support. Estranged even from our own sense of purpose. Myanmar itself was in chaos. The economy had collapsed under the combined weight of the COVID-19 pandemic and a coup by the Tatmadaw that fractured the country. Activism, sanctions, and silence swept across the business community like an eclipse.

Before I was elected president that day, before the speeches that would follow, before the milestones yet to be achieved, there was only me in a dark room with a laptop. No script. No audience. Just a quiet moment of realization that if I did not speak up, no one would. And in the darkness of that room, one question surfaced and refused to leave me. If I found my voice, could it give my people the courage to find theirs?

That question did not linger for long. It demanded an answer in action. When I stepped into the President's chair of AMCHAM Myanmar in April 2023, I had a great deal to learn and a great deal to say. The Chamber had been without a voice for far too long. My predecessor, though well intentioned, had seemingly grown disillusioned and exhausted. Somewhere along the way, I felt he simply stopped believing that AMCHAM could survive in Myanmar. Once a leader chooses apathy over belief, the rest of the organization inevitably follows that same spiral of indifference.

He rarely spoke publicly at meetings or events. He appeared uncomfortable taking the podium, retreating instead into the safety of board protocol. I could not lead that way. Myanmar was in crisis, and our business community did not need silence. It needed a voice strong enough to cut through indifference and restore belief.

That was my objective with *The Inaugural Address*, my first speech as president. It was not simply to announce my presence, but to make clear that AMCHAM was done hiding in darkness and silence. To achieve this, my speech had to have a resonant and unmistakable message.

This Chamber does not exist to advance individual businesses.

It exists to ensure the community's survival. Titles do not matter. Identity comes from purpose. In the Marine Corps, this principle is captured by the foundational concept of *unit esprit* or *esprit de corps*. The idea that the institution is greater than any individual within it. Nobody is above the unit. The same had to be true for AMCHAM. No one stands above the community.

Nowhere was that principle more important than on the Board itself. I have sat beside people on the Board far wealthier and far more accomplished than me. From CEOs leading country operations for global corporations to local tycoons. Yet after they elected me president, in a private room before I was formally introduced, I told them plainly:

"The moment you walk through AMCHAM's doors, we are all equals."

Service on the Board is unpaid. It demands time, energy, and often personal sacrifice, offered with no promise of reward beyond responsibility. Yet, that is the commitment each governor makes the moment they nominate themselves to serve. This was the role, and I expected my board members to meet that responsibility or step aside. We were the leadership of AMCHAM Myanmar, and the example had to begin with us.

I also understood that *how* this message was delivered mattered as much as the message itself. A professional, formal address centered on community over self would signal immediately that change was underway. Leadership begins by setting the example; however, the membership does not attend board meetings. They do not see the work from the planning sessions to the internal debates. What they see is what stands before them in public at official AMCHAM events.

That is why presence mattered. That is why preparation mattered. Members do not engage based on promises. They engage based on what they can see. What they saw, consistently over the years I was president, was me. Fully prepared. Properly presented. Well groomed. Suited with tie. AMCHAM pin on my lapel. Speech in hand. Standing before them not out of obligation, but out of respect for the time they gave to our community.

These could no longer be mere events. They had to become gatherings. Forums where ideas were heard, morale was restored, and belief in the community was rebuilt. *Esprit de corps* had to be visible, not just spoken about.

During my time as AMCHAM president, I never missed an event, and I never arrived unprepared. Every time I took the stage, I delivered formal remarks that were written, sometimes rehearsed, but always intentional. A leader does not speak about setting the example. A leader becomes it. That standard was set on that day in April 2023, when I delivered *The Inaugural Address.*

LEARNING TO USE MY VOICE

I may have had endless experiences speaking in front of people prior to April 2023, but I was never truly a public speaker. In the Marine Corps, you speak to your Marines all the time: weekly formations, field operation orders, the safety briefs before a long holiday weekend. I gave operational briefs to commanding officers and even generals, but that's not speechcraft. That's reporting. That's command presence. You don't rehearse a speech in front of a platoon; they'd see right through it. Marines expect you to be real, direct, and unscripted. The only time you'd deliver formal remarks was at a change of command or some high-level ceremonial event, and even then, it wasn't the norm unless you were a high-ranking officer, like a general.

The only time I ever prepared something close to a speech before AMCHAM was probably back in college, when I was president of my fraternity and had to speak at our alumni dinner. I remember writing it 30 minutes before I had to step up to the podium, with a few too many beers in me. It worked, but that wasn't speechcraft. That was improvisation, and I knew that wouldn't be enough anymore.

I wasn't a trained speechwriter. I had no formal education in rhetoric or communications. I was a Marine officer, a business owner, and a volunteer leader. I didn't have a communications team, let alone a speechwriter. Every word that's been spoken in these pages, every pause, every phrase, every breath, was mine. I wrote them all, but how?

I taught myself.

I devoured books and transcripts of great speeches, something I have always done since my formative years. I spent many late nights studying the mechanics of oratory: how to build sentences that flow, how to mix short, punchy lines with longer, lyrical ones, and how to find the cadence that carries a message regardless of the words being spoken. I practiced varying my pace and pauses until words felt alive in my mouth.

One technique I discovered early was anaphora, the repetition of a phrase at the beginning of consecutive clauses to drive home a point. I remember looking it up once, just to be sure: "anaphora is the repetition of a word or phrase at the beginning of consecutive sentences." I thought of Dr. Martin Luther King Jr., how he didn't just say "I have a dream" once. He said it eight times, like a drumbeat echoing through the soul of a broken nation. King didn't just speak truth, he carried his people with it. He built rhythm into hope and hope into action.

So, when I sat down to write my first speech as president of AMCHAM Myanmar, I asked myself: What word could anchor a fractured community? What phrase could gather, lift, and rally those who had nothing left to hold onto? What image could rise above the silence, and signal that we were still here? Bit by bit, a word took shape: flag. And with it, a motif emerged:

The Flag of American Commerce.

THE FLAG OF AMERICAN COMMERCE

In crisis, I looked for symbols to rally hope, and I found one in that phrase. The Chamber, our battered network of businesses, families, and workers, wasn't just an institution. It was a banner. A standard.

Something flying in a dark sky and without us, without our collective presence, that flag couldn't fly at all. We had to be that flag. It wasn't branding. It was strength, turned into language. It was my mantra. It was the beginning of our voice.

All these elements came together in *The Inaugural Address* in April 2023. It was my first time serving as president, so I wrote the speech slowly and deliberately, line by line. I opened by welcoming our new governors to the Board and thanking those whose nominations were not successful, something no past president had bothered to do, and then turned to our greater purpose. I wove in everything I had been learning about speechcraft: the discipline of cadence, the power of repetition, the rhetorical structure of anaphora. I placed commas, periods, and even the now infamous em dash (thanks for ruining it for writers, ChatGPT). I did this not for grammar, but for breath. For rhythm. For weight. The phrasing wasn't fancy; it was earnest, deliberate, and clear.

I asked, "What is The Flag of American Commerce?"

Then I answered it, again and again, until it stood tall on the page and even taller in the room. What I wrote wasn't just rhetoric, it was a blueprint. Every paragraph doubled as both a plan of action and a declaration of identity. I told them plainly that membership wasn't about profit, it was about people. That our presence here could set the ethical standard for responsible investment. That staying and creating jobs was providing one of the most fundamental human rights to the people of this country: economic opportunity.

The moment that still echoes the loudest from that speech, still quoted back to me by members to this day, was my "ask" to the membership:

"I ask all of you, to commit to our community, and not to ask what AMCHAM can do for you, but what you can do for AMCHAM to ensure that The Flag of American Commerce not only survives but endures."

That line wasn't accidental. It was personal. A tribute to one of my childhood heroes, John F. Kennedy. I grew up a Kennedy Democrat in California, and to this day, the Kennedy brothers remain giants to me. Their speechcraft wasn't just political; it was poetic, moral, and muscular. JFK's inaugural address line about civic duty shaped how I viewed leadership from a young age. That cadence. That conviction. That call to service.

In that moment, standing before my community, I wasn't just quoting Kennedy, I was answering him. That *The Flag of American Commerce* wasn't just a symbol. It was my promise, but to deliver that promise, to make those words live, I had to earn the right to speak to them.

By comparison, our old leadership style felt flat. Dull. Forgettable. Before my first speech as president, I realized no one expected fireworks. We were a volunteer board under siege; small, tired, used to silence. That had to change, and I promised myself then that I would always show up and speak out. However, if I was going to master speechcraft, I had to put in the work through late nights and failed drafts. I figured I'd rather stumble in front of someone I trusted than stand frozen in front of my entire membership.

That's why, from day one of my presidency, I relied on one person, Zar: my Head of Finance. Yes, the one who started out as my assistant all those years ago. From this speech to my last, she sat across from me while I paced, cursed, rewrote, doubted, and despaired. She listened while I rehearsed every line. She told me when to tear it up and when to stick with it. Every leader needs that person, someone who sees the rough drafts and still believes in the final message; someone who can accept you at your lowest point and applaud at your highest. For those of you in leadership: find that person. Find your Zar.

When I finally was done delivering my inaugural address, no frills, no slides, just my voice, something shifted. The silence in the room broke. Heads nodded. Eyes lit up. For the first time, AMCHAM Myanmar told our community: We are still here. We matter. We will not fade away. What should have been just another Annual General Meeting felt like history. That inaugural address didn't just launch my term.

It launched our voice.

THE INAUGURAL ADDRESS

Ladies and gentlemen, distinguished members of AMCHAM Myanmar,

I'd like to start off by welcoming our new governors to the Board but most of all I want to thank all the members who submitted nomination forms for governorship, competition is the very essence of American commerce, and the more members we have applying to be governors of this great Chamber in the coming years, the greater we will become. To everyone that applied, even if not elected this year, I will say this to you: Be patient.

You are wise, accomplished, and committed, and your contributions to this community are already deeply valued. It will not be long before your leadership is recognized, and when that moment comes, I have no doubt you will rise to it with the strength and grace that brought you here today.

Now I believe The Flag of American Commerce continues to play a crucial role in this economy, but why? What is The Flag of American Commerce and why is it so important? What's the point of all of this?

To answer that, I think back to my body of work for this Chamber for the past three and a half years, to times people were asking me about an AMCHAM membership or I was among colleagues and friends discussing the importance of the chamber of commerce and the number of times I have heard, "Ahh chamber memberships, those are a waste of money, how does that help my business? How does it help me?"

And of course, I would smile and shake their hand, thank them for their time…but what I really wanted to tell them?

If you are looking at the viability of your chamber membership from a profit and loss standpoint, membership with AMCHAM will never be worth it. Trying to connect your membership's value with your revenue output from sales leads generated through networking events is not only not the purpose of our networking events but not what AMCHAM is here to do.

The very foundation of this Chamber is community, but this community cannot grow without the selflessness of its members; AMCHAM is, after all, a nonprofit.

And yet, The Flag of American Commerce cannot fly without a community to support it, whether it's getting involved on committees or the Board, or even as president, we are all The Flag of American Commerce.

But that flag and this community do not just represent Myanmar, you also represent the US Chamber of Commerce building in Washington, DC, the world's oldest and largest commercial organization.

That is the flag you represent, but that flag would not exist in Myanmar without members who are willing to volunteer their time without any self-interest. Sacrifice will always be the hallmark of great leaders, and every one of you here today is not just a member, but a leader of this business community.

And so, today I ask you, I ask all of you, to commit to our community and not to ask what AMCHAM can do for you, but what you can do for AMCHAM to ensure that The Flag of American Commerce not only survives but endures to continue to give the people of this country the hope of economic opportunity.

Economic opportunity, one of the most fundamental human rights...

I see our friends from the embassy are here today to support us as usual, as they will tell you the US government remains committed to Myanmar to promote democracy and human rights in the country. One of AMCHAM's strongest relationships is with the US government and its embassy here in Yangon.

While AMCHAM is not a political organization, we can still help this agenda by simply staying here, by showing up to work and continuing to fight challenges to create jobs, but not just any jobs, good jobs with fair wages for not just those that work for us directly but for the entire supply chain that supports our investment.

Our commitment to human rights does not have to start and end at complying with sanctions, but our continued presence here sets the standard for foreign investment that is both ethical and transparent. This is a testament to our community's commitment to our people.

Our community has endured some tumultuous years recently and will most likely have many more ahead. Yet the history of American commerce is unlike anything this world has ever seen. That history was achieved by successes and failures in tumultuous markets like Myan-mar, even at times in those markets when American commerce needed to be erased and rebuilt again, AMCHAM was always the constant in that history:

This Chamber, this flag, this community. It's a part of our past, present, and future, and among those of us who have spent so many years here, it's a reminder, not only of why we stayed, but all that was great in this country and what could be great again.

So, the next time you're with friends in the business community or in your budget meetings, talking about chamber membership and if they are worth it, you tell them this, you tell them about our community and what it means to the people of this country, you tell them about The Flag of American Commerce.

God bless you; I love you. Thank you.

A VOICE RECOGNIZED

THE JULY FOURTH ADDRESS, 2023

The work creates the voice. The voice earns recognition. The recognition cements legitimacy.

Accreditation was never just a box to tick. It was our line in the sand. A chance to prove that this community still mattered. That we weren't some forgotten outpost, but a real American Chamber, carrying The Flag of American Commerce in one of the toughest business environments on earth.

The Inaugural Address was delivered at the end of April 2023 with one simple goal: to break the silence. The next major moment came two months later. On the last Saturday of June 2023, we held what became known as the AMCHAM Annual Independence Day Celebration, and with it, the July Fourth Address. This was different. It was no longer an intimate gathering; it was a full-scale event, drawing more than 255 people. It was the first truly grand stage I stood on as president, and with that scale came pressure.

By then, expectations had shifted. *The Inaugural Address* had cracked the silence; *The July Fourth Address* was meant to rally the community. It was about bringing people together and making clear that this moment, this gathering, was only the first step.

What the membership did not fully see was that, behind the scenes, structures long left dormant were being rebuilt. The first act of leadership was never asking others to work. It was demonstrating, visibly and consistently, what work looked like. That work began with committees and events.

Committees are the engine room of a chamber of commerce. They are small, sector-specific forums where members operating within the same industries surface real policy problems, pressure-test solutions, and develop the confidence to speak openly in front of their peers. This is where advocacy begins. When committees function properly, members stop behaving like spectators and start acting as participants in a shared mission.

When I stepped into the role, AMCHAM Myanmar had no functioning committees at all.

The absence of committees meant there was no structured channel for members to raise business concerns, no mechanism for external advocacy, and no pipeline for developing future leaders who could be vocal within the organization. If there was one decision my predecessor made that I not only opposed, but that nearly ruined our community, it was his decision to dismantle the committees entirely.

His justification was poor attendance.

That reasoning inverted the very purpose of leadership. The president is the face of the organization, and inspiring people to show up is the job. Empty chairs are not a reason to shut doors; they are a signal that leadership has failed to mobilize. Rather than rallying the membership, he allowed the committees to fade quietly, shielding the decision behind the claim that members preferred to keep a low profile. That explanation was as lazy as it was convenient, and it was entirely inaccurate. The problem with committee attendance was his failure to lead.

Events followed the same downward trajectory. They lacked agenda, intent, and professional execution. Poorly marketed and loosely organized, low turnout became inevitable. At the same time, a new executive director was stepping into the role. He was capable and well-intentioned, but he had no prior experience running a chamber of commerce. Without structure or direction, he risked drifting into the same fog that had already settled over the organization.

By that point, member engagement had nearly disappeared. The sense of community that once defined the Chamber was barely recognizable. AMCHAM Myanmar had become a shell, drifting steadily toward collapse, the familiar death spiral of any neglected nonprofit. There was no guidebook for revival. There was no manual for rebuilding a business community inside a country at war. So I turned instead to the only thing I trusted.

I led.

I made a deliberate decision to work harder, longer, and more visibly than anyone else. The role was unpaid and often unacknowledged, but that was irrelevant. I would never ask a member to do something I was unwilling to do myself. From the first day, my message to the AMCHAM staff was direct and uncomplicated. We would perfect the basics.

Running a committee meeting or an event on time, with preparation, structure, and clear communication, was not administrative window dressing. It was foundational. Timelines mattered. Calendar invites mattered. Promotion mattered. Agendas mattered. These disciplines were simple but nonnegotiable. A serious chamber requires seriousness in execution.

Excellence begins with the basics.

As I noted in the prologue, members pay to belong to a community. Showing up already costs them time, energy, and in Myanmar's environment, a degree of personal risk. Many members believed that attending events was no longer worth the effort. Given the quality of what had been delivered before, that assessment was understandable.

The basics of every function the Chamber performed for its members had to be respected and delivered. Once members could see that effort, structure, and professionalism returning, I knew commitment would follow. Once members saw others committing to committees, sacrificing time to attend events, sponsoring initiatives, or leading advocacy discussions, something powerful would happen.

It would become contagious (and it did).

Throughout my presidency, attendance increased. Engagement deepened. Members wanted to be present at every event, not out of obligation, but out of pride. They wanted to belong to something larger than themselves. Then as belief took hold, the organization began to change. Membership grew. Partnerships followed. Support expanded beyond basic membership to Silver, Gold, and Platinum partnerships. I wanted companies confident enough to place their names alongside ours, because belief paired with sacrifice creates culture.

That culture does not emerge from vision alone. Vision without execution is noise. Leadership requires work and execution, and execution always begins in the same place: the basics.

Within the first month of my presidency, two things demanded our full presence: chamber accreditation and the Fourth of July event. They were connected. One would get the US Chamber of Commerce to buy into our vision. The other would get our own membership to do the same.

The July Fourth Address took place at our annual Independence Day Celebration. The year before, we had laid the groundwork for a potential flagship event, but this year? I wanted it to scream America. Not politely nod at freedom, scream it.

This was my first major event as AMCHAM president, and we

needed to show members that this was a new chapter in AMCHAM event excellence, but that we were going big. KFC, donuts, balloon swords, face paint, and nachos smothered in authentic ballpark cheese that I had personally shipped in from America. It was hosted by the US Embassy at the American Club in Yangon. Kids ran wild. Adults drank beer in the pool. Yet, I knew we needed to kick off the event with a "bang." Before anyone touched a hot dog, I made the entire crowd rise for the national anthem.

Whitney Houston. Super Bowl XXV. Queued and played. If you know, you know.

Then we hit play on the soundtrack of the Republic: Tom Petty, John Cougar Mellencamp, Grand Funk, Skynyrd, Toby Keith, Kenny Loggins. *Danger Zone* blasted while burgers hit our attendees' mouths. For four hours, Yangon became a backyard in the Midwest.

That day, 255 people showed up. At the time, it was unprecedented. Even before the pandemic or the coup, we had never pulled those numbers at an event. This was our biggest crowd ever. And most of them weren't executives, they were Myanmar nationals. Our workers. And that was the point. This was a community day. A picnic for our staff and their families. A chance to show our gratitude, but they didn't just come for the food.

They came because we did the work leading up to the event. They came because we perfected the basics. They came because they believed in what we were doing. They believed in what we stood for.

Then there was accreditation from the US Chamber of Commerce. Accreditation was never a side quest. It was part of the agenda from the very beginning because it gave the membership, and the broader community, a shared goal. It was about trust and recognition from one of the oldest and largest commercial organizations in the world. Accreditation separates real chambers of commerce from lobbying fronts, private clubs, and broken associations. It ensures that when American business speaks abroad, the world knows it speaks with purpose and authority.

The July Fourth Address was my opportunity to announce accreditation as our community's main fight.

That is why the US Chamber of Commerce was mentioned in *The Inaugural Address* itself. From the moment I assumed the presidency, accreditation was understood as essential, not parallel, not aspirational, but foundational. Yet before that speech was delivered, and before the application was submitted, a question lingered quietly within the community:

Could this Board of Governors accomplish in four months what multiple presidents and boards before me had failed to do over six years?

AMCHAM Myanmar was established under the umbrella of AMCHAM Thailand in 2013, but it did not formally separate to become a locally registered association until 2017. Even after that transition, the Chamber remained unaccredited for years. When I first joined the Board, accreditation was described as a priority and an active workstream under the sitting president. Three years later, nothing had been accomplished. Two presidents preceded me. Multiple boards came and went. None secured accreditation. There was no explanation, no proof that there had ever been any follow-through, just silence. To this day, I still do not have a clear answer to why.

So, when I became president, that was going to change. The decision was simple and nonnegotiable. We were either a real American Chamber of Commerce, or we were not, and real American Chambers are accredited.

I reached out directly to the US Chamber of Commerce in Washington, DC. I briefed them on the crisis we were operating in, the risks on the ground, and the work already underway. I was direct and unapologetic. I told them exactly what I wanted.

"I want AMCHAM Myanmar accredited. Period."

There was no attempt to soften the message. I did not wait for a committee vote. I did not ask for permission or a show of hands. Accreditation became our first milestone, and I moved forward accordingly.

The process was not simple. Unlike chambers in Singapore, Thailand, or Australia, whose accreditations had been in place for decades, AMCHAM Myanmar was an open question of reputational risk. To further complicate matters, the US Chamber's leadership in Washington had to revisit its own archives and reconstruct the process for an accreditation application. I worked alongside them throughout this process, step-by-step, to determine how we would move forward.

At the same time, I placed accreditation at the top of every board agenda. Every governor understood that this was not a side project or a symbolic goal. It was the responsibility of the entire Board. Accountability became the standard. Participation was expected. When a board member failed to show up, the work continued without them. Failure to try was not an option.

After months of meetings and late nights, the application was submitted just ahead of *The July Fourth Address*.

However, my push for accreditation was not just about recognition. It was about changing a broken culture. I had learned in the Marine Corps that some of the most important lessons do not always come from great leaders. Sometimes they come from bad ones. They show you what not to do, who not to become. That was the only lesson I took from my predecessor.

Let me be clear. I did not hate the man. After one year on the Board, I was actually nominated for president in 2021, but I lost to him. He became president. I became vice president. Despite this, I supported him fully until his final day on the Board. Commitment to a cause runs deep for me, even when I disagree with my peers.

Yet again, the problem with his leadership was that he appeared to simply stop caring. Meetings no longer mattered. He would become annoyed and resort to buffoonery if he had to spend more than 40 minutes in the boardroom. He needed the AMCHAM staff to order breakfast sandwiches and coffee just to get him to show up. Honestly, he likely spent more time deciding on that breakfast order than he did preparing the meeting agenda, and it showed.

When hard decisions arose, he did not want to deliberate. He did not want debate. He wanted a quiet, stress-free environment for himself, not a functioning chamber that brought value to its members.

And that is exactly what he got. A boardroom full of silence.

ENDING THE POLITICS OF SILENCE

Ironically, when I first joined the Board as a governor, he was the one who proposed what would become the executive committee, a group of board officers (president, vice presidents, secretary, treasurer) that would meet separately from the full Board to "streamline" decision-making. He sold it as a scheduling tool; something borrowed from larger AMCHAMs like Singapore. A way to make board meetings "shorter and easier." By the time he became president, it had become a shortcut to avoid accountability.

Big decisions were previewed and pre-decided behind closed doors. Then, at the full Board session, we'd hear: "The executive committee has already decided this. Any objections? No? Okay, next."

It was all prepackaged. All performance. I sat in those executive committee meetings, as vice president, knowing it was wrong. And as much as I protested that the Board should be discussing this openly, I stayed loyal and didn't undermine him in front of the rest of the Board. Mainly, because the damage was already done. The culture of the Board was already broken.

So, when I became president, the very first institutional change I made was this: no more backroom decisions. We still held executive committee meetings. They were mandated in the bylaws. Yet I made it very clear from day one: We would not decide anything behind closed doors. Every meaningful decision would go to the full Board. We would deliberate. We would discuss. We would vote. We would do what we were elected to do.

Of course, this was also the era of remote *everything*, the lingering curse of the COVID-19 work mindset. To my predecessor's credit, he was not the only one falling victim to apathy. Other governors were logging into "hybrid" board meetings instead of showing up in person, even when they were twenty minutes away from the AMCHAM office. They would log on, mute their microphones, and disappear behind a laptop screen.

So, I drew a line immediately. Either we met in person, or we met fully virtual. But if you were on this Board, I needed you in your seat, ready to speak, ready to lead.

That did not sit well with everyone. One governor in particular, my predecessor's friend, former secretary, and now my vice president on the Board, preferred the old way. He would eventually sue me and AMCHAM. If I am being honest, I believe this decision, this shift in expectations, was what first sparked his resentment toward me.

Leadership is not just about carrying the burden. It is about sharing responsibility. I wanted every board member to feel that weight. Eventually, more than a year later, my Board voted unanimously to dissolve the executive committee entirely. We removed it from the bylaws because we had proven that real leadership does not need shortcuts. We were only 11 people. We could meet. We could talk. We could be a team. And no one needed breakfast sandwiches to show up anymore.

A STAGE, A FLAG, A PHOTO

The July Fourth Address carried real weight for me personally. Unlike the inaugural event, this speech came with scale. It was my first time speaking outdoors, at an open event with hundreds of people watching. That difference mattered, and I felt it. I was nervous. It was one of my easier speeches to write because it was also one of my shortest, yet I practiced it more than any other.

The setting amplified that pressure. The American Club in Yangon sits on US Embassy property, American soil in a sense. Like American clubs around the world, it functions as a social and community hub for diplomats and those connected to the American presence. There is a pool, a bar, basketball courts, and open space. It is informal in layout, but deeply symbolic in meaning. That was where I would deliver *The July Fourth Address*, standing before my community on American ground, speaking not just about patriotism, but about responsibility.

On the day of the event, I arrived early to greet members as they came in. Even so, an hour before taking the stage, I pulled away from the crowd and went back inside the American Club with Zar. We practiced again. I ran through the speech repeatedly, nearly to the point of memorization, wanting every line to feel natural rather than rehearsed. When I finally took the stage, I opened with The Flag of American Commerce.

"It has risen. It is surviving. It is enduring."

I announced to the membership that our accreditation application had officially been submitted and that a high-stakes interview in Washington was only a week away. Standing there, I made one thing clear. This was not performative. It was personal. We were not here to fade quietly. We were here to be seen.

We were here to rage against the dying light.

That day, I did not just talk about accreditation. I told a story about legacy and what it would mean if we were the ones to achieve it. Any other AMCHAM in Asia gets accredited? Good for them. If we got accredited, that changed everything.

It is hard to overstate how impossible that felt at the time. As I explained in the prologue, nobody wanted to have anything to do with Myanmar when it came to business. "Business" and "Myanmar" had become near oxymorons. Even multinationals were keeping their heads down, scrubbing their websites, pretending they were not here, if they had not already divested.

So, when we stood up and said we were going after accreditation from the US Chamber of Commerce, a global institution built on legitimacy, it ran counter to every instinct and every trend. That's exactly why it mattered.

If we could do it, on our budget, under these conditions, with the world's back turned away from us, then maybe, just maybe, others could too. That was the story I told. That was the legacy we were trying to write. That the hope of economic opportunity could endure, not just for American business, but for the people of this country.

As I stepped off the stage to applause and the flash of cameras, the music rose and the workers of our community began to surround me. That was when the photo was taken. The one that would later be painted by monks, inlaid with crystals, and gifted to me by the AMCHAM Myanmar staff on my ten-year anniversary later that year. The same image that would eventually inspire the cover design of this book.

The American flag was wrapped around my shoulders, and in that moment of community resilience and collective strength, it captured everything. It was patriotic. It felt almost magical. More importantly, it marked the moment our community understood what was happening.

We were starting something special.

Accreditation was never just a box to tick. It was our line in the sand. It was a chance to prove that this community still mattered. That we were not a forgotten outpost, but a real American Chamber, carrying The Flag of American Commerce in one of the toughest business environments on earth.

When we finally secured accreditation less than two months later, in August 2023, it was not just a win. It was a message. A message that commerce was still alive in Myanmar. That opportunity still existed. That AMCHAM Myanmar was here to stay.

It echoed a line that became the heartbeat of that speech and a permanent fixture of our community:

"An AMCHAM Myanmar today. An AMCHAM Myanmar tomorrow. An AMCHAM Myanmar forever."

That is what accreditation truly meant.

THE JULY FOURTH ADDRESS, 2023

The Flag of American Commerce.

It has risen, it is surviving, it is enduring.

I want to thank our good friends at the US Embassy for hosting us today and continuing to champion our flag.

Now many of you have asked me since I became president, what is my goal this year for AMCHAM?

I could talk about our new Executive Director and his successful turnover, I could talk about AMCHAM taking a financial loss this year by investing our cash reserves into its members by subsidizing members' ticket costs at AMCHAM events like this one today, I could talk to you about our upcoming AMCHAM Delegation to Washington, DC, to advocate to lawmakers to be more proactive with the country's crisis, but I'd rather talk to you about…legacy.

Accreditation with the US Chamber of Commerce in Washington, DC, is an achievement that has eluded our community since we pulled away from AMCHAM Thailand in 2017. That accreditation application was successfully submitted this month, and we eagerly await its approval, but accreditation does not just mean recognition from the world's oldest and largest commercial organization but echoes to the world that commerce is still alive in Myanmar.

Accreditation from the US Chamber is not just about the coming year, it's about the coming decade. It means an AMCHAM here today, an AMCHAM here tomorrow, and AMCHAM here forever. That's legacy.

Listen, if I'm speaking frankly, this country and its crisis are not a priority for lawmakers in the US. Most of you, if not all of you, know this already. But, if we do not continue to use our voice to advocate our cause, if we keep quiet and don't take any action, we will be dismissed, we will be erased, and everything we've done here, everything we've been through and fought for, to survive, will have been for nothing.

Any other AMCHAM in Asia gets accreditation, good for them, they're drinking champagne back in DC, talking about trade, maybe they get a trophy or plaque.

But if we get our accreditation, on our budget, with our limited resources, with all the challenges we've overcome. We change things. We can show lawmakers in the US, that there can be another way, there must be another way so we can ensure the everlasting hope of economic opportunity continues to endure for the people of this country.

So, continue to put in the work, dig in your heels, strengthen your resolve, maintain your convictions, we will not allow this country to go back to being a black hole of sanctions because we will not go gentle into that good night. Rage, rage against the dying light!

AMCHAM Myanmar today, AMCHAM Myanmar tomorrow, AMCHAM Myanmar forever.

A VOICE OF HOPE

THE RIPPLE OF HOPE SPEECH

Work creates. Action inspires. Hope ripples.

If even one factory stayed open, if even one worker remained employed, those acts could send ripples of hope through Myanmar. And together, those ripples could become a current strong enough to crash through any challenge we faced, at home or abroad.

In July 2023, I traveled to Washington, DC, as part of the AMCHAM Asia Pacific Doorknock Delegation. With our accreditation application already submitted, I arrived at the US Chamber of Commerce early on a humid summer morning. The meeting with their leadership went better than I had hoped. I knew then we were going to get it. I was right. That milestone would soon become official, marking the first phase of our campaign: recognition.

The trip began in triumph. It ended in quiet heartbreak and a brutal lesson in political reality.

For more than a week, I crisscrossed the capital, meeting with think tanks, nonprofits, congressional staffers, and senior officials from the Biden administration. Everywhere I went, the message was the same. Myanmar was not just low on the list of US priorities. It was not on the list at all. I asked questions, offered policy ideas, and challenged assumptions. No one was interested.

I remember walking a senior Biden official out of the US Chamber of Commerce building and asking him point-blank whether there was a plan to address the crisis in Myanmar. He looked at me and replied flatly,

"There is no plan, son. There's nothing that can be done in that country."

This was not just anyone. He was the president's go-to Indo-Pacific advisor and would later become one of the highest-ranking diplomats in the Biden-run State Department. If anyone had the authority to shape US policy on Myanmar, it was him. That single sentence captured everything I had seen that week. Total indifference. No curiosity. No openness. No willingness to even consider alternatives to the stale, outdated playbook of sanctions and isolation.

When I returned to Myanmar later that month, I asked the AMCHAM staff to organize a fireside chat. We called it *The President's Fireside Chat*. Fireside chats are meant to be frank and solemn by design. They strip away ceremony and force clarity, bringing people closer to uncomfortable truths. The purpose was simple. It was to debrief the community on the brutal reality we were facing. On

August 10, 2023, at the Novotel Yangon Max Hotel, I spoke to our membership and did not sugarcoat it.

"I broke through one wall," I told them, "and saw a hundred more waiting ahead."

At the time, AMCHAM's advocacy efforts were only just restarting. The committees had recently begun meeting again after being all but dissolved by my predecessor. I had established AMCHAM Myanmar's first-ever advocacy committee to bring structure and discipline to our messaging, but the community was still learning how to speak out again. The immediate goal was simple. It was to get people into the room and get them talking.

Yet after what I had seen in Washington, I knew that a committee in name alone was not enough. We needed substance. Real policy positions grounded in data, facts, and lived experience. If we were going to be dismissed anyway, then we would at least be dismissed for saying something worth hearing.

Unfortunately, fear still hung thick in the air. Fear of retaliation. Fear of visibility. Fear of being seen. Many in our community were reluctant to raise their voices, especially those operating from within Myanmar itself. I understood that fear, but what I couldn't accept was the silence around the Biden administration's foreign policy, the very policies that were gutting our businesses, emptying our offices, and stripping our workers of their futures.

Everyone in Myanmar has an opinion on sanctions. From business executives to taxi drivers, anyone who has lived through decades of US sanctions can tell you the same thing: they don't work, and they never will.

Sanctions made the powerful, both the Tatmadaw and their cronies, richer while everyone else became poorer. The brief period when sanctions were lifted had been, without question, the greatest era of economic opportunity Myanmar had known. So, coming home to Yangon, my message to the community was simple: if you want to complain about sanctions, write it down, support it with data. Tell me how these policies are affecting you. Give me something to fight with.

By the time of that trip in 2023, I was only three months into my presidency. I was still doing everything myself, every meeting, every message, every word written. There was no advocacy paper. No sector-specific talking points. No data. That had to change if we had any hope of shaping the future. And yet before I could ask others to find their moral courage, I had to ask myself: Where did mine come from? Who inspired it?

The answer led me back to the true author of a line I used in my speech:

"Moral courage remains the one essential, the vital quality for those who seek to change this country's vast array of ills."

—ROBERT F. KENNEDY, "DAY OF AFFIRMATION"

One of the handful of American speeches that has ever moved me emotionally is Robert F. "Bobby" Kennedy's 1966 "Day of Affirmation" address, delivered to students at the University of Cape Town during his visit to South Africa during the era of apartheid. Most know it by another name: the "Ripple of Hope" speech, so that's what I'll call it here. I've read it. I've listened to it. Dozens of times. But the version that truly breaks me isn't the one Bobby gave in Cape Town. It's the eulogy version his brother Ted recited at Bobby's funeral in 1968 at St. Patrick's Cathedral. Ted had woven Bobby's words into his eulogy, and in doing so, turned them into something transcendent.

That moment gave me an idea, an idea that would become my version of the "Ripple of Hope" speech. I cut lines. I moved paragraphs. I paraphrased Bobby's words and reshaped them into a Myanmar-centric call to action. This wasn't just quoting a great man, I was drawing directly from him, building something new from something timeless. I've often quoted great men in my speeches, and you'll see some of that in the chapters ahead, but this was different. I had never done this before, and I haven't done it since. In that moment, it felt right. It felt necessary.

"A great American hero once told my people," I said, quoting Kennedy verbatim, "that 'each time a man stands up for an ideal, acts to improve the lot of others, or strikes out against injustice, he sends forth a tiny ripple of hope.'"

I fully embraced Kennedy's words. He had seen those *tiny ripples* merge into a current strong enough to sweep down the mightiest walls of oppression. I told our audience the same thing. If even one factory stayed open, if even one worker remained employed, those acts could send ripples of hope through Myanmar. And together, those ripples could become a current strong enough to crash through any challenge we faced, at home or abroad.

Using RFK's speech so closely was a risk, but it was one I needed to take. It will likely be the only time in my life I allowed myself to paraphrase another man's words so directly. In that moment, my own voice was not enough. I needed history at my side. I needed one of my heroes. I needed Bobby.

Every line I paraphrased was delivered like a prayer. I leaned into repetition. Inclusive language. Cadence. Three times, just as Bobby had, I began with the same word.

"Surely, this common goal..."

"Surely, we can learn..."

"And surely, we can begin to work harder..."

I stamped the rhythm into the room.

Then I turned to my members and said plainly that I could no longer do this alone. I was not the all-knowing expert in every industry. I was a security professional. I did not know the intricacies of manufacturing, banking, or agriculture, but they did. I needed their help. I needed their voices.

If I went to Washington without them, without detailed messaging, without policy papers grounded in evidence and consequences, there was nothing I could do. That was the truth. This was not a call for help. It was a call for my people to find their moral courage.

That was the spirit I carried into the speech. I dug into that quiet space of my mind to frame what needed to be said. The theme became clear almost immediately: moral courage. In this brutal new world, with sanctions choking us and our people suffering, the easy choice was silence. To hunker down. To chase the illusion of safety and quick profit. But I knew we had to be bolder.

I spoke of our shared ambition in the language of shared duty. We save one job. We create one job. We act selflessly. Earlier speeches had centered on my own experience, but here I turned the mirror outward. I even confessed what I had once believed:

"So yes, I now believe there is nothing one man or one woman can do against the enormous array of this country's ills."

The point was clear. Our community's mission was never about one charismatic leader delivering miracles. It was about companies, workers, families, all of us, shouldering hope as one. The *Ripple of Hope* speech reframed how my community viewed my leadership. I was not promising to be a hero. I was asking each of them to become one. To be the ripple. To be the voice. There was one line I wrote that meant more to me than most, adapted from Kennedy but shaped by Myanmar's reality:

"And I believe that in this generation in Myanmar, those with the courage to enter the moral conflict will find themselves companions in this American business community."

That was the heart of the speech. It was not just about ideals. It was about belonging. I wanted people to know that moral courage would not leave them isolated. That in this Chamber, in this fragile but determined community, there were others ready to stand beside them, and at the top of that list was me, their president. In a country where speaking truth often meant risking everything, I wanted that line to feel like a hand reaching out in the dark.

In hindsight, maybe it was more than that. Maybe it was my first attempt to reach Act Three of my leadership doctrine, where belief is no longer only personal, but collective. Where the flicker of light in the darkness is not just your own, but something you pass forward, one ripple at a time.

I closed the speech with a truth that stripped philosophy down to practice:

"During this time of great despair and conflict, the greatest compassion we can give to the people of this country is to give them a job."

There was a pause. Then applause, but it was not cheerful. It was quiet, solemn, and reflective, the kind that comes when something hits too close to home. In that moment, many realized we were not just struggling. We were drowning. Yet that recognition brought not only sorrow, but a strange kind of hope. If we were going under, we were going under together.

Looking back, I can see exactly how that moment changed me. It was not about my voice being heard. It was about empowering others to speak and building a movement around conscience and moral courage.

Standing in that ballroom at the Novotel Yangon, I was no longer just Adam, the President of AMCHAM Myanmar. I had become part of something larger than myself. A story of moral courage. A story of a voice of hope.

By then, something had shifted. I had established myself as a skilled orator within the community. People were no longer attending events out of obligation or curiosity. They were coming because they wanted to listen. Events were filling up. Guests were becoming members. Members were upgrading to corporate partnerships, paying more to place their logos on our flags and banners. Behavior had changed.

The *Ripple of Hope* event itself was marketed simply as a briefing, a report back from Washington, an update on accreditation. But by that point, the speech was no longer incidental. It had become the main event. People understood that when they came to an AMCHAM gathering, they would hear a thoughtful, well-prepared, forward-looking address about the community's future and how change could be built, not wished into existence.

People did step up. They volunteered. They asked to be involved. Not everyone followed through as they imagined or as I expected, but that, too, was part of the process. Wanting to belong is not the same as being willing to do the work. Leadership means living with that tension and continuing anyway.

The Inaugural Address was about breaking the silence. *The July Fourth Address* was about rallying a community. *The Ripple of Hope Speech* marked the wake-up moment. It was somber, grounded in harsh reality, yet still inspiring. The speeches did not replace the work. They set the stage for Act Three and gave people something to believe in.

And with that, the ripples began.

THE RIPPLE OF HOPE SPEECH

Distinguished guests, ladies, and gentlemen,

I once thought I could push this community and our cause for substantial change by my very own will. I was able to convince myself that this country's enormous array of ills was not beyond my vision or control.

I believe there was pride in this thought, even arrogance, but what I have also found from this is experience and truth.

And perhaps we all can now see this truth, even if only for a time, that this community and those who work for us are not simply our employees but our people; that they too share with us the same array of ills; that they seek, as we do, nothing but the chance for their communities and children to live out their lives with both purpose and happiness.

Surely, this common goal can begin to teach us something.

Surely, we can learn that this goal cannot be achieved by the likes of a few, let alone one.

And surely, we can begin to work a little harder to bind together our time and resources in pursuit of this common goal.

The answer is to rely on moral courage.

We cannot create change successfully if those among us continue to cling to a present that is already dying, who prefer the illusion of security and short-term financial success to the realities that are coming for our people's future.

This is an extremely cruel world we live in now, and this generation in Myanmar, both in our community and throughout the country, has had thrust upon it a greater burden of responsibility than any generation that has come before us.

So yes, I now believe there is nothing one man or one woman can do against the enormous array of this country's ills.

While it is true that many of the world's great achievements and great problems were solved by the work of a single individual, few of us will change history alone, few of us will achieve the greatness of the likes of a 32-year-old Thomas Jefferson, who famously proclaimed that 'all men are created equal.'

These individuals changed the world on their own, but so can we all, together, with the work of our own hands; we save one job, we create one job. We can act selflessly to change a small portion of events that we control, and in the total of those acts, we can define this generation in Myanmar.

A great American hero once told my people that 'Each time a man stands up for an ideal, or acts to improve the lot of others, or strikes out against injustice, he sends forth a tiny ripple of hope.'

If this capsule of my people's history can teach us anything, it is that our selfless acts from this community, to collectively change what is present in front of us, can send out ripples that will build a current that can crash through any challenges we face domestically and any resistance we face abroad.

It is unfortunate that for many of us, there is still the temptation to follow the easy paths of financial success and personal ambition so graciously accepted among those who do not adhere to sanctions and our business ethics. But that is not the path Myanmar has marked out for our community.

Moral courage remains the one essential, the vital quality for those who seek to change this country's vast array of ills. And I believe that in this generation in Myanmar, those with the courage to enter the moral conflict will find themselves companions in this American business community.

All of us will ultimately be judged in the years to come, and we will surely judge ourselves at the end of our time on this earth, on the effort we have contributed to building a new society here in Myanmar, and to the extent to which our ideals and ethics have helped shape this country's new future.

I have now come to realize that this country's future lies well beyond my vision, but it is not completely beyond our community's control.

In any event, this is the legacy we will leave behind.

I spoke a lot about legacy the last time we met, but perhaps I was wrong about our legacy.

Our legacy does not need to be idealized or enlarged by certificates of accreditation or awards and trophies. Perhaps my legacy and yours can simply be known as being joined together, hand in hand; to be remembered simply as good and decent people: who saw war and tried to survive it, saw poverty, and tried to heal it, saw many great wrongs and tried to right them.

And for all of us who still love this country, I pray that we can continue to find the moral courage to shape this country's future.

As I've said many times to many of you individually

As I've said many times to this community as a whole

As I've said many times now, both here and abroad

During this time of great despair and conflict, the greatest compassion we can give to the people of this country is to give them a job.

Thank you.

INTERLUDE ONE

THE SANCTIONED AND THE STARVING

This interlude chapter is the why behind my story, behind my community's story, behind my people's story. And one day in the future, when the sun finally rises on a peaceful Myanmar, this is the story my people will tell.

Imagine you have a retired grandmother in Kansas receiving a text message about a "delinquent water bill." She taps the link, panics, and by the next morning, $2,000 has evaporated from her account. The scammer wasn't in Kansas. He wasn't even in the United States. He was inside a locked compound on Myanmar's lawless frontier, where since 2022, trafficked workers, militias, and criminal syndicates have turned a civil war into a global fraud factory.

Your imaginary grandmother is far from alone.

Between 2022 and 2025, people around the world lost hundreds of billions to scams originating in Myanmar's borderlands. Romance schemes, crypto traps, fake investment pitches, bargain-bin Rolex offers, all flowing out of a collapsed country most Americans couldn't find on a map.

Here is the uncomfortable truth Washington still avoids: The scam epidemic hitting American households did not happen simply because Myanmar collapsed; it happened because, after the collapse, the West ensured no one inside the country had the ability to stand it back up.

And this is where Washington enters the story.

To understand why my community was pushed to the brink, we must confront policies made not in Nay Pyi Taw or Beijing, but in Washington, DC. Since the 1990s, America's policy toward Myanmar has been driven less by conditions on the ground than by activist fervor and the Washington ecosystem built around it. Even those closest to Myanmar's democracy movement warned against isolation. Ma Thanegi, who campaigned for democracy at Daw Aung San Suu Kyi's side before her arrest in 1989 and endured three years in Yangon's infamous Insein Prison until 1992, rejected sanctions early and unequivocally. Writing in 1998, she argued that isolation was not a solution but a cause of Myanmar's decline. In her essay, "The Burmese Fairy Tale," she wrote:

> Burma (Myanmar) has many problems, largely the result of almost 30 years of isolationism. More isolation won't fix the problems and sanctions push us backwards, not forward. We need jobs, we need to modernize. We need to be a part of the world.

She was right then, and she is right now.

By cutting off trade, capital, and financial access, Washington's embargoes didn't punish generals, they punished ordinary people. They strangled technology, erased jobs, and handed the military a convenient scapegoat for decades of failure. The National League for Democracy (NLD) was the central civilian-led political party behind Myanmar's pro-democracy cause, led by Daw Aung San Suu Kyi after winning an overwhelming electoral mandate in 2015, and ultimately displaced when the Tatmadaw seized power in the February 1, 2021 coup.

The then Biden administration snapped back to Washington's oldest Myanmar reflex: isolation. It engaged neither the ethnic armed groups controlling the borderlands where scam centers thrived nor the Tatmadaw. As a result, there were no joint investigations, no intelligence coordination, and no pursuit of arrests or extraditions for the criminals draining US bank accounts. For nearly four years, President Biden and his government ignored the very actors who could have shared seized evidence that might have helped Western law enforcement agencies disrupt the scam networks before they globalized. That cooperation never came.

Instead, Western nations' policies severed Myanmar's formal financial system entirely, leaving the only cash still moving out of the country overwhelmingly criminal: scam center loot funneled through the black markets. The Biden administration approach focused almost entirely on restoring democracy through sanctions and barely at all on protecting Americans from the criminals exploiting the chaos.

Beijing, on the other hand, chose a very different path. Beginning in late 2023, China allowed ethnic armed groups along its border to launch a major military offensive against the Tatmadaw. The true purpose of this green light was not peace, but a crackdown on scam centers, as Chinese citizens had long been their primary victims. The contrast was stark. Chinese pressure produced raids, arrests, and real action. Washington issued statements and sanctions, and its citizens continue to be scammed.

Western governments followed the Biden administration's lead, responding with the same recycled foreign policy script that has failed Myanmar for decades. Their "maximum pressure on the Tatmadaw" strategy did not weaken criminals; it weakened the state, driving Myanmar deeper into isolation and amplifying the instability in which criminal syndicates thrive, all while plunging the country into a darker abyss of violence. Isolation neither restored democracy nor stopped the killing.

Which brings us to the core of my community's crisis.

Myanmar didn't merely become unstable; it became sanctioned, starving, and structurally incapable of policing criminal networks because of internal conflict and misguided decisions made in faraway capitals by people who never once set foot in the country. All of it traces back to two torches Western policymakers lit:

Torch 1: The "Sanctions-as-Press-Release" Playbook: Western governments, led by the US, rolled out punitive measures with the nuance of a Facebook post, crippling entire sectors without providing any guidance for legitimate business to continue. Compliance teams worldwide chose the simplest path: divest from the country.

Torch 2: Financial Action Task Force (FATF) Blacklist: Once Myanmar was blacklisted by FATF, global banks had their excuse to cut ties altogether. No courtroom. No explanation. Just silence and frozen wires.

These two torches punished the Tatmadaw, yes, but they also, incinerated the formal economy, gutted businesses, erased jobs, and hollowed out communities, making Myanmar "high-risk" for American business investors.

Picture Wall Street, the City of London, and Singapore's Marina Bay as one giant, velvet-roped nightclub. The bouncers are the banks. The dress code? "Low risk only."

Then Myanmar shows up post-coup in rumpled clothes, flip-flops, and flagged as "high risk." At first, the bouncers just frown. By 2022, they weren't just turning Myanmar away, they were slamming the doors, pulling the fire alarms, and lighting up a neon sign that screamed: Myanmar: Keep out.

That's de-risking in action, driven by sanctions and the FATF blacklist.

WHAT IN THE HELL IS FATF AND WHY DOES IT TERRIFY BANKS?

Ninety-nine percent of readers will never have heard of FATF, yet it may already rule your financial life. FATF is the global hall monitor of money: armed with a title, immense self-importance, and the belief that compliance memos defeat corruption. Based in Paris, naturally, this bureaucratic juggernaut brands itself as an "international standard-setting body" for anti-money laundering, counterterrorism financing, and proliferation controls.

In plain English: FATF writes rules no one voted on, enforces nothing directly, and expects every bank on earth to act as its unpaid security guard or face the consequences.

The method is simple: fear.

The tactic: peer pressure.

The unspoken motto: We don't freeze your account; we just make sure someone else does.

FATF doesn't need to kick down doors or freeze accounts itself. Once a country lands on its "blacklist," the banks do the work automatically. Transfers are rejected without explanation. Accounts are frozen without apology. The lucky few payments that squeeze through are condemned to the financial equivalent of purgatory: "enhanced due diligence." A polite term for months of unanswered emails, while some banker in Frankfurt demands your utility bill from 1997.

Need to wire money to pay your workers' salaries, import rice, or settle an outstanding invoice? The bank says, "No." Your only path left to survive is "hundi." Informal networks, underground cash channels, the very black-market system FATF claims to be dismantling. There is no other option.

And here's the punchline: Those black markets are often enabled, or outright run, by the same dictators and cronies Western governments claim to punish through sanctions and FATF. Shutting down legitimate financial channels doesn't starve tyrants. It feeds them. The underground economy thrives, and the cash flows uninterrupted straight into the hands of the powerful.

Meanwhile, humanitarian aid organizations, the real, ground-level non-governmental organizations (NGOs), are forced to use hundi or, worse, smuggle duffel bags of cash into the country like narcos just to buy antibiotics for a rural clinic. That's where we are: global charities laundering pocket change just to send paracetamol to a village.

FATF is a task force that claims to fight dirty money by criminalizing clean money, then acts shocked when the only road left is dirty. By severing Myanmar from the formal financial system, FATF did not stop illicit flows; it supercharged them. Scam center cash that once might have been flagged by banks moved through informal channels before disappearing into layered transactions across crypto exchanges and fintech platforms worldwide. This is precisely the kind of untraceable ecosystem FATF claims it exists to prevent. In Myanmar, FATF became the trigger for global disengagement, isolating the country financially from the rest of the world.

THE POLICY OF MAXIMUM PRESSURE: SANCTION AND FORGET

So how did sanctions become the great paradox of Myanmar policy, meant to hurt the powerful but devastate the powerless? The answer is simple. Instead of learning from decades of failure, the Biden administration repeated it. A 1990s sanctions manual was dusted off, coated in moral outrage, and packaged with a press release masquerading as strategy. Under pressure from activists and policy entrepreneurs, sanctions were wielded like a hammer against a glass house, shattering what little stability remained, while China quietly picked up the deed.

Take, for instance, the activist campaigns that from day one targeted MOGE, the Myanmar Oil and Gas Enterprise. State-owned enterprises like MOGE are how governments capture profits from foreign companies extracting national resources. After the coup, the Tatmadaw assumed control of the state and, with it, MOGE.

To the activists across Western capitals, sanctioning MOGE became the supposed "silver bullet" to drain the generals' revenue and end the war.

The reality was the opposite.

When the European Union granted those demands in 2022, France's TotalEnergies exited the Yadana gas field. Its divested shares were contractually redistributed to the remaining partners, meaning the Tatmadaw received them at no cost. MOGE's stake jumped from 15 percent to 21.8 percent without spending a dollar. Chevron followed, announcing its intent to exit while spending more than a year trying to sell its 41.1 percent stake to Thailand's state-owned oil company, PTT Exploration and Production Public Company Limited (PTTEP).

PTTEP waited them out.

Then, in December 2023, the United States imposed non-blocking sanctions on MOGE, an act of foreign policy so counterintuitive it bordered on parody. Chevron grasped the implications immediately. With no viable buyers left, the company walked away on April 9, 2024. Once again, the activist-led divestment strategy worked its magic. MOGE's stake ballooned to 37 percent, handing the Tatmadaw even greater control over one of the country's most valuable revenue streams. Sanctions meant to starve the generals instead gave them an economic lifeline.

This is what happens when policy is shaped by activist group chats, third-tier think tanks, and short-term optics rather than strategy. A smarter approach was obvious: force Chevron to hold the shares, allow pipeline revenues to decline naturally, block dividend flows, and exit only when the asset was truly worthless. Instead, Washington sanctioned, Chevron fled, and the Tatmadaw was gifted free shares once again.

The farce did not end there. Activists reacted with genuine surprise when they realized they had strengthened the very institution they claimed to oppose. In a haze of performative regret, they floated ideas like placing shares in escrow, ignoring that both TotalEnergies and Chevron had already exited, since ultimate authority over MOGE's shareholding rested with the Tatmadaw anyway. By then, every major Western company tied to MOGE was gone, leaving no one left to pressure. Yet activists clung to the fantasy that severing MOGE revenues would collapse the Tatmadaw and end the war. By then, concern for the people of Myanmar had given way to spite and vengeance, repackaged as policy.

And at the center of this misguided gospel stood its chief evangelist: Dr. Sean Turnell, better known as "Professor Sanctions."

Once an economic advisor to Aung San Suu Kyi and later imprisoned by the Tatmadaw, Dr. Steve Turnell has since emerged as the high priest of Western activist orthodoxy. He now seems to play the role of policy pope for a movement more interested in punishment than progress. In early 2025, Turnell sought to pressure the incoming Trump administration into "getting tougher" on Myanmar with a report that landed with all the subtlety of a drone strike, *The Military, Money, and Myanmar: Breaking the Nexus*. His prescription was simple: sanction everything. MOGE, the Central Bank, private banks. If it breathes, blacklist it.

That same absolutist logic assumes the MOGE "silver bullet" would work a second time, through full-blocking sanctions meant to cut off all US-dollar energy payments, including those from Thailand and China. Yet this plan ignores a basic reality. Thailand derives more than half of its natural gas from Myanmar, supplied through PTTEP-operated pipelines running directly to the Thai border. Fully blocking MOGE would be little more than an inconvenience for the generals, who would simply receive payments in Chinese yuan instead of dollars. For Thailand, however, it would gut the energy grid, effectively telling Bangkok, "Hey, sorry about the lights going out, but we're really trying to teach Myanmar a lesson." China would step in immediately with financing and energy deals, absorbing both revenue and influence, while Thailand would be left exposed or forced to accommodate Beijing. Either outcome would be a disaster for American interests in the region.

Then came Turnell's 2025 obsession with Myanmar's banking system. His plan calls for cutting off all the country's banks from the Society for Worldwide Interbank Financial Telecommunications (SWIFT), effectively isolating the entire sector. He goes further, advocating blanket sanctions against the Central Bank of Myanmar and all private banks. The problem is simple: Most Myanmar citizens still rely on these institutions to survive. Severing them even further from the global financial system would not drain the Tatmadaw's war chest; it would push ordinary people into the hundi system, recreating the same black-market dynamics the FATF naughty list imposed on Myanmar in the first place.

Let me explain what this paradox looked like with a real example: agriculture.

Myanmar's agriculture sector, roughly 30 percent of the country's GDP, was steadily strangled in the years following the coup by FATF blacklisting and US-led sanctions. Before blacklisting, fertilizer importers could place orders with overseas suppliers and pay through Myanmar's banks. Bureaucratic? Yes, but it worked. After the de-risking of Myanmar's banks, the system froze. Importers were forced to rely on middlemen brokers in places like Singapore, Bangkok, or Dubai, who could receive payments and move funds on Myanmar's behalf.

Between broker fees, currency losses, and increased risk, agriculture members within AMCHAM estimated these detours added $8 to $16 per metric ton of fertilizer. With Myanmar importing about 1.5 million metric tons in 2023, that translated into roughly $12M to $24M in additional annual costs. Those costs were absorbed by poor farmers, who paid higher prices and competed for reduced supplies, as importers simply stopped importing fertilizer rather than risk guaranteed losses.

It got worse. These broker-based supply chains offered no protection. No bank guarantees. No safety nets. If a broker disappeared or delivered substandard product, there was no recourse. In some cases, fertilizer routed through these channels was so poor in quality it was likely repackaged product from Iran. This was the paradox of US policy: in attempting to stop illicit trade, it pushed Myanmar's farmers toward the very Iranian regime it claimed to be isolating.

Ordinary workers and migrant families were not spared either. More than a million Burmese worked abroad, mostly in Thailand and Malaysia, sending money home to support their families. Before, they could remit funds through formal banking channels at reasonable cost. After blacklisting, banks treated Myanmar like plutonium. Transfers were blocked, delayed, or hit with outrageous fees by hawala-style middlemen. Families that once received $200 now saw half, if they were lucky. The rest disappeared into the black-market cash economy.

Yet even that was not enough. After choking off banking and migrant worker remittances, the activist vengeance tour shifted toward measures that would effectively trap ordinary people inside Myanmar.

Enter Tom Andrews, the United Nations Special Rapporteur on human rights in Myanmar. In his conference room paper, *Banking on the Death Trade: How Banks and Governments Enable the Military Junta in Myanmar*, formally submitted to the UN Human Rights Council on 26 June 2024, Andrews did not bother to ease into it. Right out of the gate, page three, he called on the international community to "sanction aviation fuel suppliers" in Myanmar.

Behold another "silver bullet" solution for Myanmar's endless civil war. Yet again, another elegant sanctions fantasy promising to collapse the Tatmadaw collides with reality, a recommendation that offers no explicit operational, humanitarian, or diplomatic exemptions for local fuel suppliers. None, and therein lies the problem Andrews never pauses to wrestle with:

What foreign airline would ever fly into Myanmar knowing it cannot refuel under any circumstances once it lands?

Once aviation fuel suppliers are sanctioned, there is no fuel to refuel aircraft in Myanmar. Civilian airlines are private companies. They do not debate moral nuance. They look at risk, insurance, and liability, and simply stop flying. Even worse, this would still not cut off aviation fuel from the Tatmadaw; China would see to that.

Enter Amnesty International. In January 2026, it published a bombshell investigation confirming what sanctions logic made inevitable: the Tatmadaw's jet fuel continued entering Myanmar through covert supply chains, with mounting evidence pointing to Iranian-linked shipments arriving in Yangon. To evade detection, Iranian-linked vessels disabled their Automatic Identification System (AIS), the transponder network used to track ships globally, while loading and unloading cargo. Satellite imagery, port records, and shipping data all told the same story. The fuel did not stop.

What Tom Andrews and the sanctions advocacy crowd still fail to answer is the most basic question of all: how are sanctions supposed to stop China? Even if every black-market or Iranian fuel shipment were somehow cut off, Beijing would never allow a Tatmadaw it arms and equips to be grounded. China sells the aircraft and ensures the fuel keeps flowing.

What makes Andrews' call even more astonishing is that he has probably never even set foot inside Myanmar since the coup in 2021. Instead, he has engaged the country from a safe distance, another policy pope in activist circles in Washington, DC, reportedly spinning tales of "on-the-ground" heroics while operating out of Bangkok or Chiang Mai.

This is the paradox of America's policy of "maximum pressure," driven by activists and academic do-gooders who never paid the cost of their own ideas. A policy that strangled legitimate business, strengthened black-market networks, and handed the Tatmadaw new economic lifelines.

I am not against sanctions. They can work, but only when paired with real engagement. Sanctions are a leverage tool, meant to extract something concrete from the sanctioned party.

You cannot pressure someone you refuse to speak to, and that was the fundamental flaw in the Biden administration's approach.

Most revealing was the failure to sanction the major armed groups that enable and at times run scam centers. Those actors were not designated until the Trump administration entered office in 2025. By the end of Biden's presidency, sanctions policy had become largely symbolic, even as scam centers actively robbed American households. The Trump administration shifted course, using sanctions as a homeland-security tool rather than a morality play, targeting transnational scam networks instead of trying to redesign Myanmar's internal politics from afar. This created immediate pressure on the Tatmadaw to dismantle the remaining scamming super-complexes, while signaling to Beijing that scam enforcement in Myanmar was no longer dictated by Chinese pressure alone.

Myanmar paid the price for the former approach, and so did the American homeland.

THE FOG MACHINE OF POLICY: USAID PURGATORY AND THE DIASPORA

The other pillar of the Biden administration's Myanmar policy was the United States Agency for International Development, USAID. From 2021 to 2024, the United States allocated more than $800 million in aid to Myanmar, almost all of it through USAID. Virtually none of it reached us inside the country.

Globally, USAID had long been criticized for becoming a fortress of the American contracting industrial complex. According to a Center for Global Development review, nearly 80 percent of USAID's funding went to US companies, while less than 10 percent ever reached local organizations in the countries it claimed to help. Its "localization" figures (confirmed by DevelopmentAid and USAID's Office of Inspector General) showed that in 2022 only $1.6B of $15.7B in total awards went directly to local entities, rising to just $2.1B of roughly $18B in 2024. The rest circulated through Washington's closed loop of Beltway contractors.

Three firms, Chemonics, DAI, and Tetra Tech, dominated that loop, repeatedly winning multibillion-dollar contracts to deliver the same generic programming across continents. Oversight reports from the USAID Inspector General revealed that about 30 percent of total project spending was absorbed by administrative overhead, while roughly 40 percent of grants achieved less than half of their intended results. Nowhere was the dysfunction clearer than in USAID's $10B Global Health Supply Chain project, led by Chemonics. Investigations by Reuters and Foreign Policy found that in its worst year, only 7 percent of medical shipments arrived on time, and in 2024 the company paid $3.1M to settle federal fraud allegations.

In practice, USAID became a scam for private-sector consultants. It was a chain of middlemen paying middlemen, enriching contractors while countries remained poor. That is exactly what I saw in Myanmar: staff and overhead based in Bangkok, not Yangon; contractors subcontracting repeatedly just to reach local NGOs. A system with no accountability, no visibility, and no meaningful impact on the ground.

Here is the part rarely acknowledged. Most of the so-called Myanmar-based or Myanmar-focused organizations receiving USAID funding were not operating inside Myanmar at all. They were based safely across the border in northern Thailand, clustered around the border town of Mae Sot, otherwise known as "Little Burma." It was a floating archipelago of expatriate activists, journalists, aid workers, and academic elites, all claiming to serve Myanmar without ever setting foot inside it. Endure five minutes talking with these freaks and you would think they were orchestrating covert operations from exile.

The truth was far less romantic. Thai military intelligence knew exactly who everyone was. None of it was covert; it was tolerated. Northern Thailand had become a staging ground for an entire aid theater, a managed ecosystem of undocumented migrants, underground networks, and foreign NGOs performing what amounted to geopolitical cosplay, aid edition, on Thai soil. Everyone knew what USAID had built there. No one said a word.

Even at the height of USAID's mission under the civilian-led NLD government from 2016 to 2020, American companies failed to win a single serious infrastructure bid. Roads, solar grids, energy projects, and development zones all went to China.

Where was this "goodwill" USAID was supposed to buy America? Where was this fabled soft power?

While Washington sent humanitarian funds wrapped in consultants and capacity-building manuals, Beijing signed Belt and Road deals and poured concrete. One side brought workshops. The other brought bulldozers. If the United States wants to compete with China in Asia, it cannot keep showing up with talking points and grant agreements. It needs machinery and real investment.

When President Trump and the Department of Government Efficiency (DOGE) office finally exposed this reality during USAID's dismantling, I had no sympathy. Millions of American taxpayer dollars had been funneled into aid programs that barely reached the country. Even today, I have not seen a clear accounting of where that money went or whether serious audits were ever conducted. While USAID staff and contractors circulated between hotel lobbies like the Athenee in Bangkok and "field visits" to Chiang Mai, China was methodically tightening its economic and political grip on Myanmar. That is USAID's legacy in Myanmar: an abyss of wasted tax dollars, missed opportunities, and PowerPoint slides.

Which brings us back to the activists.

At this point, it is hard to pretend they did not treat the livelihoods of Myanmar's people as expendable. They were willing to torch the entire house if it meant winning a moral argument about the purity of their boycott-and-sanctions doctrine in some Georgetown coffee shop. In the process, they reduced an entire country to a slogan, elevating one buzzword into a ritual, a kind of password for entry into their strange little Muppet club.

"Diaspora!"

In Washington, activists invoke that word like a sacrament. Whisper it over a lukewarm Americano and suddenly they are credentialed enough to design a Southeast Asia–focused microloan bank from a WeWork in Dupont Circle. For decades, *diaspora* was their magic summoning spell. Say it twice and you might land a USAID grant. Say it three times and you would get invited to speak at a UN-sponsored Rohingya event.

"Diaspora! Diaspora! Diaspora!"

Never mind whether the story was grounded in reality. Washington did not care. What mattered was whether the narrative could extract sympathy on Capitol Hill before the next symbolic sanctions vote.

Only after President Trump returned to office did these same activists suddenly "discover" scam centers. For more than three years, they dismissed transnational crime as inconvenient, off message to the approved "diaspora narrative." The moment scam syndicates became the only topic likely to secure a meeting with a Trump-era official, they became overnight experts. Suddenly everyone had "urgent intelligence" and a fresh moral crusade.

Funny how none of these America-hating liberal activists cared about President Trump's America First politics until their relevance depended on it. Yet even today, any time they need a panelist, a press quote, or an op-ed, the reflex is the same: "Get someone from the diaspora." That's right. Say it out loud one more time, readers:

"Diaspora! Diaspora! Diaspora!"

It's like the *Beetlejuice* summoning chant for Beltway freaks. Say it three times and a Brookings fellow appears with a George Soros grant, while Samantha Power's book descends like a haunted HR memo.

By late 2025, the diaspora disconnect reached peak absurdity. Rumors spread that the congressional hearing, *No Exit Strategy: Burma's Endless Crisis and America's Limited Options*, was a last-ditch activist blitz. The goal was simple: pressure the Trump White House through Congress to squeeze out one more round of sanctions, revive USAID-era funding pipelines, and reinstall *diaspora* as the guiding star of Myanmar policy. The strategy worked on several offices because staffers were deeply intertwined with the same activist networks, a dynamic that extended into Republican offices that helped organize the hearing.

Republican lawmakers shocked that Make America Great Again (MAGA) voters doubt their America First credentials should start by checking their own staff rooms. Their aides were parroting globalist talking points instead of defending US interests. The hearing itself exposed the rot. Not a single witness addressed the scam-center industry that flourished under Myanmar's post-coup instability, the one development directly threatening American households. It was Myanmar policy reduced to its annual fifteen-minute performance, delivered by think tank analysts masquerading as experts with "on-the-ground" insight that amounted to little more than talking points recycled from Washington's diaspora bubble.

"Diaspora" has become the fog machine of Washington's Myanmar policy. Pretty to watch. Useless in reality. While activists chant identity mantras, sanctions grind real livelihoods into dust. They don't work and never will. They fed the Tatmadaw, handed China the keys, and crushed the very people they claimed to protect. That failure demands clarity, not more moral theater.

You want a real plan for Myanmar?

End policy-by-echo-chamber and say publicly that responsible businesses feeding the people of Myanmar should stay. More importantly, America must accept the hard truth about Myanmar. Re-engagement will not restore democracy or dislodge China overnight. It will not be clean or satisfying. But it will defend concrete US interests, dismantle scam centers that robbed billions from Americans, and maybe, just maybe, give the people of a broken country a chance at peace.

America may have lost Myanmar to China, but she doesn't need to abandon her.

THIS IS THE WHY

Now, I know what you're thinking. *Adam, are you really going to just blame America for Myanmar's collapse?* Of course not.

But let's be clear: This isn't a book about the civil war that has raged in Myanmar since 1948. This isn't the story of the long, violent legacy of the Tatmadaw or the ethnic rebels they've fought, and sometimes quietly enabled, through decades of conflict. Nor is it the story of how China, playing both arsonist and firefighter, has armed the Tatmadaw to the teeth while birthing and nurturing the very ethnic armies they battle. I will write that book one day. It deserves its own reckoning, but this isn't that book.

This is the story of AMCHAM Myanmar.

I wrote this interlude chapter not out of bitterness, but as a witness. This chapter, this interlude, was always about something else. It was about naming the real culprits behind the siege on my community, not just the coup-makers in Nay Pyi Taw, but the policymakers in Washington, the Beltway consultants working from hotel desks in Bangkok, and the activist-industrial complex that made it fashionable to paint us as enemies. This was the battlefield we inherited, crafted by the Biden administration's foreign policy, powered by a morality cartel, and enforced by a sanctions regime that punished my people while empowering their oppressors.

The legacy of President Joseph Biden's foreign policy in Myanmar is not measured in grand speeches or aid pledges. It is measured in empty factories, shuttered classrooms, and the haunted eyes of children whose parents struggle to feed them each night. In the wreckage left behind, I set out to build something different, a legacy of quiet resilience and moral courage for my community, whose strength endured even as Western policies sanctioned and starved them.

This is the why and this is the who.

Why our community was demonized.

Why businesses fled.

Why even today, my people's voices are still being choked out by bureaucrats and activist bullhorns thousands of miles away.

This interlude chapter is the why behind my story, behind my community's story, behind my people's story. And one day in the future, when the sun finally rises on a peaceful Myanmar, this is the story my people will tell.

We stayed. We fought with no applause. We kept the lights on because no one else would.

SURVIVE THE CRUCIBLE

HOLD THE LINE. FACE THE FIRE.

What separates the strong from the weak isn't perfection; it's how they respond when the plan falls apart. You don't abandon the plan, you adapt it. You don't panic, you pivot. You take what you've built and use it to fight forward.

Every leader who puts in the work earns a season of grace. You show up. You deliver. You lead with purpose, and for a while, the people let you lead without distraction.

That's the honeymoon phase. That's Act One. Usually defined by your first three to six months, in my case, six. Yet, leadership doesn't end with the first milestone, because the moment you set a precedent, the moment you show what's possible, the real test begins.

Not everyone applauds when you succeed. Some grow resentful. Some feel threatened. And some don't just doubt your leadership, they try to tear it down. That's exactly what happened next.

Even after we secured accreditation...even after we stood shoulder to shoulder with hundreds of jubilant members at our events...the fire still came.

A former board member, unwilling to accept the Board's direction or the membership's will, challenged my leadership. He didn't just dissent. He turned it into a constitutional crisis. Legal threats. Lawsuits. He sued me. He sued the Board. Three governors resigned, some out of fear, others because they didn't want the drama. After all, this was a volunteer role. So how do you lead through that?

You do what you've always done. You do the work. You face the crisis without flinching. And you stay true to the vision that brought you here in the first place.

That's the crucible.

Every leader, no matter how prepared, eventually faces a moment they didn't plan for.

And what separates the strong from the weak isn't perfection; it's how they respond when the plan falls apart. You don't abandon the plan, you adapt it. You don't panic, you pivot. You take what you've built and use it to fight forward, but this internal challenge of a constitutional crisis and a disgraced board member was just one front.

Outside the Chamber, a different kind of pressure was rising. Since the 2021 coup, Myanmar's business community had been trapped between two forces: a military government on one side and a growing activist movement on the other. For many activists abroad, the message was simple: if you had not shut down your business, you had betrayed the people. We were shamed publicly with threats, accusations, and name-calling. I was targeted. My members were targeted. For years. It did not matter how carefully we walked the line, how constructive or quiet we were, how many jobs we saved or families we fed. We were all targets.

This is the crucible.

The strong do not break; they push forward. Because through it all, the work never stops. And in my second act, there was only one way forward:

Keep building.

That was the answer. We stayed the course and built what we always intended. We launched our most ambitious milestone yet: the Social Impact Donation Fund. One hundred thousand dollars in 100 days.

Bold. Unrealistic. On paper, impossible. But we did it, and we did it with a smile. And the activists, the ones who shamed us and dragged our names through the town squares of social media, said nothing. If saving jobs and protecting livelihoods were not enough, we did something they could not imagine doing.

We raised $100,000 for real social impact projects across underdeveloped communities in Myanmar.

We launched the campaign. We rallied the membership. We hit our goal and silenced the critics.

Yet even after proving what was possible at home, the broader policy landscape remained frozen in silence, apathy, and paralysis.

I returned to Washington, DC, for the second year in a row and found the same indifference. Not just toward the people of Myanmar, but toward my people, our business community, on the brink of collapse. The Biden administration, never missing a chance to underwhelm, resigned itself to sanctions and silence, leaving us stranded in the same failed US–Burma policy vacuum.

Back home, Myanmar's economy was suffocating under regulatory overreach. Imports stalled. Factories closed. The currency drifted in constant disarray.

So, I made a decision.

If no one would speak for us, we would speak for ourselves.

I had already reactivated our committees back in Act One, reminding members they still had a voice. Now, we turned those whispers into a chorus. We gave them a platform to speak plainly about real issues: financial constraints, currency chaos, trade bottlenecks, reputational risk. We gave them a safe space. We gave them a voice. Then we made those voices endure.

That work became the "AMCHAM Policy Paper," an honest, independent message grounded in member reality, not outsider assumptions. The paper, and the process behind it, laid the early foundation for what would later become the US–Burma Economic Forum in Act Three.

It reinforced a simple truth of leadership: You don't always need to build something new to solve a new problem. Sometimes the answer is already in your hands. We took what we had built, our committees, and pivoted them into a new solution. Lead with discipline through crisis, and you often emerge stronger than when you began.

But here's what no one tells you.

At some point, the metrics stop mattering. The data. The dashboards. The progress reports. You can show all of it and still feel morale draining from the room. That's when leadership has to change. You can't always lead with a firm hand. You can't always lead by being the smartest person present.

My role was no longer to prove leadership. It was to embody it.

That shift came into focus at the launch of the philanthropy fund with the *Awakening Speech*, a moment we'll return to later. Its impact was immediate. That single speech raised more than 30 percent of our fundraising goal in one night, but it marked something else entirely:

A turning point for the Chamber, and for me.

I stopped trying to explain every decision. I stopped trying to solve every problem. I stopped trying to earn my role through milestones alone. I stopped caring about those who would doubt me and only seek to tear me down, because my people didn't care about any of that. They needed courage. They needed strength. They needed to believe in themselves again.

That was the real transformation of my leadership's crucible in Act Two. Not the crisis itself, but what it revealed. That leadership is never just about doing the work. It's about becoming the kind of leader your people can believe in, especially when nothing makes sense anymore. That's how we survived the crucible. Not just with milestones, but with meaning and that's how we began the quiet shift into Act Three.

Not with another campaign, but with something harder to measure, a gift that only comes when a leader lays bare his heart and soul to his people:

You give them something to believe in.

A VOICE CHALLENGED

THE GOVERNORS DINNER SPEECH 2023

Success invites challenge. Challenge
incites conflict. Your crucible begins.

*That's the irony of leadership in crisis. You can spend
weeks preparing a speech about community pride,
economic opportunity, and national transformation,
pouring your heart into every word, only to walk
offstage knowing you'll have to confront a constitutional
crisis the very next morning. A crisis conjured not
from principle, but from ambition. Manufactured
from thin air to challenge your authority at the very
moment your leadership was meant to be affirmed.*

There was no confetti. No fireworks. No orchestra swelling in the background. Just a freshly printed accreditation certificate displayed in glass, a trophy that meant everything. That night on October 27, 2023, we didn't gather in black ties or ball gowns.

We gathered to celebrate our community...finally.

Nearly 200 of us. Suit jackets pressed, business cards in hand, conversations flowing. For the first time since the coup, AMCHAM Myanmar held a proper event to celebrate our community. Not a rally. Not a briefing. Not a panel. An event to finally celebrate out loud.

This alone was radical. For more than two years, even the idea of gathering in one room, in semi-formal wear, with purpose and pride, felt foreign, if not dangerous. We had cancelled the annual black-tie gala during the 2020 pandemic and quietly shelved it altogether after the coup. The reputational and security risks were too great, the mood too fractured.

Yet now, something had shifted. We had momentum and it was time, not just to celebrate, but to help our people start believing again...or at least begin that journey towards belief.

Just a few months earlier, I had given *The July Fourth Address* at one of the largest Independence Day events in our Chamber's history, with 255 attendees, a raucous celebration of survival. Yet that survival did not just happen. It was made possible by the members who stayed.

Many small and medium-sized enterprises had shut down or exited the country altogether. Those who remained, especially large employers and multinational players, did more than hold the line. They elevated their commitment through visibility, not just words. They contributed more financially to the Chamber by deepening that commitment.

That moment marked the rise of corporate partnerships for our Chamber. Unlike regular memberships, corporate partners do not just join; they stake their brand with the Chamber. Their logos appeared on our flag, our banners, our website, and at every event. It was belief, printed in bold and flown high.

Accreditation had finally come through from the US Chamber

of Commerce. The elusive goal we had chased since our break from AMCHAM Thailand in 2017 was no longer a hope. It was framed on the wall.

I wanted our community to see it that night, and more than that, to feel what it meant. From that point on the more we showed the work, the more that commitment to endure grew. That was the turning point. Our total membership numbers may have dipped, but our backbone strengthened. The night of an event called the Governors Dinner was meant to honor exactly that: the ones who stayed, who stood tall, and who were proud to have their logos next to ours.

This is how the Governors Dinner was reborn.

Now we had done a humble version of it the year prior; quiet, intimate, barely 50 people. This version of the Governors Dinner was different. This was a declaration. Not just that we were still standing, but that we were building something lasting. The concept was straightforward: a formal networking night for our business community to look its best, speak honestly, with a formal ceremony to celebrate what we had all accomplished together. Not as survivors, but as leaders.

Yet I knew from the beginning, I couldn't let that moment become a passive victory lap. The worst thing that could happen to a community like ours was to treat accreditation as the finish line. It wasn't, it was only the beginning. So, when I set out to write the speech for that night, I anchored it around a single, repeating question, drawing on my love of anaphora in speechcraft:

"Is this a time for American commerce?"

It wasn't just a catchy line. It was the question, one I'd been asked point-blank in Washington, DC, and one that lingered in every investor's hesitation, every policymaker's raised eyebrow, every journalist's cynical write-up. In essence: *Is there still a place for American business in Myanmar?*

The answer, of course, was yes, but it couldn't be a blind or naïve yes. It had to be a defiant, reasoned, resolute yes.

That was why I pivoted the tone in the final stretch of the speech.

Celebration alone wasn't enough, not that night, not in Myanmar, not with what we were up against. I turned to the audience and asked them something harder:

"What do they really know about our community?"

What did the world that so casually judged us actually understand about what we had endured, what we had survived, what we were still navigating just to be in that room together?

That question only worked because, for the first time, I made the speech personal. I revealed my own story, not just as president, but as a person. I spoke about arriving in this country with no money, drowning in student debt, angry at the world. I shared how Myanmar had given me what no other place had: a second chance. A reason to believe. That vulnerability wasn't performative; it was a challenge. I wanted them to know I wasn't above the struggle. I was forged by it, too.

That's when I gave them the line that would echo through every crisis we faced as a community, including the earthquake that would strike nearly a year and a half later:

"It's the hardest challenges that make the toughest people. Add sacrifice, dedication, and the will to survive that runs generations deep in every last one of our people. That's who we are. That is our story."

The message landed. The room felt united, but even as the speech ended, something deeper, and far more personal, was unraveling.

WHAT THEY DIDN'T SEE

What almost no one in that ballroom knew was what had unfolded just hours before. While tables were being arranged upstairs, I was downstairs in a board meeting fighting for the Chamber's very survival. Four months into my presidency, my treasurer and I had flagged a looming crisis: We were on track to run out of cash by the end of March. The end of March was the end of memberships, every year renewals for membership go out at the beginning of March and last till the end of June. The issue was that the Chamber gets the majority of its revenue and in turn, cash in the March to April timeframe. We were not going to last that long.

It wasn't that we were spending irresponsibly. On paper, the Profit and Loss (P&L) Statement looked fine. The problem was cash flow. The previous Board, led by my predecessor, had approved a draft budget that failed to account for Myanmar's fractured financial reality. We were operating in an economy with three exchange rates, a central bank that set conversion rules, and a growing gap between local-currency revenue and US-dollar expenses.

One clear example was staff compensation. The executive director leads the team that runs the Chamber's day-to-day operations. It is a full-time paid position accountable to the Board. Yet AMCHAM had been paying its executive director in US dollars while collecting nearly all membership dues in Myanmar kyat. The result was a monthly exchange loss that was simply unsustainable.

So, we made hard calls. We transitioned all chamber expenses, starting with the staff salaries, into local currency. We slashed unnecessary accounting and advisory fees that had been bleeding us (in some months, we'd paid $1,000–$2,000 for little more than a Profit and Loss Statement download). We stopped hosting every board meeting, which came at a cost at the AMCHAM office, and definitely stopped subsidizing the catered breakfast sandwiches that the previous president loved. Every expense that didn't serve our core mission had to go. We also phased out the complacency of "hybrid" meetings: if you were on the Board, you were expected to show up and take ownership, plain and simple. These decisions restored a measure of fiscal discipline that we desperately needed.

Not everyone appreciated these moves. One board member in particular, formerly the secretary of the previous Board and then serving as my vice president, began challenging nearly every decision. He appeared to place responsibility everywhere but on himself, pointing fingers at the treasurer and at me, framing the crisis as a failure of current leadership rather than the legacy he had witnessed. From my perspective, it felt less like problem-solving and more like an effort to dominate the room, including reprimanding our full-time AMCHAM staff and derailing the discussion with pedantic arguments.

What he failed to grasp is something every effective leader eventually learns: In a volunteer-run community, authority only exists if people choose to give it. Nobody follows a bully. He lost the room that day. The votes passed, the cost-cutting measures and the plan to raise membership fees in the coming year were approved. On that tense afternoon, we narrowly pulled the Chamber back from the edge of financial collapse.

Then the fallout came.

Following the vote, that same board member moved to reassert control by triggering a constitutional crisis, the first in the Chamber's history. He suddenly insisted that the Board of Governors' terms expired in January, not July. His argument rested on a prior bylaw amendment that aligned the fiscal year with the Myanmar government calendar (April 1), which he now claimed had inadvertently shortened the Board's term. It was a technical oversight by the previous Board, one on which he had served not only as secretary but seemingly as the former president's de facto legal advisor. He had never raised the issue before. Its timing made his intent clear; this was his power play.

The deeper issue wasn't just this legal technicality; it was the old culture of the Board that had allowed it to fester. This board member had long thrived on a perpetual obsession with the bylaws, poring over technicalities to divert meetings away from substantive issues. Under the previous president, such idiosyncrasies were indulged. Together, they would often hash out decisions in private, behind closed doors, even before the executive committee or full Board convened. Governance by backroom consensus became the norm. Bylaws were wielded less as safeguards of good governance and more as tools of influence disguised as procedure. Accountability suffered in that shadowy "boys' club" of theirs.

When I assumed leadership, I brought that era to an end. No more arcane debates to stall action. No more procedural detours. No more special arrangements or perpetual hybrid attendance for a favored few. Every governor would show up, in person, and do the work in full view. Transparency and accountability were no longer optional. I dismantled the system that had protected the politics of silence.

It seemed he did not simply resent the change; he saw it as a threat.

It did not escape me that this board member, my own vice president, had not attended a single board meeting in person or any in-person event in the six months since the AGM at which he had nominated me as president. His absence was not merely symbolic. It spoke volumes about how he viewed leadership responsibilities.

So, when I mandated that board members physically attend milestone events like the Governors Dinner, it was not just a procedural adjustment. For me, it was a line drawn in the sand. Rather than meet it, he chose retaliation, in what appeared to be an effort to challenge a leadership structure he could no longer quietly control. And this challenge came just hours before a night when we had something far more important to celebrate.

That's the irony of leadership in crisis. You can spend weeks preparing a speech about community pride, economic opportunity, and national transformation, pouring your heart into every word, only to walk offstage knowing you'll have to confront a constitutional crisis the very next morning. A crisis conjured not from principle, but from ambition. Manufactured from thin air to challenge your authority at the very moment your leadership was meant to be affirmed.

Yet, that paradox is what made the 2023 Governors Dinner so powerful, not just the speech, but the event itself. It wasn't just a celebration; it was a turning point. Accreditation had given us recognition. Now we had to prove we were worthy of it. Even as one board member tried to divide us, even as trust frayed behind closed doors, we had to show our community that we would not let dysfunction derail our path toward belief.

Yet, moving forward, the politics inside our boardroom would begin to look a lot like the politics that our community was facing outside of the country. The very questions I was preparing to ask on stage that night had already been answered in real time by what we had done that day.

"Why am I still here? Why are we still here?"

We proved that the hardest challenges forge the strongest people. It was through sacrifice, commitment, and a Board willing to shoulder the burden, not run from it, that we met our challenge head-on that day. Our leadership held firm. Our community endured.

That night, this speech, this moment, was a microcosm of everything I had come to believe about leadership: that it is not defined by the ease of your victories, but by how you carry the weight of struggle. Even with one man's selfish belligerence trying to derail everything we had built, even with the weight of a crisis just resolved and a new one already forming, I stood tall. I raised my voice, and I delivered this speech without a flinch.

For it was a time for American commerce, not because it was easy, but because it was necessary.

And in that moment, we had chosen to lead it, fully aware that even greater tests awaited us beyond the celebratory spotlight of that wonderful October night.

THE GOVERNORS DINNER SPEECH 2023

Distinguished guests, excellencies, ladies, and gentlemen,

This is a day of celebration, a celebration of opportunity.

We stand here in the name of the American Chamber of Commerce.

We stand here with their blessing as their accreditation shines here before us: "Is this a time for American commerce?"

A question that was asked of me, as I stood before the Chamber in Washington, DC.

"Is this really a time for American commerce to be recognized and celebrated in Myanmar?"

I did not hesitate with my answer, because at the heart of American commerce is the belief that the individual, the child of God, has the inherent right to economic opportunity and that all societies and states exist for that individual's opportunity.

"Is this a time for American commerce?"

Investment into Myanmar will go ahead, whether America joins in it or not. But for this community and The Flag of American Commerce we bear so close to hearts, we not only mean to be a part of it, but we also mean to lead it. So, when the eyes of the world turn to Myanmar, from Yangon to states and regions beyond, they will see our flag and this community, whose leadership in technology and industry, whose hopes for peace and security in this country, whose obligations to our people as well as their communities, require us to solve the challenges of this country, and not just for wealthy, not just for those of a particular religion, not just for those of a particular ethnicity, but for all people in Myanmar.

"Is this a time for American commerce?"

More than any time in our community's history, our future is not of our own choosing. We did not expect, nor invite, a confrontation with challenges we face today. Yet the true measure of our community's strength is how we rose to master these challenges when they did arrive.

Eighteen companies have elevated their membership to the corporate partner level since 2020. From 23 members in 2019, to 41 members as of today; that's a 78 percent increase in corporate partnerships. Many of those corporate partners sit here tonight, who after hearing the heartbreak of COVID, a coup and conflict, ran towards adversity to ensure that this community not only survived but endured.

Ran towards adversity.

"Is this a time for American commerce?" They asked me, and I acknowledged, that the real intent behind their question, behind their doubts, disbelief, is the why: Why am I still here? Why are we still here? Are we truly making a difference given the risks, given the challenges?

I think back to when I took a chance on Myanmar. Another unemployed combat veteran of America, drowned in student debt, furious with the world. But this country took a chance on me, embraced me, empowered me with the opportunity to rise above my challenges. In my darkest time, this country was my great hope, and I believe that American commerce must continue to be a guiding beacon of hope for this country in its darkest hours.

So, I had a question for them. What do they know about our community? What does this community that's been to hell and back know about American commerce? Well, I'll tell ya. More than most other countries.

You see, it's the hardest challenges that make the toughest people.

Add sacrifice, and dedication, and the will to survive that runs generations deep in every last one of our people. That's who we are. That is our story.

Now it's probably not the one that they've been hearing in the media, the story being told by folks who have never even been here, who don't know what we are capable of, because when it comes to American commerce it is not as much about the country it is in, more so than who it is helping.

So yeah, we're part of the America Chamber now. But this isn't Washington, DC, or Europe, or Japan, or Malaysia, or Thailand. And we're certainly not Singapore.

This is Myanmar. And this is a time for American commerce.

A VOICE TESTED

THE "14 MONTHS" SPEECH

Face the fire. Embrace the crucible.
Prove you're worthy.

From that point forward, AMCHAM Myanmar would no longer be defined by backroom agendas and meetings, it would be defined by the will of its members. Power had returned to where it belonged, in the hands of our people. The crisis, disruptive as it was, revealed our strength. We didn't avoid conflict. We confronted it together and in doing so, we proved that unity and shared values outweighed any one individual's ambition.

The Chamber's constitutional crisis began quietly with a technical question. Yet it quickly escalated into one of the most consequential internal battles in AMCHAM Myanmar's history. It started during a Board of Governors (BOG) meeting held just before the 2023 Governors Dinner, a meeting that, in hindsight, cast a long shadow over everything that followed. The question was simple:

"Had the Board's term already ended?"

This question was raised by a single board member, stemming from his review of our constitution. He argued that a previous decision to align our bylaws with the Myanmar calendar year meant our board terms had already expired. At first glance, it appeared to be a good-faith concern. However, the timing, and the tone, told a different story.

Rather than a sincere exercise in oversight, his move felt like a gambit, an attempt to assert relevance and claw back influence at a time when his standing had grown weaker. During that October board meeting, his behavior became increasingly erratic and combative, leaving many governors frustrated, and some even alarmed.

By the time we reached our December board meeting, the frustration that had quietly built behind closed doors finally boiled over. We had convened our usual monthly meeting, but this time, the gloves came off.

One by one, governors began to speak out.

Their objections went far beyond constitutional technicalities. In challenging his approach, their responses revealed what I had long suspected. This was not a constitutional crisis. It was a power play. A calculated attempt to destabilize the Board and seize influence through chaos. Just as clearly, the governors made this known that day through their positions and, more importantly, where their trust lay.

With the president. With me.

In a time of national political instability, economic collapse, and institutional fragility, their response spoke volumes. The overwhelming support they gave me reflected what they believed effective leadership looked like in a crisis. Several noted, without needing to say more, that I had carried the lion's share of the Chamber's advocacy work. I had drafted every letter to policymakers, engaged officials directly, and funded my own trips to Washington.

That same support also revealed how they viewed the leadership dynamics on the Board. Their confidence rested on presence, contribution, and accountability. By those measures, the contrast was apparent. Until the Governors Dinner, the vice president had not attended a single in-person chamber event. He had not contributed meaningfully to AMCHAM's survival. He offered no financial support for advocacy trips, sponsored no events, recruited no members, and gave nothing beyond his own dues.

It was through that lens that his proposals to resolve the constitutional crisis at that December 2023 board meeting were received. When he put forward ideas to address the dispute, none received a vote. Not because of their technical merit, but because governors recognized the risk they posed. In their view, adopting such measures would have alienated the very members we were struggling to retain. No one's business was thriving. The economy remained in crisis. Members were already stretched thin, financially and emotionally. At that moment, the Board, and in turn the Chamber, did not need disruption. It needed steadiness.

What we needed most was not just revenue. We needed belief. We needed members to see their higher calling and recommit not just with their dues, but with their hearts. To stand up and say, *Yes, this Chamber still matters*. This community still matters. His proposals would never inspire that. If anything, they would have driven members away at the very moment we needed them to stay. Adopting his plan might have checked a procedural box, but it would have set the Chamber on fire. So, I offered the Board a different path.

Let the people decide.

Our constitution did include a clause empowering the Board to extend its own term. Yet if invoked unilaterally, without member consent, would have looked and felt like a raw power grab. This was never just a legal question. It was a question of legitimacy. I was determined that any resolution would happen in the open, with the members themselves as arbiters of our fate.

When the Board voted, he abstained. Every other governor present voted in favor of my proposal:

Call for an Extraordinary General Meeting (EGM), gather the full membership, and ask them to vote on whether to extend the Board's term to resolve the funding crisis. We would put our fate not in the hands of legal interpretation, but in the hands of those we served, the members.

Yet, when the moment came to resolve the crisis through a board vote, the very board member who had ignited this crisis and pushed us to the brink chose, at that critical moment, to abstain from voting on any proposed solution.

He didn't vote against it. He didn't dare oppose a democratic process outright. Yet he wouldn't support it either, not even voting in favor of his own earlier proposals when offered the chance. In the end, he simply sat on his hands.

This was *his* crisis, his challenge to the Chamber's governance. But when it came time to solve it, he refused to take a stand.

A week later, when the official minutes of the meeting were circulated, they included the frank comments governors had made toward him that day. His absenteeism. His failure to contribute as vice president. His unwillingness to lead when it mattered most. The truth was laid out, in black and white.

He took offense.

Just days before Christmas 2023, less than a week after that meeting, he formally resigned from the Board by email. Rather than stay and see the crisis through, he chose to walk away.

His resignation should have marked the end of the drama. In truth, it was only the prelude.

THE EGM

The Extraordinary General Meeting (EGM) convened in late January 2024. The question we put before the membership was simple:

Should the current Board of Governors' term be extended until May 2025 to realign elections with the fiscal year and ensure continuity during an ongoing national crisis?

It was a straightforward fix to an awkward technical issue and yet, it was also far more than that. This was a turning point, not just legally, but philosophically. We weren't asking members for a procedural adjustment. We were asking for something deeper:

Trust.

Trust in the Board to lead during one of the most fragile moments in our history.

Trust in the Chamber's direction.

Trust in the president.

Trust in me.

That day, I delivered what would come to be known as the *14 Months* speech. It wasn't a legal brief. It wasn't a recitation of bylaws or constitutional precedent. It was a moment of truth, a show of strength and a reaffirmation of our community's will to survive together.

I did not shy away from the controversy that had brought us there. I leaned into it. Because leadership isn't about hiding behind lawyers or clinging to technicalities. It's about standing before the people and being accountable to them, no matter how uncomfortable that may be. So, I stood there, in front of the membership, and said clearly:

"We have serious problems, and we need serious people in charge to solve them."

By this point in my tenure, I had begun to find my voice as a speaker.

Repetition had become one of my signature devices, a rhetorical tool I used deliberately in every major address. I had come to learn that when used with intention, a simple repeated phrase could become a kind of drumbeat, echoing long after the speech itself had ended.

In this speech, that idea crystallized around a single phrase: "Fourteen months."

WHY 14 MONTHS?

It was the amount of time the membership was being asked to grant us, and, in truth, to grant *me*. It was the runway members would vote on that day, carrying us from that moment of crisis to the next scheduled elections in May 2025.

What many didn't know, however, was that I was the only board member facing immediate term limits under our constitution. Had the extension failed, I would have been automatically "termed out" at the end of that month, forced to step down and barred from running again for at least a year.

In other words, our now former board member's sudden, convenient reinterpretation of the rules wasn't just about governance. It was a calculated maneuver to remove me from the presidency, and to block me from any future leadership at all.

He saw the extension as my lifeline, and he intended to cut it.

What he didn't understand was that I had no intention of making this about me.

I refused to stoop to that level, to frame this vote as a referendum on my presidency or plead for my own survival. That kind of desperation would have only validated the very tactics I was standing against.

Instead, I knew I needed to give the members something greater to believe in. Something that transcended the noise of internal politics. I needed to deliver a speech, not to save myself, but to inspire my people. To remind them what was at stake, not for me, but for the Chamber itself.

The "14 Months" Speech itself unfolded in three deliberate phases, each with its own tone, cadence, and purpose.

PHASE ONE: COUNTDOWN TO "14 MONTHS."

I opened by hammering that phrase into the hearts and minds of everyone in the room out of responsibility. This wasn't a threat. It was a transfer of ownership. I was telling them the clock was ticking, for all of us, to prepare the Chamber's future before it was too late. I wanted every person listening to feel the urgency.

Fourteen months to strengthen the Chamber.

Fourteen months to prepare new leaders.

Fourteen months to prove our model of resilience could endure.

Each repetition built momentum:

"Fourteen months...14 months...14 months..."

I said it again and again, drawing their focus into the narrow window of opportunity we had. I closed that phase with a direct appeal:

"But you need 14 months and your work begins today."

PHASE TWO: SHIFT FROM COUNTDOWN TO CONFRONTATION

Time wasn't our only challenge; credibility was on the line. I laid out some hard truths. Our community had grown complacent. Committees were stagnating. Engagement was fading.

I warned. Advocacy was "falling short of expectations." The problem wasn't numbers, it was silence. Too few voices. Too little candor, and so I called on everyone in that room to speak up, to help us fight back.

Then I turned to the broader threat: the suffocating regulations imposed by the military government, policies choking our businesses. I was blunt. No leadership, mine or anyone else's, could make up for a community that chose to stay silent.

I didn't hold back.

I called out the government's overregulation and announced our boldest advocacy campaign yet: a full-on push to unlock critical imports, member by member, meeting by meeting, whatever it took. None of it would matter if the Chamber didn't survive.

We were entering renewal season. Dues were increasing, and I didn't sugarcoat it. This wasn't just a financial ask; it was a moral one. A stronger AMCHAM meant a stronger future, but only if our members had the courage to invest in that future now, when it mattered most.

PHASE THREE: INSPIRE

I didn't want to end the speech dwelling on problems or critiques. I wanted to lift the room, to give them something to believe in. So, I turned to storytelling.

I told the story of one of our own board members, someone who embodied the very best of our community. Dr. Greg Hedger. A lifelong educator. A fellow governor. A man who had poured his heart into helping young Myanmar students. I spoke of the scholarship fund he helped build for underprivileged youth, and how, together, our Chamber had channeled over $30,000 toward that cause. Through Greg's example, I wanted everyone in that room to see what was possible, even in crisis.

Even now, amid the turmoil, we were capable of acts of generosity. We were capable of building something bigger than ourselves. We just had to decide to do it. As I spoke, I gestured to Greg in the audience, acknowledging him by name. The room responded. You could feel it shift. With that momentum behind me, I broadened the lens.

I reminded everyone that heroes were not out there somewhere; they were us.

Our businesses were keeping hope alive in Myanmar, providing livelihoods across the country, from the heart of Yangon to far-flung corners racked by conflict. Then, in a final tonal shift, I reached beyond my usual rhetorical influences from the Kennedys, and invoked a voice I had rarely drawn upon in the prior AMCHAM speeches:

President Ronald Reagan.

Specifically, I found myself channeling Reagan's first inaugural address in 1981.

Reagan's cadence, his clarity, and his resolute tone guided my final words, imbuing them with a familiar spirit of determined hope. That moment marked a turning point in my speechwriting journey, stylistically and, in some ways, spiritually. I wrote the climax of this speech to connect our little gathering in Yangon to something much larger:

The American spirit that now lives abroad.

ORACLE OF OBSTRUCTION

Yet just as I wrapped up and the room seemed to breathe in the message, something absurd unfolded. Our hard-won clarity was nearly hijacked, literally, by a performance so ridiculous it could've won *Best Supporting Actor in a Fictional Crisis* at t*he Annual Gala of Manufactured Outrage.*

I opened the floor for EGM proceedings, and a proxy voter sent by our former board member sprang into action. Too fragile to face the membership himself, my now resigned former vice president had dispatched this chosen disruptor to do it for him. I've since dubbed this individual the "Oracle of Obstruction," the kind of guy you find at every expat happy hour, waxing poetically about constitutional law, while conveniently forgetting he lives in Myanmar, not the halls of the Supreme Court.

He wasted no time launching into a dramatic monologue: the EGM was invalid, the Constitution violated, the vote illegitimate, the Board corrupt. If you didn't know better, you'd think he was exposing a global scandal, not objecting to a term extension vote at a chamber meeting. Still, we addressed his claims, one by one. I even handed the mic to several members who calmly, firmly rebutted his points.

Yet, no logic, no process, no peer input could stop him. He kept interrupting, standing, waving, refusing to yield, as if auditioning for a courtroom drama. By then, it was clear: This wasn't about principles. It was about disruption. He wanted to derail the vote, to deny the membership their voice. That realization angered many in the room, members who had shown up to be heard, not silenced by someone else's tantrum. So, I turned to the membership and, keeping my tone as calm as I could manage, asked them directly:

"Shall we remove him?"

Hands shot up across the room in an emphatic yes. The people had spoken. I had all the justification I needed to eject him and move on, and yet I chose a different path. Perhaps out of principle. Perhaps to prove a point. I motioned for him to stay. I would allow even this disruptive voice to cast a vote, because true leadership means protecting the process, especially when someone tries to turn it into theater.

I refused to let our hard-fought commitment to member participation be tarnished by stooping to his level. If he wanted to vote "no," then so be it. We would absorb the dissent and show the strength of an overwhelming consensus beside it. With order restored, I called for the vote. Ballots were cast and counted in short order. The result was decisive:

All but one member voted to extend the Board's term till May 30, 2025.

Naturally, the lone dissenting vote came from our intrepid disrupter, still red-faced and fuming, still huffing and puffing as if he might somehow blow AMCHAM's house down with sheer indignation. He did not succeed. Despite the theatrics, our constitutional crisis was resolved and what we gained went far beyond a technical fix. That day marked the restoration of something deeper:

Faith in our democratic process.

From that point forward, AMCHAM Myanmar would no longer be defined by backroom agendas and meetings, it would be defined by the will of its members. Power had returned to where it belonged, in the hands of our people. The crisis, disruptive as it was, revealed our strength. We didn't avoid conflict. We confronted it together and in doing so, we proved that unity and shared values outweighed any one individual's ambition.

The vote to extend our term became more than a procedural vote; it became a vote of confidence. By giving us those "14 months," the members gave themselves a chance to carry forward the mission. A voice challenged had become a voice tested.

I had been measured in the fire and had been found worthy. What emerged was something far more powerful than survival:

A renewed mandate to keep fighting for a brighter tomorrow.

THE "14 MONTHS" SPEECH

Ladies and gentlemen,

Fourteen months.

Fourteen months till the election committee will gather nominations to elect a new Board of 11 governors by the end of May 2025.

Fourteen months for those of you who have board aspirations, and for the few who are shying away from it, to answer this higher calling of service.

Fourteen months for you to showcase your selfless commitment to our Chamber's cause and to the future of this American business community.

Fourteen months to make this next election one of the most successful and competitive cycles of new governors to take this leadership mantle.

As I said when I first took the presidency, competition is the foundation of greatness, the essence of industry, the spirit of American commerce; the more members we have applying to be governors in the coming years, the greater we become.

But you need 14 months, and your work begins today.

Committee attendance is falling short, and we have observed that the advocacy from those committees is also falling short of expectations. This advocacy shortfall is not due to membership attendance, but a lack of communication from members at these meetings.

We want your ideas. It's up to you as industry experts to tell AMCHAM what issues you are facing as a business. This makes you and your voice an invaluable ally. AMCHAM has and will continue to use your voice to advocate change both here and abroad...and that continues today.

Tomorrow morning, I am sending to UMFCCI a call-to-action

letter for the government's consideration to support the bulk approval of AMCHAM members' import quotas for the remainder of 2024. It is, by far, the most aggressive effort we have made to ensure our members keep jobs alive. The other issue is the regulation surrounding foreign currency for said imports. As of today, they need to throw it out, the current framework is not working. You cannot address import challenges without getting rid of the current regulations importers face to acquire the US dollar. I consider both these issues one and the same and I will go member to member, hold countless meetings, and do whatever it takes, and we are going to get the imports.

We have serious problems, and we need serious people in charge to solve them, because this is what we do here at the American Chamber of Commerce.

Yet none of this can happen if this Chamber does not survive financially. We need your renewal this coming month. AMCHAM must increase its corporate partner memberships; if you are not a corporate partner, upgrade to Silver. If you are Silver, upgrade to Gold, if you are Gold upgrade to Platinum, and if you are Platinum, renew your Platinum membership, and I hope to see you fighting your Platinum peers to sponsor every event we have.

A stronger AMCHAM means a stronger future for all of us, and we have seen glimpses of this bright future already. As our executive director said, in just nine months since this Board convened, this community has secured accomplishments both domestically and abroad.

If we look to the answer as to why, in such a short time, we achieved so much and helped keep jobs alive, it was because here in this community, we unleashed the freedom of individuals to speak up about their issues. Freedom to express your concerns has been more available in our Chamber, in our committees, than in any other place in this country.

The price for this freedom at times has been high for this Chamber and its leadership, but as your president, it is my top priority that this Chamber will always be your haven for free speech and thought.

As to those who say that we are not on the right path, to those who say there are no positives in our community, to those who say this Chamber lacks the leadership and heroes this country needs, I say to you, you just don't know where to look.

The commercial prowess of this community with its thousands by thousands of employed Myanmar nationals; each one of your employees adds up to only a tiny fraction of the value chain you bring to this country. Each one of you who stands here with me today is a testament to the kind of hero I speak of.

Your business brings value to people in places like Yangon, the Ayeyarwady, from Bago to the road to Mandalay, and halfway around the country in places like Sittwe, Myitkyina, Taunggyi, Dawei, and across a thousand conflict-riddled farmlands of a place called the Bamar heartland.

With us today is one such hero of our community, Dr. Greg Hedger, a governor, an educator, and a leader of young minds. His school's partnership with AMCHAM to ensure underprivileged youth can receive higher education is just the tip of his selflessness. Through his leadership, his organization has brought charity to an orphanage, an animal shelter, and rural schools around the country; his pledge to selflessness is a model to the pledge that we must ask of ourselves as a community: We must work, we must sacrifice, we must endure. And as Greg has done, you must continue to cheerfully fight every day, as if the solution to our entire struggle resides with you and you alone. Thank you, Greg.

We must realize that the crisis we are facing today does not require the kind of ultimate sacrifice that so many civilians in Myanmar have paid since 2021. That is not what is needed from us. It does require, however, our best effort, and our willingness to believe in ourselves and to believe in our capacity to perform great deeds; to believe that together, we can and will resolve the problems which now confront us.

Let this be understood by those who doubt our agenda today, who doubt the future of American business in this country, who doubt that this country has a future. We will remind these doubters today and onwards that the everlasting hope of economic opportunity for the people of this country is the highest aspiration of this Chamber. And as your president I will continue to negotiate for it, sacrifice for it, and together, we will not stop fighting for it. Let's vote!

INTERLUDE TWO

THE MIRACLES OF BELIEF

God had never asked me to fix Myanmar. He had asked me to follow Him. I was not sent to Myanmar to suffer for my sins, but to serve His will. Not to live in the darkness of His shadow, but to be His light in the darkness.

The story of why I came to Myanmar has already been told, but how I actually left for Myanmar is a different story. That story does not begin with a vision. Or a dream. Or even a plan. It begins with a laptop case. A laptop case that vanished into the night.

It was August 2013, the night of my departure for Thailand. I was 27 years old, a US Marine Corps veteran who had come home from war to find no direction, no steady job, and a growing sense of anger with nowhere to go. I had nothing left to lose except a one-way economy ticket out of LAX.

Before heading to the airport, my mom and I made one last stop. A final goodbye at my grandmother's house in Los Angeles. My family lived in Riverside, California, but my grandmother still lived in the same house where she had raised her children, including my mother, and helped raise her grandchildren, including me. That house had always been a place of warmth and tradition. Even today, every time I leave America for a long journey abroad, I still stop by to see her before I go. On that night, though, it was not just tradition. It was something deeper. A sendoff filled with unspoken worry and love.

My grandmother. My mom. My aunts. My cousins. All gathered in that house. All of them knew what this trip meant. They knew I had been struggling, unemployed, uncertain, just trying to hold on. This trip was not about chasing opportunity. It was about survival. I needed to go, not because I had it all figured out, but because I did not. I needed to find something. Anything.

After the laughs, the hugs, the goodbyes, my mom and I returned to the car and drove toward LAX. I had only one carry-on bag, but inside that bag was everything: my passport, cash, laptop, and all my school documents. All of it was zipped securely into a small laptop case I was obsessive about guarding.

As we pulled onto the 605 freeway, something gnawed at me. Call it instinct. Call it anxiety. Call it a whisper from above. Something made me unzip the bag and reach inside, just to check. Just to be sure.

Nothing.

The laptop case was gone. My heart stopped. My chest tightened. My breath disappeared. No passport. No cash. No laptop.

I panicked. I told my mom to turn around. We raced back through the Los Angeles night toward my grandmother's house. I tore through every room, every bag, every cushion, every chair. I moved in a haze, driven by desperation, almost outside myself. My mom would later describe it as madness. It was, because it felt like this was the final blow, the world telling me:

"No, you don't get a second chance."

Everything hinged on that laptop case. The flight. The journey. The escape. The hope. If I did not get on that plane, everything might collapse. Given the state I was in, I did not know if I would ever find the courage to try again. Eventually, I slumped against the wall of my grandmother's living room in silence. I could not speak. I could not scream. I could not cry. I felt like a dead man.

My family stood around me, helpless. No one knew what to do. I did not either. How could I have been so careless? How could I lose the one thing that meant everything? After everything I had been through, was this how my journey would end? Before it even began?

My mom watched as her son, her baby boy, sat broken and defeated in the very house where she had been raised. She said nothing, but I saw it in her eyes. Sorrow. Helplessness. And then something else.

Resolve.

She turned to my aunt and said, "Let's take one more drive around the neighborhood." It made no sense. It was late. It was dark. We had already searched the house, the car, and the street. Still, they left.

You need to understand something about my mother. After my grandmother, she has the deepest faith in God of anyone I have ever known. It is not loud or performative. It is instinctual. Quiet. Intimate. Unshakable. In that moment, with her son collapsed in despair, she turned to something higher. She later told me she felt something.

A whisper. A nudge. A voice.

She did not know why she turned down that particular street. It was not logical. It was not mapped out. She just knew. It was a road she had driven thousands of times. The street she had grown up on. Where she rode bikes as a little girl, walked to school, played with cousins, and later drove her own children every Thanksgiving and Christmas. Yet this time, something inside her told her to go.

Then, beneath the soft yellow glow of a streetlight, she saw it.

The brakes slammed. She jumped out of the car. In the middle of Los Angeles Street, a busy two-way road feeding into the 605 freeway where cars and commercial trucks barrel through at all hours of the day was the laptop case. It was just sitting there. Untouched. Undisturbed. She opened it. Inside was everything. My passport. My documents. My cash. My laptop. Not a single item was missing. Not a scratch. Not even dirt on the case. It was as if someone, or some power, had placed it gently there, exactly where she would find it. Waiting.

Waiting for faith to arrive.

What my mother must have felt in that moment, seeing the answer to her prayer lying in the middle of the street while knowing her son was sitting broken just blocks away. It must have been overwhelming. Yet I know what she believed. She believed it was a miracle, and she was right.

Back at my grandmother's house, I was still sitting silently against the wall when the door opened. My mom walked in, smiling and victorious, holding up the laptop case.

"It's a miracle!" she cried.

"A miracle!"

My grandmother, herself a woman of deep and unwavering faith, proclaimed the same. Their voices echoed through that little house, now filled not with despair, but with awe. I did not say a word. I was stunned. In minutes, I swung from hopelessness to disbelief to overwhelming gratitude. The same floor I thought I would never rise from now felt like the threshold of grace.

Yet there was no time to celebrate. I had less than two hours to make the flight, and LAX was nowhere near close. This was Los Angeles traffic, not divine teleportation. Still, somehow, we had a shot. My grandmother rushed over, stood above me, and without hesitation traced the sign of the cross on my forehead. Her hands were gentle and deliberate, blessing me one last time. Then we were off again.

My mom drove like a woman possessed, but this time it was not fear behind the wheel. It was faith. An unshakable certainty.

"This is meant to be," she kept repeating. "God wants you on that flight, Adam."

She was right.

She dropped me off at LAX, and I moved through the airport in a blur. I checked in, cleared security, and reached the gate with ten minutes to spare. The plane boarded. I sat in my scuffed economy seat. The laptop still worked. The passport was there. The cash was still in my pocket. Everything was there.

I was on my way to Thailand.

Somehow, by grace, not logic, the path had been made clear. I was being allowed to go. It was not because of problem solving. It was not grit. It was a mother's faith.

A mother who believed in her son when he no longer believed in himself.

A mother who placed her trust in a plan greater than either of them could understand.

A mother who heard a whisper from God and followed it.

Through my mother's faith and God's grace, that low point became the foundation of everything I would one day believe. That was the first miracle of my life. Not why I left. Not even where I went, but how I arrived there. Looking back now, I wonder if that was the point all along. If the first miracle was getting me onto that plane, the second miracle was what transformed me into a servant of God's plan.

A vessel of faith, built in exile, tempered in darkness, carried by belief.

FACING A RECKONING

To understand the second miracle, you need to understand what was happening behind the scenes in the American business community in Myanmar in the months that followed. What was unfolding across AMCHAM. What was happening inside my company. And what was quietly unraveling inside my own mind.

After the Extraordinary General Meeting in late January 2024, the one that extended our Board's term, things appeared to settle, at least on the surface. There was no public rupture. No explosion. Just a low murmur of discontent. When our Annual General Meeting arrived in May, we kept it modest and intentional. No stage. No speeches. No drama. A short online session, a routine embassy update, a financial report, and a reaffirmation of course.

Yet beneath that calm, pressure was building.

By mid-April, the legal threats began. They came from one person, that same former board member who had resigned and failed to derail the vote to extend our board terms. Formal legal notices started arriving, not just to me or the Board, but everywhere. To my company. To international business partners. To the US Chamber of Commerce in Washington. To anyone he thought might flinch.

The accusations were broad and relentless. Constitutional violations. Procedural fraud. Defamation. Anything that might delegitimize what we had built. One notice was sent directly to the legal inbox of my business partner's headquarters in Paris. Their response was immediate and blunt:

"Who is this person? And what is he talking about?"

To them, it was absurd. To me, it was corrosive. This was never really about legal risk. It was about reputation. Humiliation. A scorched-earth effort to tear down what he could no longer control.

His demand was born out of spite and aimed at destruction. He wanted the Board to call for elections to select a new Board. And yet, electing a new Board was never about governance. It was about erasing the vote of the people. My extension came from the membership alone. I was already term-limited and barred from running again. New elections meant only one outcome: my exit.

So, resign quietly, or be dragged through court.

At the same time, activist groups began to circle. Not yet openly targeting AMCHAM, but close enough to feel the heat. On another front, our Myanmar national members were already being harassed. Decent people, unsanctioned, targeted simply for continuing to operate businesses in Myanmar.

Meanwhile, every member was dealing with their own crisis. Import licenses stalled without explanation. Regulations multiplied. Entire factories hung in the balance. We intervened quietly where we could, behind the scenes, ministry by ministry, company by company, just to keep operations alive. Yet no matter how hard we worked, it was never enough, and it never stopped.

The pressure wasn't just external; it was personal.

Then two board members, both Myanmar nationals, resigned quietly. Not because they opposed the EGM. They had supported it. They voted for it, but they simply didn't want to be dragged through court. I understood their decision. I did not blame them. Still, it stung. We replaced them. Our morale held, but the internal toll was mounting.

What no one could see was what I carried behind the calm statements, the steady presence at board meetings, and the polite composure at member events. Yet, behind closed doors, I was also facing a reckoning about my own company. My multinational business partner since 2016 had been slowly looking to withdraw from Asia for years. After COVID-19, they never bothered sending anyone from their side back to the country. After selling off their other Asian assets, Myanmar was the last piece left. For them, it was too complicated, too isolated, too radioactive.

So, we entered quiet, civil discussions. There was no animosity, but there was finality. I told them directly, if you want out, name your price or divest. After months of negotiation, we reached a deal. I agreed to buy them out entirely, taking 100 percent ownership of the company I had built from scratch. This marked the moment I fully stepped into the role of founder and owner. There would be no fallback. No partners to blame. No safety net. This company was 100 percent mine now, for better or worse.

By the time the agreement was signed and the rebranding began, the pressure from all around me had already reached its peak. Activists. Lawyers. Regulators. Scrutiny from within and without. Our members were being labeled traitors. I was being slandered. Still, my leadership did not pause. All of it layered into something heavier than any single blow. For the first time, I began asking questions I had been avoiding.

"What were we actually changing? What was I changing?"

In the middle of all of this, I moved forward with one of our boldest initiatives in the Chamber's history. A philanthropic campaign with a single goal. To raise $100,000 in 100 days. The launch event date had been set long before the lawsuits and resignations: June 20, 2024. Locked in and unmovable.

What had once been planned as a simple event to raise money had now carried the full weight of everything we had endured. I knew I would have to speak. Not to welcome the crowd, but to lead them. To inspire them to donate to a cause they believed in. To donate because they believed in me. It would be my first public address since the EGM and everything that followed. This was not a moment for safe lines or easy applause. It demanded something deeper. The speech needed to reset the narrative. Restore belief. Turn silence into strength. It needed to remind people why AMCHAM still mattered.

In truth, I wasn't ready to give a speech, let alone write one.

Mentally, I was scattered. Emotionally, I was running on fumes. Physically, I was exhausted. The months leading up to that moment had been relentless. Holding the community together had consumed every ounce of energy I had left. I began to question my faith in God's plan, the same plan that had carried me years earlier, on the night faith put me on a plane and set this journey in motion. I was not rejecting that plan, but I was struggling to see it.

By May 2024, I was not hopeless. I was just unclear. There is a difference. Hope is what keeps you showing up. Clarity is what keeps you from burning out. By then, I had lost clarity. Inspiration felt impossible. I could not rally others until I found a way to restore it.

So, I made a choice. At the time, it felt like a retreat. In truth, it made everything else possible.

I took a holiday.

THE SECOND MIRACLE

For the first time in more than two years, I stepped away from work on May 26, 2024. Ten days. That was all I allowed myself. I booked a trip to Koh Phangan, Thailand, an island most people associate with full moon parties, cheap alcohol, and backpacker chaos. That was not where I was headed. I went to the west of the island, where the jungle meets the sea and the energy shifts. Yoga enclaves. Detox spas. Meditation retreats. A strange ecosystem of seekers and healers.

Not exactly my natural habitat.

I had a reason for going. An old friend named Warren. A decade earlier, we had bonded when we both arrived in Myanmar, two men with Afghanistan in our past, each still carrying that weight in very different ways. I wore the scars like a badge of honor. He chose a path of yoga and spiritual discipline. Over time, Koh Phangan became his sanctuary. When I told him everything, the legal threats, the activist campaigns, the institutional abandonment, he did not flinch. He listened, then said simply:

"Brother, you are not going to solve anything if you can't see straight. Come get your clarity back."

He was right.

I had not realized how deep I was in it until I finally stepped out of it. Months of giving everything I had. Fighting for members. Holding the Board together. Keeping the lights on.

And yet, all I could think about was the people who hated me. The ones who whispered. The ones who slandered. The ones I could not win over. The truth was, I had the Board's trust. I had the love of my community. The EGM had proven that. Still, I could not let go of the idea that not everyone loved me.

That was where I was broken. That was my flaw.

Not the pressure. Not the critics. It was the belief that if I worked hard enough, gave enough, loved deeply enough, everyone would support me. That is not leadership. That is delusion, and it was eating me alive.

As soon as I arrived on the island, the detox began. Seven days in total. Two days of fruit and raw vegetables, followed by five days with nothing but water. Warren assembled a small group of teachers and practitioners to help turn the trip into something more than rest. It became a mission to reclaim clarity. Most days were spent alone, walking, riding a motorbike through jungle roads, practicing yoga, doing breathwork, and submitting to treatments I would have laughed off just a few years earlier. Acupuncture. Herbal compresses. The whole kit. The only work permitted was dialing into AMCHAM's online AGM. Everything else was stripped away until only stillness remained. That was the point. I had come to Koh Phangan to bleed out the noise, drain the chaos, and reset my mind.

Then, on June 1, 2024, I almost lost my life.

That morning, deep into the fast and already physically depleted, I had a bodywork appointment at a small spa on the far side of the island. I took a motorbike, because in Koh Phangan there is no other way to get around. The treatment itself was gentle enough. Yet, afterward, something felt off. My body felt too light. My head was clouded. My balance was just slightly off. Still, I just wanted to return to the quiet little villa I'd rented by the beach. So, I kicked the engine to life and started the ride back.

That's when everything went sideways.

Maybe I hit the curve too fast. Maybe it was my depleted energy from the fasting. Maybe it was something else entirely. I do not remember much, only the moment my bike lost control and the pavement rushed toward me.

I skidded 20 feet across the road. The asphalt shredded my palms and scorched my legs. Somehow, still gripping the handlebars, I managed to push off at the last second, just before the bike slammed into the front steps of a Thai restaurant.

I was still standing.

The bike was upside down. The restaurant crowd froze. Then a swarm of yogis and shirtless hippies rushed out towards me, shouting,

"Oh, my goodness! Oh, my goodness! Are you okay? Are you okay?"

I was not sure. My palms were torn open. My legs were scraped. My toes were bloodied. Yet nothing was broken. No fractures. No torn ligaments. I was bruised and bleeding, but alive. As I stood there, dazed and shaking, one thought rang louder than the pain.

How did I survive that?

I should have been impaled. Flipped. Crushed. Thrown into a tree or into the restaurant of hippies standing in front of me. I was not.

I was still standing, feet planted on the hot asphalt, blood dripping from my palms, and all I could do was look up. Around me, the hippies and yogis shouted over one another, trying to help, trying to make sense of what they had just seen.

That's when I saw her out of the corner of my eye.

At the edge of the restaurant patio, a young woman stood from her table. Unlike the others, she did not rush. She moved calmly, almost serenely, weaving through the chaos with a single bottle of water in her hands. I told her I was fine. That I did not need anything. She said nothing. She simply handed me the bottle and softly whispered,

"It's for your wounds."

Then, without hesitation, she gently poured the water over my hands, washing away the dirt, gravel, and blood. She did not ask for thanks. She did not wait around. She turned and walked back into the restaurant. I never saw her again.

To this day, I believe she was an angel. Not a metaphor. A real one. I do not know her name. I do not remember her voice. Yet I will never forget her hands as she poured that bottle of water over mine, cleansing my wounds with quiet grace.

Eventually, I made my way back onto the motorbike, wrapped my palms with whatever cloth I could find, and rode to the nearest 7-Eleven. I bought gauze, antiseptic, tape, anything that might hold me together. From there, I rode back to the villa and stepped into the most excruciating shower of my life. Every wound burned. Every scrape screamed. I poured alcohol over my skin, biting down on a washcloth to keep from yelling.

It was only later, standing in front of the mirror, that I noticed something else. A wound on my ribcage, just beneath my right chest. I had not felt it during the crash. It must have come from the slide, the fabric rubbing against raw skin. At first, I assumed it was just another abrasion. The longer I stared, the more it felt like something else. Not a scrape. Not an accident. A mark. A message.

And then, almost as if to underline it, the island broke open.

A massive tropical storm swept across Koh Phangan. The wind howled. The windows shook. My friend Warren came over to check on me and began strapping down anything that might fly. The power went out across the island as I drifted in and out of sleep. Waves breached the pool deck. Fish from the sea flung themselves into the saltwater infinity pool outside my villa.

And yet, I was not afraid. I was not anxious. I felt something else entirely. Stillness.

It was in that stillness, my body broken while the storm raged outside, that I finally heard Him. God did not arrive with thunder or command. He came with clarity. A revelation, unmistakable and complete, of the path I had lost sight of. The road to who I was meant to become was not waiting beyond Myanmar. It had always run straight through it. I was not called to escape the chaos. I was called to walk through it. With faith, not fear. With purpose, not pride.

As I lay on the bed of that darkened villa, torn, aching, and wide awake, I saw it clearly for the first time in months. Faces came to me in flashes, uninvited yet unmistakable. Not of the critics or doubters, but the believers. My people. The ones who had stood by me from the beginning.

With them came a clarity I had not felt in a long time. The same clarity that had guided me when I first set foot in Myanmar, back when there was no roadmap, only conviction. Before the noise. Before the politics. Before the war. That clarity had once built something from nothing. Yet, somewhere along the way, I had lost it, buried beneath responsibility, distraction, and pride.

I had been trying to carry everything at once: the crisis, the Chamber, the members, and my own reputation. I was surviving my crucible of leadership, my Act Two. Yet the very fire that allowed me to survive that crucible also trapped me within it. Survival became the focus, and in doing so, it prevented me from seeing beyond it. That was the wall keeping me from reaching Act Three. It was not that I had lost my belief, but that my belief had become misguided. I believed that if I worked hard enough or gave enough of myself, I could somehow fix everything. That was never the assignment.

God had never asked me to fix Myanmar. He had asked me to follow Him. I was not sent to Myanmar to suffer for my sins, but to serve His will. Not to live in the darkness of His shadow, but to be His light in the darkness.

When I finally emerged from that slumber and stillness, I looked down at my hands, bandaged, raw, and trembling, and then at the wound on my ribcage. In that moment, a realization settled into my mind, and I thought of the Roman spear that struck beneath the ribcage of Christ. I was not comparing myself to Christ, and I knew better than to do so. Yet the symbolism was unmistakable. God had spared me that day, when I should have died. He had marked me not to punish me, but to awaken me. To remind me of the wounds borne through His Son's suffering. To remind me of the sacrifice Jesus Christ had made for all of us.

This was the second miracle of my life.

When the storm finally passed and the island fell quiet, I stepped onto the patio of that villa and stood there, letting the rainwater wash over my face. The bruises, the cuts, and the soreness in my limbs were still there, but the fog had lifted. And with my arms stretched toward the sky, I felt something I had not felt in a very long time.

Peace.

I had survived my crucible of leadership, my Act Two. I had endured the pressure, the attacks, the isolation, and the weight of responsibility. God had never stopped believing in me, even when I had stopped believing in myself. The path He had set before me had never disappeared. I had simply lost sight of it. With that realization came something deeper, the understanding that this suffering was not random, that it had meaning, and that a purpose was still unfolding.

Act Three had arrived.

Leadership was no longer about surviving the fire or proving my worth. It was about opening my heart again to the people I was called to lead, not by force and not by fear, but by belief.

As I limped back inside the villa, I opened my laptop and, with the battery fading, began to write my speech. The words came clearly and without hesitation. It was a declaration, an unapologetic call to break the silence and awaken belief. Belief in our Chamber. Belief in our community. Belief in ourselves.

And on June 20, 2024, those words would become more than a message. They would become a moment.

A moment in time that would come to be known as "The Awakening."

A VOICE AWAKENS

THE AWAKENING SPEECH

From strength, belief survives. From sacrifice, belief awakens.

What began as a speech to raise funds for philanthropy became a declaration of belief. No rehearsals. No gimmicks. Just my heart on the podium, my vision made flesh, my soul awakened.

On June 20, 2024, at the Park Royal Hotel in Yangon, my community gathered in person to launch the AMCHAM Myanmar Social Impact Donation Fund, which would later be known simply as the SID Fund. We called it "$100,000 in 100 Days." It may have sounded like a generic slogan, but it was far more than that. It was a declaration.

At a moment when most businesses were downsizing, fleeing, or retreating into silence, we chose a different path. We asked our members to give. Not for public relations. Not for optics, but for real impact. The SID Fund was a deliberate philanthropic initiative I spearheaded while still in my crucible of leadership. The Chamber was under pressure from every angle, yet I knew that regardless of the drama, this fund had to move forward.

The air that night still carried the weight of the previous months. The legal threats had not disappeared. Activist shaming campaigns had not faded. The gossip never stopped. No rational observer would have picked this moment to try something bold. And yet, that was precisely why it mattered.

The idea itself had been born over a year earlier in Bangkok, over coffee, during a brainstorming session between our then executive director and a small group of USAID officers posted there. By that point, most of USAID's Myanmar team had already relocated across the border. While our executive director would later leave AMCHAM, the concept she helped shape became her parting gift to our community, one last quiet act of belief in what this community could still achieve.

The idea was simple. Could the private sector lead a philanthropic fund? Could AMCHAM, with its network and credibility, serve as a bridge between donors and impact, channeling resources into communities that needed them most?

USAID agreed to partner with us. They had the systems, the contacts, and the infrastructure. Through them, we could access a vetted network of NGOs and civil society organizations, supported by monitoring and evaluation tools. We would bring the energy. They would help with the mechanics.

At first, it worked.

We moved quickly, built the framework, and scheduled the launch. Quietly, I hoped this might signal a new kind of collaboration, one where US government support reinforced private leadership rather than constrained it.

Then came the catch.

What began as a partnership gradually took on the tone of a purity test. USAID did not simply want to support the SID Fund. They wanted to control who was allowed to support it. Every AMCHAM member had already been screened against US sanctions lists, but that was not enough. They did not trust our standards and insisted on conducting their own version of due diligence.

This was not due diligence in any formal or professional sense. I say that as someone who conducts background checks and investigations for a living. What USAID pursued instead was ideological filtering, driven by optics rather than facts.

The core problem lay with certain local national staff at USAID, who operated less like development professionals and more like ideological gatekeepers, deciding which local organizations and individuals were deemed acceptable to participate in the humanitarian space. Quietly, through embassy channels, I was told that some of these staff members harbored deep hostility toward the private sector, toward AMCHAM, and toward me personally because of my insistence on moving the initiative forward without being "blessed" by an activist purity test. In practice, USAID's local national staff's loyalty appeared to rest less with development outcomes and more with activist networks they treated as untouchable authorities.

What followed was no longer surprising. USAID staff began combing through our members' social media accounts, primarily Facebook, and pressuring us to disinvite certain members who failed their version of "due diligence." Not for any wrongdoing, but for vague associations and allegations taken out of context. A group photo. A rumor. A comment thread accusing someone of having "close relationships" with the Tatmadaw. That alone was enough. I found the hypocrisy impossible to ignore. Individuals who not only bore no risk, but should have been helping us achieve our funding goal, were passing judgment on business leaders still operating on the ground. This was the reality of how USAID operated in Myanmar: transforming development work into a reputational tribunal where performative virtue mattered more than practical outcomes.

For me, this was the line they crossed.

I was not going to allow USAID, or any government agency, decide which of our members were morally acceptable enough to donate to a philanthropic fund. We were trying to raise $100,000 in 100 days during an economic collapse to help real people in real communities. We were not going to shame donors, and we were not going to let unelected local staff blacklist contributors based on gossip. This was our fund. If you were an AMCHAM member, you were welcome to donate. Period.

So, I pushed back. Not publicly. Not theatrically. Directly.

USAID never issued a statement or made a scene; they simply stepped away. Privately, I was told that the SID Fund would now proceed as an AMCHAM initiative, without USAID's public involvement. Their logo remained on the June 20 launch materials because everything had already been printed and published, but they avoided group photos and declined to take the stage. Instead, they had some senior diplomat from the US Embassy to read prepared remarks on their behalf. The message was clear.

This would be the last time USAID stood beside me, AMCHAM, or the SID Fund.

To their credit, they did not sabotage the effort. Several staff members who had supported the initiative from the beginning attended the event and continued to offer quiet guidance behind the scenes. Some local hires who were still working in Myanmar genuinely believed in what we were doing and provided informal feedback and insights.

Institutionally, however, USAID had washed its hands of us. There was no press release. No website mentioned. No public acknowledgment that the SID Fund even existed.

It was as if they were embarrassed. Embarrassed to be associated with a private sector initiative they had helped design. Embarrassed that our donors did not conform to ideological filters. Embarrassed that we refused to bend.

What the SID Fund eventually financed was not ideology, not slogans, and not performative compassion. It funded real work over a full year, beginning in October 2024. Through nine initiatives, AMCHAM member funding supported projects implemented across Yangon, Bago, Mandalay, Kachin, Shan, Kayin, and the Ayeyarwaddy Regions. One hundred percent of member donations were disbursed directly to project activities, with all initiatives completing agreed outputs and documented early outcomes.

USAID showed little interest in that long-term potential from the very start. Even before a single dollar was raised, the agency had already made a quiet decision to retire the program that supported the groundwork for the SID Fund, the Responsible Investment and Trade Activity, commonly known as RITA. A pre-COVID-19 relic, it was allowed to fade as priorities shifted away from economic resilience toward activist programming centered on democracy or inclusivity. As if I needed another reason to feel no sympathy when USAID was dismantled under President Trump in 2025. So as senior leadership at USAID looked toward a post-Biden transition and openly hoped for a Harris administration, they allowed RITA, and in turn the SID Fund, to drift into silence.

We didn't get the memo.

Even as the partnership dissolved publicly, the mission remained intact. We still had the SID Fund. What we needed now was belief, and of course the money to turn that belief into action. And yet, on the night of June 20, it fell to me to give that belief a voice.

To this day, I consider *The Awakening Speech* the greatest speech I have ever written and delivered. Others might disagree. Some point to *The Peace Speech*, or to one of the Governors Dinner addresses, and I understand why. This was a speech delivered in an intimate setting, not a grand ballroom filled with hundreds of people. It was spoken to a small group who believed they could do more than stand by as communities across Myanmar suffered. *The Awakening Speech* has always been different for me. I did not revise it. I did not rehearse it. I did not need to.

It came from some place deeper.

I had just returned from Koh Phangan. From the crash. From the storm. From the moment of clarity that followed. From wounds that did not break but remade me. I was no longer wandering, no longer burdened by doubt or the need for approval.

My soul had been awakened.

I knew from the start that the SID Fund was more than a fundraiser. It was our answer to the chaos, the lies, the pain, the defamation, and the fear that had surrounded us for months. It was an act of defiance and a statement of what we believed in.

I also knew that I could not ask my community to believe in me without reminding them why any of this mattered in the first place. So, I opened by speaking about my company's recent rebrand, using it to set the stage for what truly mattered. I told them that I had finalized the buyout of my multinational partner and now owned the company outright, the first time I had spoken publicly about that transition. The point was never to talk about myself. It was to honor the people whose belief in me gave life to my journey in Myanmar.

It had always been about my people. The workers who stood with me from the start. My general manager. My head of finance. My people. That night, they sat front and center in the audience, living proof of the community we had built together. Then I told them the truth I had spent months avoiding.

"It's about them: my people, my workers, the workers of Myanmar. I cannot solve the problems of this country, nor is it my place or my right to do so. They must find the answers to the problems of this country."

I cannot fix Myanmar. I am a tourist here, but maybe, just maybe, I can inspire the ones who will. In the end, a Myanmar problem needs a Myanmar solution. My job is to lend my strength to those who lack it. It is what I have done my whole life.

STRENGTH THROUGH SACRIFICE

Looking back on that night on the island, writing this speech by the light of my dying laptop, that was the moment I realized it. The theme of my speech, and what became the new motto of my newly rebranded company:

Strength Through Sacrifice.

I spoke those words over and over again that night, *Strength Through Sacrifice,* not just as a theme, but as a gift. Then I looked out at my American business community, ready to hand them something many had forgotten they still carried.

Their dignity.

I reminded them of the sacrifice they had already given over the years: time, money, stability. They were not in Myanmar to profit. Most were barely breaking even at that point. They were still in Myanmar to keep what they had built alive, to keep jobs alive, to keep the communities built around their businesses alive. They kept going when everything around them told them to quit.

And yet, for all that work, for all that sacrifice, they were shamed. They were vilified online. Accused of profiting from war. Branded as traitors by Facebook activists who had no idea what they had endured. So, I told them plainly that it was time to stop apologizing for trying. It was time to stop apologizing for surviving. We were not fighting to keep our businesses alive because of politics. We were still fighting for our people's future. So, I asked them to donate to the SID Fund, not out of guilt or pressure, but out of this very belief. From the clarity that comes when you remember who you are and why you are here. That night, I told them:

"Today is a time for choosing."

The phrase had been etched in my mind for decades. I first heard it in Ronald Reagan's 1964 "A Time for Choosing" speech, a call to stand firm in one's belief. On June 20, I was not quoting Reagan for effect. I was living my own time, choosing my own time, and so were my people.

I had arrived at the turning point of my speech, the moment

when everything that followed would depend on what we chose right then and there: resilience, belief, community. I told them I was done spending my time and energy on those determined to tear us down, the online shamers, the whisperers. Their time was up. And so, I addressed those naysayers in my speech, simply and defiantly:

"God bless you; God bless you. I have nothing in my heart but love for you."

Love thy enemy. That is what Jesus preached to his followers, and if I had truly been saved by God, I had to live by that truth. Then came the climactic line, a moment that would go on to be one of the most quoted from any speech I have ever given:

"I am awake, ladies and gentlemen, and I see before me the best of this country. Willing, able, and ready to lend the people their strength."

What began as a speech to raise funds for philanthropy became a declaration of belief. No rehearsals. No gimmicks. Just my heart on the podium, my vision made flesh, my soul awakened. I had walked into that room with no donations pledged. I walked out with over $40,000 committed, nearly half our target in a single night. That was the moment everything changed for me as a leader. I had entered my Act Three, and I had delivered.

As I wrote in the prologue, not everyone experiences all three Acts of leadership. Many never make it past Act One, where you show up every day to do the work while nobody is looking. Even fewer survive Act Two, the crucible, when the attacks come, legal threats emerge, shaming intensifies, and collapse feels inevitable. I barely made it through Act Two, but I emerged still standing.

Very rarely does a leader unlock an Act Three, but for me, *The Awakening Speech* was the key that opened that door. God may have shown me the path to the door, but belief in His plan is only part of it.

You have to become that belief. You have to stop letting belief live as a slogan and allow it to become the force that carries everyone who follows you.

From that night forward, I was no longer just leading a chamber. I was leading something bigger. A movement powered not by bureaucracy or politics, but by belief. The belief that even in darkness, our community could still choose to be the light.

Oh, and that $100,000?

It was raised.

THE AWAKENING SPEECH

Ladies and gentlemen, my dearest members,

Today is a time for choosing, and today I am asking all of you to donate to our social impact fund; but why?

Will it solve the problems of this country? No. Will it solve the problems this business community faces? No. But is that our purpose? Is that what we can control?

For months I have pondered this, my mind enslaved over these questions. For the first time in a while, I questioned my leadership: Am I truly making a difference? Why am I even doing this?

I recently took a holiday, my first real one in two years, and what I found was clarity; I have spent so much time trying to solve the problems of this community, the problems of this country, that I forgot where it started, what I first believed in.

A Myanmar Problem needs a Myanmar Solution: that's where it started, that's the idea I built my company around.

Now, speaking of my company, many of you and others have asked why I have recently changed its name and rebranded. I would like to address that now if I may.

My other shareholder is a multinational company based in Europe who will be selling their shares to me by the end of the year. I think for too many years, even before conflict, coup, and COVID, I had let them put their trust and belief in me, not in my company, the country and even the people. And you see therein lies the problem: it is not about me.

It's about them: my people, my workers, the workers of Myanmar. I cannot solve the problems of this country, but it is not my place or right to do so. They must find the answers to the problems of this country. Whether I leave this country in the coming years or die here of old age,

I am a tourist here. Everything I build with them, a company, assets, wealth, will eventually fade to dust. What I leave behind is a community that I helped build with them. What I leave behind for that community to endure is not money: it is the example I set for them every day, the willingness to sacrifice my strength for others.

Strength through sacrifice.

Words I have lived by. Words that I have not only built my company around, but my community of employees and their families: my people.

But I am not alone in this; every one of you in this room has built your own communities. You all have this same story to tell, whether you represent a major investment or you're an entrepreneur, you all have made your mark on this country through the communities you have built. And when we come together here at this Chamber to combine our collective strength, that is the power of AMCHAM, that is the power of community. That is what is everlasting, that is what cannot be destroyed, and even if our people cannot solve the problems of this country, we give them strength to endure them, to grow and nurture what we started together.

And so today I am asking you to sacrifice your strength again by donating to others who need it, because that is the example we must continue to set for our people: we sacrifice, and sacrifice, and sacrifice, and when we are tired, we sacrifice some more. That's what leadership is.

And I know, I know you've sacrificed so much already; I know you have already been pushed to your limits, and you're tired. I am tired. Since 2021, you have sacrificed the wealth of your companies, your personal wealth, you have sacrificed relationships, time with your loved ones, all for the preservation of jobs. And even through all of this, were you thanked? No, because you then had to sacrifice your dignity because of those who wish to shame you both directly and indirectly due to your continued presence here.

Every one of you has your own tale of harassment: somewhere along the way a perversion has taken place. The natural right of a citizen of this country to pursue economic opportunity for their families and communities is now considered to be an alliance with the military and its government.

The freedom of commerce has never been so fragile as it is right now: the right to provide jobs and livelihoods to the people of this country has never been so close to slipping from our grasp. Yet if we were to abandon our pursuit of free commerce due to the challenges we face from the current government, due to stone throwing of those who have no solutions for the millions of people in the country who just wish to carry out their lives in peace, then we leave only one future for this country: economic ruin.

Our activist friends seem unwilling to debate this issue. They want to make you and I believe that there are only two sides; that we must choose between two ultimatums: divest or be a traitor.

Well, what of this economy that they would destroy, and in destroying, they would destroy the jobs our companies create, and in turn, the very communities of workers that you and I hold so dear? Today is a time for choosing and today I am saying no to ultimatums. Today, I am taking this pledge to show the world that there can be another way. There has to be another way!

And I ask all of you today to join me in that pledge. Donating today is not just a choice; it is a commitment to the future of our collective communities, to this American business community. It is a pledge of our continued willingness to believe in our strength and to believe that together, we will resolve the problems which now confront us by continuing to sacrifice our strength to those who need it.

Strength through sacrifice.

Now to our naysayers, to those who continue to try to drag us down, who continue to offer only criticisms of our belief in our path, today I say this to them: God bless you; God bless you. I have nothing in my heart but love for you. You have made us bleed but guess what? We are still standing here stronger than ever, and your 15 minutes are up. Today, we take a pledge!

And our donations are not just about social impact but our continued journey on the path that has been laid before us. Your pledge today signals to this world that we only know one way, and that way Is forward!

I am awake, ladies and gentlemen, and I see before me the best of this country. Willing, able, and ready to lend the people their strength.

So let us pledge today to stop focusing on the past and remain present, in the here and now, to what we can control. Let us present to this country an American business community that is powerful, commercially and morally. An American business community that has a cause, a vision of a future when all people of this country are free from prejudice in their pursuit of economic freedom; a country where they are beholden to no one.

Strength through sacrifice. Thank you.

A VOICE RINGS

THE JULY FOURTH ADDRESS, 2024

A voice doesn't whisper forever.
Eventually, it rings. Let it ring.

*It was just us against the world now, and
believe me, the world had it coming.*

The American Club in Yangon was electric that day: June 29, 2024. More than 300 voices filled the air, 335 attendees, the largest crowd our Chamber had ever brought together, a record that still stands. It didn't feel like a business networking event; it felt like a rally, alive with the American Spirit abroad.

Under the wide metal roof of the basketball court, shielded from the monsoon rains but wrapped in the heavy, steamy humidity of July, the space pulsed with energy. Red, white, and blue framed the stage. For three hours in Yangon, we had our own Fourth of July spectacle, a celebration of survival and defiance.

This alone felt radical. Not long ago, the thought of gathering so openly, with pride and purpose, would have been unthinkable under the military's shadow. The year before, AMCHAM's July Fourth gathering had begun to shift something in our community. Now, with accomplishments behind us and fear giving way to resolve, we stood unafraid.

What followed was not another speech, but the first test of whether our voice could move power beyond our own community.

On that hot, humid Saturday afternoon, I stepped to the microphone calm and clear-minded. *The Awakening Speech* had been delivered just weeks earlier, and my focus had never been sharper. Before me was not a ballroom of executives, but the beating heart of our community, mostly Myanmar nationals: workers, mid-level managers, and their families. Children waved miniature American flags, parents wore patriotic shirts, and the smell of hot dogs and burgers hung in the air. It was festive, yes, but beneath the revelry was urgency. This wasn't just a holiday gathering. It was a declaration.

The July Fourth Address in 2024 was more a rallying cry than a speech, a battle hymn signaling we would no longer wait for rescue. We were ready to raise our voices, with or without the world's permission.

"I don't know about all of you, but I am tired of being forgotten about here in the dark. I am tired of being told I cannot try, I cannot even try, to help this country. I am tired of being told I must sit here and rot away in silence."

Cheers erupted. Even the more reserved company bosses pumped their fists. Years of frustration at being marginalized, ignored, and written off were finally being spoken aloud. It hit home.

I pressed on. I told them I had taken a holiday recently, and in that quiet, I had found clarity. I repeated it again and again: From the stillness, I saw a vision.

"I have seen a vision of this country's future, a vision too often ignored by this world. I have seen a vision of this country, of you, its people, unafraid, pushing back against the darkness with courage."

The crowd was silent except for scattered cries of "Yes!" and "That's right!" at each pause. They were with me. Finally, I reached the crescendo. I raised my finger high and roared into the microphone:

"We will rage against the dying light, your voice will not die here in the dark, your voice will be heard by the world, and soon the world will know your pain...the world will know our pain."

Right on cue, Zar was waiting behind the stage, listening to every word, making sure the delivery matched the speech. As I closed the last line, she immediately hit play. "Wild Thing" by X tore through the humid air, the opening riff cutting clean and loud.

The crowd exploded.

Cheers. Applause. That electric crackle that tells you something has shifted. People were on their feet, dancing, shouting, fists raised. In that moment, our spirit surged. We were done being quiet. Our voice was ringing, loud and unafraid, finished with asking permission to exist.

It was just us against the world now, and believe me, the world had it coming.

When I stepped off the stage, the crowd surged forward; handshakes, hugs, people shouting "thank you" over the music. Chaos, but the good kind. I had turned that AMCHAM Fourth of July celebration into something that felt like a MAGA rally...deliberately so. The event had been planned (at my direction) to mirror the raw energy of the Trump rallies happening across America at that moment, right down to the unfiltered defiance.

That energy turned into action almost immediately. Conversations shifted from congratulations to strategy. Donations began flowing in on the spot. Our "$100,000 in 100 Days" Social Impact Donation Fund received a surge of pledges. A member pulled me aside with an additional contribution. Another member promised to personally chip in more. By the following month, we had smashed the $100,000 target, hitting it in under 90 days instead of 100.

Yet the euphoria couldn't mask the truth: Myanmar was still in crisis, and I had a flight to catch. Ahead of me stretched a journey into the swamp of Biden's Washington, DC, where I expected more shrugs than solutions, but this year I was coming to kick down doors no one expected me to open. The administration had walked away from Myanmar. If we were going to break through, my next steps had to be harder, unapologetic, and rooted in America First.

The shift in my political tone had already begun. On June 27, 2024, just days before our Fourth of July event, Biden's implosion on the debate stage confirmed what Americans had feared for years: the country had incoherent, absent leadership, a perfect reflection of US policy toward Myanmar under his watch. If we wanted action, we'd have to go find it, and I knew exactly where to look.

A DIFFERENT KIND OF WASHINGTON

The contrast with my past trips to Washington could not have been sharper. For years, I'd joined the annual AMCHAM Asia-Pacific Door-knock delegation, that ritual where business leaders from all over Asia dressed up in suits with name tags shuffle between conference rooms, hand over polite policy wish-lists, and get rewarded with canned smiles or quick dismissals. We spoke in platitudes; they answered with rehearsed nods. Zero impact. I came home from 2023's trip weighed down by Washington's indifference.

Not this time.

I had just delivered *The July Fourth Address* the week prior, announcing our refusal to wait for rescue. I meant every word. This

11-day trip was built around my agenda, not AMCHAM Asia-Pacific. The official Door Knock events remained on my calendar, but they were background noise. While my peers sat through agency briefings and panel discussions, I slipped away to run my own playbook, one aimed at the people and power centers that could move the needle.

Washington, DC, in mid-July was sweltering in heat and politics. Biden's disastrous debate had already set the city buzzing, and whispers of his withdrawal were everywhere. The MAGA movement was riding high on Trump's triumph, and then, on July 13, halfway through my trip, came the shock that rattled the nation: an assassination attempt on President Trump at a rally in Pennsylvania.

A gunman fired from a distance, killing one supporter, injuring others, and grazing President Trump's ear. Instead of fear, the attempt ignited a surge of resolve and defiance:

Fight!

Walking the halls of Congress that week, I felt a current of defiance, and I recognized it. The MAGA base, like our business community in Myanmar, had been ignored, written off, and told to accept their fate. The Biden White House and its allies had twisted the justice system into a political weapon: not to uphold the law, but to crush opposition, bleed Trump's momentum, and strangle any chance of his return to power. President Trump and his movement had been pushed to the margins, and decided to push back.

Sound familiar?

In Myanmar, we had found our voice. In America, a former president and his movement were fighting to keep theirs. That shared refusal to be silenced cemented my conviction: America First was where I needed to be. I wasn't in Washington as a supplicant anymore. I was there to fight for my people's future, and for America's.

My first stop wasn't the State Department or the US Trade Representative. It was AFPI, the America First Policy Institute, exiled across the river in Arlington, Virginia, like political outcasts plotting their return. Inside a glass-walled conference room overlooking the Potomac, I sat down with AFPI policy thinkers, the people quietly drafting the foreign policy framework for a future Trump administration. They didn't need convincing that Biden's Myanmar policy was a disaster. What I gave them was proof: factories shuttered, an economy in freefall, banks cutting ties, and China seizing every inch of ground the US had surrendered.

They saw the political opportunity instantly, another "America Last" failure to hang around the Biden administration's neck. For me, it was about making the strategic case: They believed in putting American interests first; I showed them that keeping a foothold in Myanmar to counter Beijing's ambitions was one of those interests.

From there, I took the fight to Capitol Hill. Backed by fresh AFPI connections, I worked through days of back-to-back meetings with lawmakers and staff, from the House Foreign Affairs Committee to the Intelligence Committee. This time, doors that had been locked a year earlier swung open. Republican offices that had ignored me before, some never even replying to my emails, were now calling me in. One Senate office even reached out before I could request a meeting.

In one meeting, I didn't waste words: "If this continues, there won't be any American business left in Myanmar, and China will take everything we leave behind." That landed. For the first time, I heard the question I'd been waiting for:

"What should Washington do differently?"

I told them straight: Stop treating Myanmar like a morality play and start treating it like a strategy. Stop trying to sanction everything; that policy is failing. Keep responsible businesses in-country so jobs survive. Engage the financial system, don't freeze it out. Stop letting China turn Myanmar into its rare-earth fiefdom. Bring every armed actor into peace talks, especially the ethnic groups US policy has long ignored. If Washington wants stability, everyone with a gun and a constituency must be at the table.

For the first time, it felt like the message didn't just land; people were actually starting to listen.

In meeting after meeting that week, I sensed the tide beginning to turn. We didn't solve Myanmar's crisis in those few days, but for the first time, AMCHAM's agenda was in the hands of policymakers and policy thinkers who were taking it seriously. I left behind copies of our AMCHAM advocacy paper, drafted by our advocacy committee and me, with input from every member, a blueprint for stabilizing Myanmar's economy so jobs could be saved and workers protected. It began circulating through think tanks, congressional offices, and policy advisors who, in years past, wouldn't have given me a second glance.

This trip was different. It wasn't just me, alone in DC, trying to figure things out. The conversations I had and the people who began to approach me quietly signaled something new. Some were already in my network; others had been watching from the sidelines until now. In one group discussion and a series of one-on-one meetings, an idea began to take hold that maybe this work could grow into a sustained advocacy effort. A campaign with the weight and focus to influence the outcome of one of the longest-running crises in modern history. It would require more than a yearly trip or a flash-in-the-pan initiative; it had to be organized, disciplined, and relentless.

Those who rallied around me shared a deep frustration. They were done with the same US–Burma policy voices that had dominated Washington for decades, recycling stale talking points, serving as little more than mouthpieces for activist networks, and mistaking noise for strategy. They wanted a new voice, a different face for the fight; someone who could cut through the echo chamber and make the case with strategy, not slogans. They saw that my voice came from my people, from a community that had asked me to be their shield and advocate. That bond, coupled with my readiness to take the fight directly into Washington's halls of power, gave me credibility they hadn't seen in years.

By the final days of my trip, the idea had shaped into a framework, one that would grow into the US–Burma Economic Forum: a permanent, organized advocacy platform under AMCHAM Myanmar, built to challenge the stale orthodoxy and force a new conversation.

From the stage in Yangon to the power corridors of Washington, our voice had carried farther than ever before. What began as a rally under the heavy monsoon air had become a message moving through think tanks, congressional offices, and policy circles that once acted like we didn't exist. It was no longer a faint plea from the margins; it was a defiant demand echoing in the heart of American power.

With the political tide shifting and the hope of an America First revival on the horizon, a voice forged in the storms of Myanmar was now ringing, carried on the conviction that freedom belongs to those willing to fight for it.

Freedom was calling. Freedom was ringing.

THE JULY FOURTH ADDRESS, 2024

Members! My people! Hear me now!

Now. Today. I want to hear your voice, and I want to hear you get loud.

And for those of you who want to know what's different about me today, well...I went on a holiday recently, and what I found was clarity.

Clarity that you, the people, the workers of Myanmar, are truly what matters to us businesspeople.

So, I need you all to help me right now. Go talk to all your bosses here today and ask them if your company has taken the AMCHAM pledge, the pledge of donating towards social impact. And to all you bosses in the crowd that haven't donated yet: What are you waiting for?

Maybe you need a holiday, because I went on a holiday recently and what I found was an awakening.

You see our donations. Our pledges signal to our communities, this country, and this world that our light here is not dying.

Because I don't know about all of you, but I am tired of being forgotten about here in the dark.

I am tired of being told I cannot try, I cannot even try, to help this country.

I am tired of being told I must sit here and rot away in silence.

I was so tired that I went on a holiday recently, and there...I made a promise to God.

That for as long as I breathe, I will do everything in my power to help you; but I need your voice. I need your voice like I need my strength.

And that voice is about to be carried with me on this journey I'm about to start, there, just there, four hours from now, my first stop will be Bangkok, then on to California, United States, because I need to kiss my momma before I get shamed again for not coming home enough, then that voice will come with me to Washington, DC where I will make that voice heard, from Capitol Hill to Georgetown to Ben's Chili Bowl. Your voice will be heard. Why?

Because I went on a holiday recently.

And what I found was a vision.

I have seen a vision of this country's future, a vision too often ignored by this world.

I have seen a vision of this country, of you, its people, unafraid, pushing back against the darkness with courage.

But I can't see that vision without your voice. I cannot continue to lead this journey we are on without your voice. I need the voice of my people, I need it like oxygen to give me strength, and if you're afraid to use that voice, let AMCHAM be your shield, and I will hold that shield for as long as you let me, for as long as I am able to.

We are awake, my friends.

And I promise all of you right here and now, we will rage against the dying light. Your voice will not die here in the dark, your voice will be heard by the world, and soon the world will know your pain, the world will know our pain!

So let it ring, let it ring! Let freedom ring!

GIVE THEM SOMETHING TO BELIEVE IN

INSPIRE THE SPIRIT. LEAD FROM WITHIN.

True belief doesn't come from what you know. It doesn't come from what you endure. It comes from who you are.

Leadership does not end with the plan. If you have done the work and survived the fire, your role must evolve. Your people do not need another campaign or committee meeting. They need something deeper.

Belief.

That belief does not replace what came before. The work continues. The fire does not disappear. By the time Act Three began, we were still delivering on the promises of Acts One and Two. The Social Impact Donation Fund, our $100,000 in 100 Days campaign, moved into its next phase by awarding grants to grassroots NGOs and nonprofits in some of Myanmar's most underdeveloped communities. The momentum had to continue, and it did.

We brought in new partners. Amazon Web Services joined the Chamber and helped launch AWS Community Day, a flagship event that trained and empowered the next generation of Myanmar coders and cloud engineers. What began as a membership win became something larger. It became a long-term investment in human capital and in the future of Myanmar's youth.

Then came the US–Burma Economic Forum, a formal advocacy platform born from the crucible of Act Two. What started as a committee-led policy paper became an organized voice in Washington, DC. It was deliberate, disciplined, and member driven. It proved that belief does not require reinvention. Sometimes it simply asks you to stay committed long enough for the plan to bear fruit. Then everything changed.

On March 28, 2025, Myanmar was struck by a devastating earthquake.

In an instant, everything we had built was tested, but it did not break. We were ready, not because we predicted disaster, but because we had built the foundation. We pivoted the SID Fund into a new Rebuild Fund focused on long-term recovery. We partnered with the US Chamber of Commerce and the US-ASEAN Business Council to launch the Tri-Relief Coalition, which delivered emergency supplies from Thailand to Myanmar. Members distributed those supplies through trusted CSR networks.

This was not luck. This was infrastructure. Born in Act One, refined in Act Two, and activated in Act Three.

That is why *The Awakening Speech* does not formally begin Act Three. The speech was delivered to a room of 50 people. It had not yet been proclaimed before the entire community at a flagship event. After *The Awakening Speech*, we were still in the crucible. We were still responding to the crisis. The lawsuit from a former board member did not fully emerge until September 2024. The critics and doubters had not vanished. The fire was still burning. And yet, something inside of me had shifted during my crucible, and it began with the Awakening.

When I first became president of AMCHAM Myanmar, I quickly realized the most urgent challenge was not political, financial, or logistical. It was cultural. In the darkness that had settled over Myanmar, my community had lost something essential. Locals and foreigners alike had grown ashamed. Ashamed of working here. Ashamed of building lives here.

I heard it constantly.

"Because of my country's situation..."

It became the preamble to every excuse, every apology, every doubt.

That was what I wanted to change most. Not just the Chamber, but the culture of the Chamber. Not just the structure of the community, but the spirit of the people within it. To lead in Act Three meant something different. It meant reaching into quiet despair and lighting a spark. Helping people stand up straight again in their own lives.

Belief starts inside. No one can believe in your leadership until you believe in yourself.

This was not the kind of leadership I learned in the Marine Corps. There, confidence was assumed. Every Marine believes they are the alpha in the room. Here, people were tired and wounded. To lead them, I had to become more than a strategist or planner.

I had to become a symbol.

And so, I wrote differently. I spoke differently. About hope. About staying. About peace. Some of my most memorable speeches came from Act Three, because they captured the moment. Take *The Peace Speech*, delivered on International Women's Day. It wasn't written to check boxes. It was written to speak to the unheard. Yes, I used that moment to elevate women, to celebrate their resilience, their leadership, their right to be heard. Yet I also used that moment to speak to something far greater.

The struggle of women in Myanmar is not an isolated one. It's a reflection of what has happened to everyone in this country, ethnic minorities, religious groups, everyday citizens of every background, marginalized not by identity alone, but by a war that has stolen their future. A war that has erased opportunity, crushed hope, and left entire generations to wonder if they still matter. So, I didn't just speak about gender. I spoke about peace, the one thing that could restore what violence had long stolen from this country:

Belief that there was a future for all people in Myanmar.

Public speaking isn't just communication; it's connection. You don't talk to remind people of the crisis they are experiencing every day. You talk to remind them of their strength. Every time I spoke, I knew if I wasn't prepared, if I hadn't done the work, my people would know it. Preparation alone isn't enough, though. A great speech doesn't just explain what you're doing. It reminds people why it matters, because when belief is fragile, facts won't carry you. Only conviction will, and if you want others to believe, you have to believe it yourself.

That is what makes Act Three different. It's not just another phase. It's another dimension a leader must ascend to. In Act One, you lead with your mind and muscle. You build. You organize. You prove you can do the work. You show them the foundation. In Act Two, you lead with strength. You fight back against the world as it tries to tear down that foundation. You survive the crucible.

In Act Three, however, you're not just building anymore. You're not just battling anymore.

You're reaching for something deeper. True belief doesn't come from what you know. It doesn't come from what you endure. It comes from who you are.

The truth is, most leaders never reach Act Three. Some never move beyond doing the work. Some rise in crisis but burn out soon after, because to truly lead through darkness, not just with strength, but with light; you have to reach a part of yourself most people never touch. You have to lead not from your head or your hands, but from your heart.

For me, that meant returning to the core of who I've always been: a man of faith. I am a lifelong Catholic, but during these years of crisis, through COVID-19, coup, and conflict, that faith in God's plan began to fade. I still prayed. I still talked the talk, but inside? I was tired, alone, and felt abandoned by His grace. I began to wonder if any of it was still real, but in the deepest part of the crucible, on the island of Koh Phangan, when I had exhausted every other strength, I found something again. I found God's grace.

Not in a vision. Not in a moment of revelation, but in the quiet realization that He had never stopped believing in me, even when I had. That the path He laid before me was still there, I just stopped believing it. That belief, that feeling that this suffering was not random, that there was a plan for me, a purpose to all of this, that's what gave me the strength to open my heart to the people I led.

That's what allowed me to stop trying to prove myself to everyone and start leading with presence. To stop commanding attention and start inspiring it. To stop protecting myself and start giving myself. That's what Act Three requires. It demands that you give more than your effort or your expertise. It asks for you and for leaders reading this, whether or not you share my faith, to believe this moment can still belong to you too.

You don't need to believe in God to find your Act Three, but you do need to believe in something. Something that is yours. Something you hold sacred.

Something that can break you open, so that others can see your light inside.

Whatever it is, find it, but here is a helpful tip: It's probably already in there. Buried beneath the noise. Beneath the burnout. Beneath the armor you've been wearing for too long.

Act Three is not about being strong. It's about being open. Open enough to lead with vulnerability. Open enough to let your people see your heart and believe in it. If you can do this, they'll follow you anywhere. That's the real secret of this final act. Not plans or speeches, or applause: just one soul speaking truth to another.

That's how you give people something to believe in.

A VOICE SHINES

THE GOVERNORS DINNER SPEECH, 2024

Belief shines brightest when it no
longer belongs to one voice.

*I was only the mirror and the messenger. The real
strength came from those who chose love over
fear, generosity over indifference, and gave others
something to believe in when belief was hardest to
find. I learned that when a voice truly shines, it
doesn't overpower, it reveals the light already burning
in others, so they can see it for themselves. If there
is one truth, I hope my people carry away from this
night, it is that a voice shines not by banishing
the dark, but by daring to speak light into it.*

I sat before a blank page in the late hours of an October night, the city outside wrapped in the heavy grip of monsoon season. Rain had been falling for hours, steady, relentless, turning the streets of central Yangon into slow-moving rivers. In just a few weeks, I would stand at the podium for our third annual Governors Dinner, an evening dedicated to celebrating our community and spotlighting the generosity within it, most notably through the presentation of our Corporate Social Responsibility awards to members whose charitable work had brought light into some of Myanmar's darkest days.

The question before me was not how to fill the page, but how to fill the moment. What could I say that I hadn't already said in seven speeches before? This year felt different. The mood called for something more than a rallying cry; it called for tribute, for praise, and for stillness. I knew this speech had to be something different from my usual addresses: a quiet reflection, almost a prayer, offered to a room hungry for hope.

Crafting it tested me in ways no other speech, briefing, or policy address ever had. I could usually hammer out a fiery address in one sitting, heart racing, words tumbling forward in a surge of conviction. This one resisted me. I wrote draft after draft, discarding each attempt. One felt overly inspirational. Another leaned too far into the spiritual. The balance I sought, a tone of sober hope, remained just out of reach.

After days of circling the problem, I picked up the phone late one night and called my older sister. She wasn't a speechwriter; she was a former educator with a PhD, someone who could hear the emotions between the lines.

"I can't get this one right," I told her.

"It's supposed to inspire hope, but everything I write feels forced and preachy. It doesn't sound like me."

She listened quietly as I spoke about our members, the fundraising campaign, the awardees we would honor, and the heaviness pressing on all of us in Myanmar. When she finally responded, her words were precise. I had been writing with urgency and anger when the occasion called for love and light. The speech, she said, needed the voice of a caring elder or a storyteller by a campfire, not a general rallying his troops. Then she began to edit my draft, deleting lines, reworking passages, and adding a few of her own. One line became the speech's North Star:

"The opposite of fear is love; the opposite of darkness is light."

Mission accomplished, big sis.

From there, the speech unlocked itself. The words began to flow. I framed it not as a manifesto, but as a meditation on moral courage, generosity, and small acts that can hold back the dark. I wrote through the night, my sentences softer than usual, my tone stripped of rhetorical armor. By dawn, I had a draft that finally felt true. Reading it back, I felt a lump in my throat. It was honest. It was human. It was exactly what I had hoped to deliver: a homily.

THE GRAND BALLROOM

The Grand Ballroom of the Meliá Yangon glittered on the evening of October 25, 2024. Chandeliers spilled warm, golden light over tables set with precision. Nearly 250 members and guests filled the space, diplomats from several Western embassies, including the US Embassy's Chargé d'Affaires, top corporate leaders from our membership, and their guests. It was a guest list that reflected not only the reach of our Chamber, but also the trust and respect our community had built through years of uncertainty.

This year felt different. People weren't there simply to make an appearance or quietly support the event from the shadows. They came ready to celebrate openly, unapologetically, and together. The hesitance that had so often defined gatherings in Myanmar's tense environment seemed to have lifted, replaced by something more defiant:

Joy.

The night had been building toward the moment everyone was waiting for: the CSR Excellence Awards. One by one, names were called, and applause rolled through the ballroom as plaques were handed out. There were three tiers of recognition: ten companies received the Silver Level *"Captain of Industry Award,"* six earned the Gold Level *"Champion of Commerce Award,"* and, at the very top, two stood apart with the Platinum Level *"Spirit of American Commerce Award."* Those top honors went to a leading local bank and Coca-Cola Myanmar, both recognized not just for their resources, but for the way they had stepped up when it mattered most.

When the last name was read, the Platinum honorees moved to the center of the stage. Gold and Silver awardees fanned out to their sides, creating a living tableau of the people and companies that had carried our Social Impact Donation Fund to life. The US Embassy's Chargé d'Affaires took her place between the two Platinum winners, smiling as the cameras flashed.

The applause lingered for a moment before fading into a quiet stillness. The master of ceremonies called my name, and I rose from my seat. As the awardees remained on stage, the audience's attention followed me. I stepped up, crossing to the far right and taking my place behind the podium. From there, I could see the entire line of honorees stretching from center to stage left, faces that had shaped the very story I was about to tell. This was their moment as much as it was mine, and it felt right to speak while they still stood in the light.

"Distinguished guests, ladies, and gentlemen…"

I began, my voice carrying across the hushed hall. After the formalities, a pause lingered, the kind of sacred quiet before the first note of a song. Into that silence, I spoke of the darkness we had all endured in recent years, both personal and shared. As my words settled over the room, I felt the weight of our collective experience, finally spoken into the open, before shifting to why we had not broken, why despair had not claimed us: moral courage.

"Through the work of our own hands and simple acts of kindness, our community's collective acts have sprung light where there is dark, fostered hope where there is despair."

We all needed that reminder, that even the smallest acts can matter in the face of overwhelming darkness. I turned to the story of our "$100,000 in 100 Days" campaign, a stand we had taken together that would help heal and lift thousands across the Golden Land. My gaze moved to the CSR awardees in the front row, shifting modestly in their seats. These were the people who had given their time, resources, and energy when it mattered most. I told them their efforts mattered, not because they could solve everything, but because they kept the flame of hope alive. Each act was a light in the darkness, and together those lights were bright enough to guide the way forward, proving the cynics wrong through sheer perseverance and unity.

"Embrace the fellowship," I urged, *"for all the problems and challenges we face, we hear the sounds of our future, not the echoes of our past, a future of everlasting hope that fills the unknowing air of this country."*

It was poetic language, almost unexpectedly so for me. In another setting, it might have sounded grandiose, but in that ballroom, it landed as an aspirational truth. We could choose fellowship over fear. We could choose to listen for the sounds of a hopeful future rather than the echoes of a painful past.

Threaded throughout my words was the imagery of light against darkness, a theme that had been alive in my heart for months. What the audience didn't know was that it came from one of my favorite authors, J.R.R. Tolkien. In *The Lord of the Rings: The Two Towers*, Samwise Gamgee speaks of holding onto the good in the world even when times are dark:

> It's like in the great stories, the ones that really mattered. Full of darkness and danger, they were. And sometimes you didn't want to know the end, because how could the end be happy? How could the world go back to the way it was when so much bad had happened? But in the end, it's only a passing thing...this shadow. Even darkness must pass. A new day will come. And when the sun shines, it will shine out the clearer.

Those words had stayed with me since adolescence, shaping how I understood struggle and the will to endure. As I wrote this speech,

I returned to them, not as a nostalgic nod to a favorite story, but as a well I had drawn from in my own darkest hours. They had once given me hope, and now I wanted to pass that hope to others. Even leaders need voices outside their own to help them speak the truths their hearts already know. This was one of those moments.

As I neared the climax of the speech, I spoke softly, but the room was so still that every syllable carried.

"In the end, this is only a passing thing, even darkness must pass. A new day will come. And when the sun shines, it will shine upon the light of this community."

By the time I reached my final lines, a heartbeat of silence lingered, the kind that hangs when an audience returns from a deep emotional journey. Then came the warm greetings and applause as the dinner music swelled. Walking back to my seat, I felt unexpectedly vulnerable. That speech had taken something out of me. I hadn't stood behind my usual armor of strength, fire, and policy points; I had laid my convictions bare. The reaction wasn't just for me, it was for us, for the spirit in that room. It felt as if a weight had been lifted from everyone's shoulders, replaced by belief, hope and possibility.

As the evening went on, members stopped me one after another to share what it meant to them. A longtime local businessman said:

"Tonight, I am proud, proud of us, proud to be part of this."

Friends abroad began messaging me. Social media filled with photos and clips from the night. I had given many speeches before, but this one felt different. It wasn't about a clever phrase or a sharp policy point. It felt like our community had rediscovered its belief.

In the busy weeks that followed, I noticed the change. People stood taller at events. Conversations carried more confidence. That night revealed the quiet power of reflection in leadership. I hadn't announced a strategy or launched an initiative. I had simply held up a mirror, showing my community its own courage, generosity, and resilience. In seeing themselves clearly again, they remembered who they were and why they were still here.

Act Three had begun. Not just for me, but for my people.

THE COST OF VULNERABILITY

Even still, I carry that night with a certain heaviness. Many members, even my own staff, still call it their favorite speech. I'm deeply grateful for that, yet inside I feel a knot of pride and unease. I don't hate this speech, in fact, I love it, but in the way one loves a hard truth. It required me to reveal parts of myself I usually keep guarded: my hopes, my fears, my beliefs.

Leadership is often measured in deals closed, reforms achieved, or speeches that shift policy. But how do you measure a moment of pure emotional honesty? I'm proud of what that night accomplished, the belief it restored, the unity it strengthened, yet it stands in a category of its own. Perhaps because it was born from the deepest well of fear and love I had ever drawn from. Writing it meant confronting my own doubts and faith; delivering it felt like standing unshielded in a storm, trusting conviction to protect me. It was exhausting in a way no other speech had been, because I had poured every drop of emotional energy into those words.

This speech was more of a homily instead of a battle cry, and it reminded us that no matter how dark the night is, a single candle, or a single speech, can be enough to show the way. A voice doesn't shine by outshouting the darkness, I realized, but by steadily illuminating what is good until the darkness recedes. Leadership in crisis had taught me that sometimes the bravest act is to be still, to be vulnerable, and to let others see you as human. Not every challenge calls for charging forward; sometimes the moment demands giving people something to believe in. That night, my aim was to spark that belief, to remind our community why we endure and what we are capable of. I offered words instead of directives, recognition instead of demands, choosing inspiration over instruction.

The Governors Dinner Speech in 2024 remains the hardest speech I have ever written, and the only one I have ever rehearsed ceaselessly, until the words themselves all felt unshakably right. When the moment came, I understood why: It was never just my speech. It was a voice meant to shine for everyone in that room, reflecting their own light back at them. I was only the mirror and the messenger. The real strength came from those who chose love over fear, generosity over indifference, and gave others something to believe in when belief was hardest to find. I learned that when a voice truly shines, it doesn't overpower, it reveals the light already burning in others, so they can see it for themselves. If there is one truth, I hope my people carried away from this night, it is that a voice shines not by banishing the dark, but by daring to speak light into it.

Light up the darkness.

THE GOVERNORS DINNER SPEECH, 2024

Distinguished guests, ladies, and gentlemen,

I want to thank you all for your attendance here tonight. To the CSR Excellence awardees, on behalf of our community, we thank you.

These past years, in moments of personal and communal darkness, we have anguished over how Myanmar could possibly go back to the way it was, living through a period of such upheaval, violence and dread that would surely burden even the bravest. And it is my worry that this fear that consumes us risks breaking our bonds as a community.

Growing up, I was often told that the opposite of fear is love, the opposite of darkness is light. Light can take many forms: love, kinship, and for our purposes tonight, generosity.

I have aspired, like many of you, to pledge these qualities to fight off the darkness which now eclipses our future. And, like many of you, my optimism sometimes wanes when I am overwhelmed by this fight. How can we possibly summon our most personal resources, our wealth, our time, our very hearts, when this tidal wave of strife seems so... unyielding?

The answer is of course to rely on our moral courage, the one essential, the vital quality of this community who seek to change a country that yields most painfully to change. And I believe that it is the shaping impulse of this community that neither fate, nor nature, nor the irresistible tides of conflict will determine our destiny. But through the work of our own hands and simple acts of kindness, our community's collective acts have sprung light where there is dark, fostered hope where there is despair.

And in our defining moment, when this community's moral courage was tested, when we were called upon to lend to others in need our strength, we not only answered this call but successfully raised $100,000 in less than 100 days. Charity that will go towards the urgent revival of the health and spirit of thousands of communities of this here place they once called the "Golden Land."

The awardees today should not be idealized or enlarged beyond who they are, but simply serve as a reminder of this community's moral courage and of course, the legacy we will leave behind, a legacy of being joined together, hand and hand: being simply remembered as good and decent people.

For when the cynics doubted this call of charity, you answered. For you are the true leaders who know while we may have wealth and purpose, we have nothing if this country lacks peace and longevity. So, fear not the struggle but embrace the fellowship, for all the problems and challenges we face, we hear the sounds of our future, not the echoes of our past, but a future of everlasting hope that fills the unknowing air of this country.

A future of one people, one community dedicated to the dream of economic and spiritual freedom that exists in every human heart. And it is our calling, now and tomorrow, to pass this dream onto the future generations of our community.

So, in those times of great fears and doubts, in those moments of despair when you no longer can see a light at the end of the tunnel, when you ask yourself if any of our work matters, why these awards matter, how this country could possibly go back to the way it was when so much bad as happened.

Because know this my friends, in the end, this is only a passing thing, even darkness must pass. A new day will come. And when the sun shines it will shine upon the light of this community.

That is why these awards matter, that is why your work matters. It means something, even if you think it is too small to understand why. So, praise them, praise them, and while you praise them, I want you to look outwards and praise each other and let our light continue to shine, so this country may continue seeing the goodness of our work.

And in this time of great darkness, when most lights seem fading and few eternal, know that our community is forever.

Thank you, God bless you, and God bless this country.

A VOICE BELIEVES

THE BELIEVE AGAIN SPEECH

Belief in a time of survival. Strength in a time of belief.

Belief was not sentimental optimism; it was survival, the only path left to us. It meant refusing to bow to bullies, whether a disgruntled former insider or a distant official who presumed to know better. It meant serving the people beside us, not our own pride. It meant fighting for the freedom to live and work with dignity, trusting free men and women over bureaucratic decrees.

It had been just over two weeks since Donald Trump's second election victory in the United States, a win every America First supporter had seen coming. The news didn't surprise me. It energized me. Not even four months earlier, I'd been walking the halls of Capitol Hill, office to office, telling anyone who would give me two minutes:

"If America abandons Myanmar, China wins!"

By then, I was making real progress, deliberately tying the cause of Myanmar, the cause of my community, and the cause of my people to the America First agenda. I had bet everything on Trump winning, knowing that a Kamala Harris presidency would mean four more years of calamity. Now, the landscape had shifted. The age of America First had arrived, bringing with it the promise of a blank canvas for US engagement with Myanmar. I was determined to paint our cause across that canvas in bold, permanent strokes. This was the moment I had been waiting for: a rare chance to rewrite Washington's approach from the ground up.

To nobody's surprise, I embraced the outcome, perhaps more openly than any American Chamber president was "supposed" to. By that point, I had no patience for the whispers or side glances from my peers in the AMCHAM world. Too many of them, especially across Asia, wore their loyalty to liberal Democrats like a badge while pretending their chambers were somehow "nonpartisan."

So, on November 21, 2024, in a meeting room in the heart of Yangon, I said it plainly, right there in front of my people, that for the first time since I was eighteen, I was a registered Republican. In that moment, I made it clear where I stood and where I was headed. I planted my flag in one of the unlikeliest places on earth, not just as a Republican, but as someone fully aligned with the MAGA movement. Not as a slogan. Not as a soundbite, but as a doctrine I intended to live by, fight for, and carry into every battle ahead.

That admission hung in the air, met with raised eyebrows and curious stares. I couldn't blame them. For most of my life, I had been a California Democrat, an idealist kid convinced that government could solve any problem so long as the "good guys" were in charge. My ideals back then were unquestionable, absolute.

I'd rallied behind Barack Obama's promise of hope and change in 2008, starry-eyed and inspired. I even carried those ideals with me into uniform as a US Marine, deploying under Obama's command to Afghanistan. But reality has a way of upending youthful certainty. Living in more conservative corners of America in my early years of military service opened my eyes. California wasn't the center of the universe after all, and not everyone who thought differently was ignorant.

Over time, I began to see that my own side's arrogance and elitism were part of the problem. Too many California liberals spent their lives mocking and belittling anyone who disagreed with them, branding them as bigots or idiots. I'll admit, in my youth, I'd done it too. That self-righteous echo chamber eventually left me disillusioned with my own party.

In my early and mid-twenties, I still clung to the hope that I could bridge the widening divide between the coastal liberals I grew up with and the rural conservatives I came to know in the Marines. I spent years trying to persuade old friends back home to listen; to understand the people on the other side, to respect opposing viewpoints for the sake of the country's unity. Yet no matter how calmly or reasonably I argued, nothing changed. My words bounced off hardened beliefs. The younger me, who once believed goodwill and logic could transcend politics, was slowly waking up to a harsher truth.

Then came my time in the deserts of Helmand Province, Afghanistan with a very formidable enemy: the Taliban. Every Marine I served with in Helmand knew which villages were under Taliban control, yet we couldn't touch them. The Taliban already had the hearts and minds of the locals by the time I arrived. We promised food, medicine, education, yet they were already getting all of that from the Taliban. Unlike us, the Taliban weren't tourists; the villages knew they were the permanent presence.

Another major reason we couldn't simply clear those areas was the intense focus on avoiding civilian casualties. The year was 2012 and the Afghan forces were set to take over offensive operations in the coming year; we were ordered to adopt a more passive posture. Every combat engagement was stringently audited and positive identification (PID) was everything. Rounds were logged before leaving the wire, logged again upon return, and every shot accounted for. Any round fired required a report, an interview, and an answer to the same question:

"Did you have positive identification before engaging the target?"

On the ground, we followed these meticulous rules, straining to win hearts and minds by avoiding even the perception of reckless fire. Meanwhile, Barack Obama's drone program was eliminating entire families thousands of miles away, operations that often lacked accurate intelligence, genuine positive identification, or any regard for the lives obliterated when flawed targeting data hit weddings, homes, and marketplaces.

The hypocrisy was staggering.

This was not an anomaly; it was the operating standard. Per a 2017 report from the Council on Foreign Relations, just three days into his presidency, on January 23, 2009, Obama authorized his first drone military action: two strikes, three hours apart, in Waziristan, Pakistan, killing as many as 20 civilians. Newsweek reported in 2012 that by the time he accepted the Nobel Peace Prize in December 2009, he had already authorized more drone strikes than George W. Bush had approved during his entire presidency. Over the next eight years, Obama would authorize a reported 542 drone strikes worldwide, compared to just 57 under Bush.

Some strikes were so reckless they read like tragedies ripped from a novel. In September 2012, a drone strike in Yemen, later investigated by Human Rights Watch, killed twelve civilians, among them three children and a pregnant woman. Not a single alleged militant died that day. The Yemeni government quietly paid restitution to the families, but the Obama administration never offered an explanation.

Three years later, in 2015, another "targeted" strike on the Afghanistan–Pakistan border turned into a diplomatic disaster. The compound wasn't housing terrorists at all, it was holding two civilian hostages: American aid worker Dr. Warren Weinstein and Italian national Giovanni Lo Porto. Both men were killed instantly. The incident was so damning that President Obama took to national television to apologize. As usual, he carefully measured his words to mask the failure of his drone program.

The human toll of the drone war wasn't limited to foreigners. In September 2011, a drone strike in Yemen killed Anwar al-Awlaki, a US-born cleric turned terrorist. While Awlaki certainly needed to be brought to justice, this was the first time in our country's history that an American citizen was marked for execution abroad by his own government without trial. Two weeks later, a second drone strike killed his 16-year-old son, Abdulrahman, a Denver-born boy eating dinner at an outdoor café. The Obama administration claimed they hadn't known the boy was there.

One human rights investigation found that in trying to kill 41 male targets, Obama-led drone strikes killed an estimated 1,147 people, including women and children, often striking the same target multiple times and still missing. In Pakistan alone, 24 men were targeted at the cost of 874 lives, 142 of them children; in Yemen, 17 men were targeted, 273 people killed, and at least four of those men survived the attempts on their lives.

By the time his presidency ended, Obama's list of bombed countries read like a morbid stamp collection: Afghanistan, Iraq, Syria, Libya, Pakistan, Yemen, and Somalia. In his final year alone, American aircraft dropped more than 26,000 bombs, nearly three bombs every hour. According to the Bureau of Investigative Journalism, between 384 and 807 civilians were killed by Obama-era strikes in Pakistan, Somalia, and Yemen, countries we had no formal declaration of war against. Hundreds of innocents who had nothing to do with terrorism were lost beneath the blast radius of Obama's "precision" war.

Infamously, Obama reportedly told senior aides in 2011, "Turns out I'm really good at killing people. Didn't know that was gonna be a strong suit of mine."

The reality of Obama's drone war, its hypocrisy, its innocent dead, turned my stomach and left me seething with disgust. I had voted for him to end the neo-conservatives and their bloodlust for forever wars; I never imagined he would become one of them. The Adam Castillo who went to Afghanistan never came home. The young liberal idealist in me died there, replaced by a pragmatist, perhaps even a cynic. By the time I left, I carried a deep scar of disillusionment. I had learned that the greatest evil is not a particular party or ideology; the greatest evil is war itself. War, and the ego that drives it, will destroy everything it touches, even the world.

I came home from that deployment with zero trust in my old party, or in any of my country's leaders. My lifelong faith in the Democratic Party was shattered. I skipped the 2012 presidential election, faced with a choice between the murderous "Drone King" or a neo-con elitist with weird hair, who, according to polls, 2 percent of adult Americans genuinely believed was named "Mittens." In the year that followed, I drifted away from the political discourse entirely, driven by the disillusionment born in Afghanistan and the reality of being a discarded, jobless veteran, both gifts courtesy of Barack Hussein Obama.

I thought my faith in the Democratic Party had already bottomed out. I was wrong.

As I first moved to Asia, I watched California, the bluest of the blue, collapse under its own failed experiment of one-party politics. By 2024, an estimated 187,000 Californians were homeless, nearly a quarter of the nation's total, lining streets, parks, and overpasses from San Diego to San Francisco. Between 2018 and 2023, the state dumped nearly $24B into over 30 homelessness programs across nine agencies, yet a state audit found almost none of them had meaningful tracking or measurable results.

Meanwhile, billions were squandered on a bullet train that was never built, median home prices soared past $900,000, and gas prices, thanks to the liberal demonic tag team of President Biden and Governor Newsom, spiked above $6.40 a gallon by mid-2022. California was no longer the economic engine of America; it was operating at a loss, bankrupted both economically and socially.

California used to be the promise of America, not a cautionary tale. Now it felt like a moralized wasteland, an economic engine throttled by crushing regulations, strangled under some of the highest taxes in the nation, and papering over waste, mismanagement, and decay under the banner of "social justice." Innovators and jobs fled, families were priced out, basic infrastructure collapsed while Sacramento patted itself on the back. California burned, literally, every year. That collapse mirrored my own journey overseas: the slow death of idealism, first in foreign policy, now in the domestic governance of my home. After Afghanistan, I was already done with politics. After watching California's implosion, I was done with the Democratic Party, but not yet ready to wear the Republican label. Instead, I drifted through political no-man's-land, disillusioned, independent, and unsure what to believe in anymore.

Fast-forward to the 2020 US presidential election; I cast my ballot as an Independent for a female president, Jill Stein. When Joe Biden took office in 2021, I had no expectations, and he met them. Two disasters would soon define his presidency for me.

The first was the chaotic withdrawal from Afghanistan, a country where I had served, where Marines I knew had fought, bled, and died. To Biden's credit, the withdrawal hot potato did land in his lap; we should have pulled out of that country during Obama's last term. In 2012, I was part of the last Marine Corps–led offensive, and by 2014 Helmand Province had been abandoned, essentially handed back to the Taliban.

What were we still doing there for another seven years?

By the time Biden took over, we had already ceded much of the country back to the Taliban. The Afghan forces Washington was counting on either didn't exist or lacked the capability to fight. This wasn't just poor execution, it was one of the most catastrophic intelligence failures in modern US military history. The withdrawal was as disastrous as it was humiliating for America.

The second disaster unfolded in Myanmar. After the February 1, 2021, coup, I spent nearly three years trying to work with the Biden administration on the issues that mattered most to my community. As I wrote in the prologue, I spoke directly to a senior White House official, only to be brushed off. I knocked on doors in Democratic offices on Capitol Hill, only to be ignored. I even tried the donor route, buying access to a Democratic senator's fundraiser through the organizing lobbying firm's invitation, only to have the senator skip the event entirely. His staff gave me less than a minute, offered a perfunctory handshake, took my brief sheet, handed me a business card, and walked away. My follow-up emails were never answered.

It was abandonment, plain and simple; the moment the last thread of my tolerance for the Democratic Party snapped.

By 2024, the Democrats had completed their descent into madness. That year, I registered as a Republican for the first time in my life and founded the first Republican Overseas chapter in Myanmar. With that, I proudly cast my absentee ballot for my first Republican presidential candidate: Donald J. Trump. This wasn't about party loyalty; it was about lived experience. I had tried enough, been ignored enough, and seen enough to know the old status quo was broken beyond repair. There was no going back.

All of this was the prologue to the central announcement in my speech. If I was asking my community in Yangon to trust me, to follow my lead through the crisis we faced, then they deserved to know exactly who I was, what I believed, and why I believed it.

NO ONE IS ABOVE THE FLAG

On November 21, 2024, in the ballroom at Lotte Hotel Yangon, I gave my first and only speech at a hybrid event during my presidency. Every committee was present, fresh from a joint meeting to discuss the twin challenges battering us from both sides: US policy on one flank, the Myanmar government's economic decisions on the other. Before I even touched the microphone, AMCHAM's lawyer briefed the room on a lawsuit filed by a former board member, now expelled, marking the first time that fight had been laid bare before our membership. It was the opening act to what I was about to say.

When I stepped to the podium, I began not with policy, but with my own story, the journey from liberal idealist to pragmatic conservative, and why that shift mattered to everyone in that room. At its core, that moment wasn't about politics; it was about demonstrating we could disagree without tearing each other apart and still stand shoulder to shoulder when it mattered most. This was the fundamental issue at the heart of AMCHAM's legal challenge, remaining united despite deep disagreements.

Even as a new dawn broke in Washington, Myanmar remained in the dead of night, with our American Chamber of Commerce, our haven of enterprise and camaraderie, under siege from forces beyond our walls and betrayal within them.

I laid this out plainly to my people. What began as a procedural dispute over the membership vote to extend our board terms had escalated into the absurd. We voted as a Board, overwhelmingly, and he lost. Instead of accepting the outcome, he walked out. Then he sent a proxy to crash our January EGM, turning a routine vote into a sideshow. The only "nay" in the room came from that proxy.

Even then, we tried to reconcile. Again and again, board members reached out to meet face-to-face, to bury the hatchet, to put the Chamber's survival above one man's pride. Each olive branch was slapped away. Dialogue gave way to threats, until he crossed the Rubicon and sued his own Chamber in a Myanmar court.

Everyone in that room knew what that meant. It wasn't just about legal fees. It was about time, morale, and unity, resources we could not afford to waste while the business community was already bleeding.

"No one is above the flag," my voice hardened.

I would not let one man's ego undo what dozens of us had bled, literally and figuratively, to sustain. That's why our Board took the unprecedented step of expelling him. The first expulsion in AMCHAM Myanmar's history. I told them I hadn't made that decision lightly. This was the same man I once called a friend, the man who had nominated me for president.

"God bless him, I wish him all the luck," I said, "but if he wants to talk, he can talk to the lawyers now."

This was the point where I finally leveled with my people. For nearly two years, I had made it my mission to be AMCHAM's shield, absorbing the blows, keeping the drama at bay, and protecting our members so they could focus on their work and our advocacy. That night, however, I laid it bare. Since taking office in 2023, I had been threatened, sued, slandered, and defamed, not only by one bitter ex-colleague but also by outsiders who didn't even live in Myanmar. They came after us for one reason: We refused to bow, stay quiet, or let the American business community here be erased from the map.

The indignation in me sharpened as I recounted one of the most absurd examples of the outside pressure we'd faced. Months earlier, the United Nations Special Rapporteur on Myanmar, Tom Andrews (yes, him again), living comfortably in Maine and working from what might as well have been a college office half a world away, had sent a letter to our executive director. In it, he instructed us to bar certain member companies from sponsoring our events and even AMCHAM itself, not because they had violated any US laws or sanctions, but simply because he personally disapproved of them.

This was his priority?

The United Nations Special Rapporteur on Myanmar, in all his self-anointed glory, decided the best use of his time was to come after a volunteer-run organization in Yangon. Not the generals. Not the war. Definitely not the jobless and starving. No, his big crusade was shutting down AMCHAM Myanmar's "Culinary Journey Dinner" event.

Maybe, for dessert, he'd go after the Rotary Club's bingo night.

If this man truly believed there was a legitimate problem with one of our members, why not take it up with the Biden White House, the Treasury Department, the State Department, heck even the US Embassy in Yangon? He'd rather strong-arm a nonprofit organization on the ground in Myanmar? That wasn't just unfitting, it was beneath the pay grade of his office. AMCHAM Myanmar has one rule:

If you're not on the US sanctions list, you can be a member.

The Andrews letter was never just about one dinner; it was a test of whether we would surrender our independence. No government, whether flying the flag of activism, wearing the badge of the UN, seated in a foreign capital, or even sitting in Naypyidaw, has the right to tell us how to run our businesses or our community. Other American chambers in the region bent under that kind of pressure, choosing silence over confrontation. We chose our own path. Where others whispered, we roared. Where they hid from controversy, we faced it head-on. That same defiance would soon be aimed at our number one target:

Government overreach.

Our Chamber existed for one reason: to defend the freedom of our community to work, trade, and grow without interference. We were not an arm of government, and we were not a political pawn. We were the voice of American commerce in Myanmar, and that voice would not be silenced.

"Government does not solve problems, it creates them."

That truth was impossible to ignore. Overreach wasn't some distant policy debate; it was the barricade we faced every single day. Everyone in that room knew it: trade permits vanishing into the quicksand of bureaucracy, a bureaucracy corrupted by design. Price controls imposed overnight that turned months of planning to ash. A tangle of regulations that made even the simplest project a war of attrition. This wasn't theory. It was the air we breathed.

That was why our Chamber could never yield; because the moment we did, we would stop being a chamber at all. This is why AMCHAM Myanmar was always different. For others across the region, AMCHAMs or other business groups grew too comfortable with government compromise, trading their independence for compliance. They muzzled their own voices in the vain hope of earning goodwill, settling for a seat at some irrelevant conference table or a photo at a meaningless trade forum that would never deliver.

We in Myanmar had already stared down the worst. We had been stripped of peace, robbed of prosperity, and pushed to the brink by a system built on control. We endured because we said "no" when it counted, no to the stone throwers, no to the regulators, no to the corrupted, no to anyone who dared to think they could write our destiny for us.

It was at this point in the speech that I paused. I leaned forward slightly and lowered my voice, as if we were huddled together around a campfire on a dark night, sharing a story, waiting to remember what we had forgotten.

"We have forgotten how to believe," I said calmly.

A hush fell over the room. Heads tilted, brows furrowed, as if they too were leaning in closer to the fire. And so, I laid bare the crisis that had weighed on me since the day I took up this mantle of leadership:

"You know when I first became president of the American Chamber, of all the challenges we faced, it was not conflict, or economic ruin or petty member disputes that worried me the most, it was your loss of belief. And it was not that you had lost your belief in the promise of this country, or that you lost belief in our community or even each other. It was that you had lost belief in yourselves."

I let the words settle before pressing on. Over the past year, I had come to recognize a pattern. My people, my workers, my local members, always began a conversation the same way, as if rehearsed:

"My country's situation..."

A fatalistic shrug that seemed to justify every setback as inevitable. The phrase carried everything: weariness, shame, even apology. It was the excuse for every obstacle, the explanation for every failure, the curtain pulled down before hope could even enter the room.

The locals among us, our Myanmar members, spoke it as though they had to apologize for their own homeland, as if being Myanmar demanded an apology. Even the foreigners in our ranks had grown sheepish about admitting they lived and worked here, as though trying to build something in this place was a mark of shame. The spark in our community's eyes had dimmed to embers. Pride was hidden. Too many of us were glancing aside, hoping not to attract the world's disdain for daring to believe in Myanmar.

We had not just lost our confidence. We had lost our belief.

I looked out at them and said quietly, "You don't have to hide anymore."

Here in this community, under the shelter of our shared purpose, we should feel safe to be who we are and to stand tall. Outside these walls adversity raged: conflict, repression, economic collapse. Inside this Chamber, we would be each other's safe haven. And if I had to carry the weight of protecting that space, then so be it.

I BELIEVE

I could not ask them to believe again without sharing my own belief, yet to do that I first had to look inside myself. In the stillness of reflection, I asked why my path had led me here, to this country, to this moment. Over time I came to see it as no accident. The miracles that shaped my journey, the grace that guided each step, all pointed toward a single task: to carry forward the cause of America, the cause of freedom and human dignity, into places where those things seemed lost.

If America's cause was truly the cause of the world, then Myanmar's cause was inseparable from it. The values I cherished at home, individual liberty, free enterprise, the simple right to work and provide for one's family, were universal. Here, those very values were under attack. To defend them in Myanmar was to stand for something larger than ourselves.

I admit that many reading this book may dismiss that as grandiose. I call it truth and in the climax of *The Believe Again Speech,* I gave that truth a voice:

"I don't care what anyone else believes. I believe!"

I believe.

That is all that matters, now and forever.

In that moment, I understood the only accomplishment that would ever matter to me anymore was for my people to rediscover their belief again. It had to be chosen, deliberately, defiantly, as both shield and sword in these dark times. Belief was not a soft optimism for when it was easy. It had to be a weapon they carried and an armor they wore every single day.

When I wrote this speech, I knew it had to bring everything together. This was, after all, the longest address I had ever given, as well as the most multifaceted. As I've written in these pages before, very few leaders ever reach an Act Three of leadership. If *The Awakening Speech* was the moment that unlocked mine, then *The Believe Again Speech* was where the door fully opened, where belief stopped being a slogan and became my mission as a leader. To make that real, I had to give them more than conviction; I had to give them myself. A leader can only ask for belief if he first shows why he is worth believing in. For me, that meant opening the chapter I least wanted to revisit, the most vulnerable moment of my life:

Afghanistan.

I had joined the Marine Corps, determined to fight in a war, so certain in my convictions that no one could tell me otherwise. I believed in a president, in a mission, in a cause. That belief carried me into a war that demanded of me the unspeakable in God's eyes: to take another man's life. That is what war does. It strips everything down to black and white. You wake up and you live, or you die. There is something profoundly human in that simplicity, and profoundly tragic.

With time, I came to see the war for what it was, not a struggle for survival or freedom, but a struggle of ego. Leaders too proud to admit mistakes. Armed groups too certain they alone were right. Politicians too stubborn to compromise. The price of that arrogance was paid in blood, American blood, Afghan blood, and here in Myanmar, Myanmar blood. The true victims of war have always been, and always will be, the innocent: young men, women, and children who never had a say in the battles waged over their heads.

Afghanistan taught me that wars driven by ego destroy everything. It nearly destroyed me, and in Myanmar I could see it destroying everyone around me.

Yet belief offered another path. It was the force that could turn collapse into survival, the spark that could allow a fractured people to stand together when everything else was falling apart. That was why I ended the speech with a warning and a choice:

"If we don't come together, right now, and start believing in ourselves again, believing in the opportunity we have right now in this moment to change things, however small a chance that may be, then we too will be destroyed, our community collapsed into nothing, forgotten, just like the rest of this country."

I meant every word. Belief was not sentimental optimism; it was survival, the only path left to us. It meant refusing to bow to bullies, whether a disgruntled former insider or a distant official who presumed to know better. It meant serving the people beside us, not our own pride. It meant fighting for the freedom to live and work with dignity, trusting free men and women over bureaucratic decrees. This was the heart of what others later called the Castillo Doctrine, though I never gave it that name myself. I preferred to call it what it truly was: *The Believe Again Speech.*

More importantly, I understood that in the moment I gave this speech, I was no longer just a spokesman of my community or even a leader caught in the tides of crisis. I had become the living embodiment of the ideals I championed.

I was, at long last, a voice that truly believes.

THE BELIEVE AGAIN SPEECH

Members, ladies, and gentlemen,

First, I want to congratulate our colleagues at the US embassy not just for their work as civil servants helping me and other US citizens vote, but for being fellow citizens of our Great Republic. As everyone here today knows firsthand, elections should not be taken for granted, and so

I want to congratulate the American people and President Trump for a very successful election cycle. To that point, to our committees, as I told our membership last August after my trip to Washington, DC: We will never have a better chance to affect US foreign policy change towards Myanmar than we do right now, with a completely new government whose agenda here is frankly, a blank canvas, but a blank canvas that can be painted.

To nobody's surprise here, I am extremely happy about my country's election results, maybe too happy. But to the surprise of many of you, this is the first election, the first year of my life since I turned 18, that I am officially a registered Republican.

You know, I was a Democrat most of my life, maybe a moderately liberal Democrat, but still a Democrat. And of course, like most young people, nobody could tell me I was wrong; my ideals and beliefs were the sun and the moon to me. And while I was still very young, I noticed that other people didn't believe in these same ideals as I did: Republicans, conservatives.

Fast-forward a decade-plus: when I joined the military, I had the opportunity to live in conservative states and to understand people's ideals, their issues, their culture, and what I realized then was maybe California wasn't the center of the universe, something most Californians spend their whole life not realizing.

But then I realized something else after living outside of California: those Democrats, liberals, and even myself when I was younger were just rude to others who didn't hold our same ideals, our same beliefs. They laughed at their way of life, called them uneducated or bigots, became outraged over the thought of a conservative argument counter to what they believed in. And so, I began to adjust my ideals to find a way to mediate the gap between liberal and conservative, the moderate center, where I spent many of these past years as an independent voter. I tried very hard to convince the people I grew up with that they needed to understand everyone's ideals and opinions more for the sake of progress. Yet, as the years went by, nothing changed. So, I tried harder. And after a while, I realized it wasn't that I wasn't trying hard enough; it's that no one was listening.

Asking someone to believe in your ideals unconditionally based on what you believe is morally right, however comforting, isn't a moral thing to do. It's cruel.

And some people would label that statement as arrogant, even ignorant.

Well, it's about as arrogant as telling someone what to believe in, and if they don't accept it, no matter how open-hearted or honest their dissent, that they're a bad person, they're a racist, a criminal, a dictator. Well, that doesn't sound very moral or right to me, does it?

And therein lies the foundational issue this Chamber is facing with this legal action brought against AMCHAM by our former member. A former board member who rightly brought up that the Chamber faced a constitutional crisis, to which the Board rightly gave him the opportunity to present a solution to solve that crisis. But when the Board voted overwhelmingly in favor of another solution, instead of working with us, working with the team to put aside our opinions of what we think is right, to do what is best for the team, what is best for the community, that former board member instead chose to resign and abandon us.

He then sent his colleague to make a spectacle and disrupt our extraordinary general meeting this past January, a meeting where this Board gave you, the members, you the people the opportunity to vote on the solution this Board voted for: to extend the current board members' terms till the end of May 2025. Not surprisingly, the only dissenting vote was from this colleague of our former board member.

Yet, once again, this Board had sought to work with our former board member to put aside our differences and do what's right for the future of this community. Instead, he chose to send us legal threats, which dragged out now to him trying to sue us in court, all because he couldn't find a middle ground to talk to us, to agree to disagree to focus on the higher purpose that every governor on this Board must have: the lasting preservation of this community, not the individual, the community.

I have spoken a lot about The Flag of American Commerce over the years, which drapes around the heart of this community; well, nobody is above that flag, not even me. And so, given the negative impact of this situation on AMCHAM's brand, image, and reputation in Myanmar due to the detrimental conduct of our former member, this Board called an expulsion hearing for our former member and voted to expel him from our community, which is the first time an expulsion has ever happened in our Chamber's history.

No one is above the flag, and I wish our former board member the best of luck. I am eternally grateful for his service to this Board. He was the board member who nominated me for president back in April 2023. God bless him, I wish him all the luck, but he can talk to the lawyers now if he wants to have a conversation.

Yet this is not the first time this year we have faced adversity behind closed doors since I became president. I have been threatened, sued, shamed, defamed, and not just by former colleagues, but by activists that don't even live here, and why? Because I refuse to lie down and shut up, because I refuse to be forgotten about here in the dark. Because nobody in the business community can try to help this country. God forbid!

Tom Andrews!

Tom Andrews, the UN Special Rapporteur, sent our Executive Director a letter, trying to shame us into not letting some of you, our members, sponsor our events.

Well, I didn't even dignify that with a response, because we have one rule and one rule only here to be a good-standing member in our Chamber, stay off the sanctions list. Until that happens, there's nothing to discuss. You are my members, you are my people, I die with you before I let somebody that doesn't even live here try to dictate our lives.

And is that not the very essence of why we are here today, why our committees are so important, why our Chamber is so important, because a chamber of commerce is a community that should believe in one thing: Government needs to stay out of our lives, government needs to stay out of our businesses. We are the experts that drive commerce, we are the creators of economic growth, not government and their ceaseless regulations, and where in the world is there not a better example of this than right here in Myanmar?

At the very heart of every one of your issues is government and, you know, we have a saying in America: From my cold dead hands! Never stop speaking out against government overreach, even here, a country where if we import something that isn't even blocked or tariffed, we have to still go through layers of regulation that are drowned in bureaucracy, a bureaucracy that is corrupt in nature and even if we manage to get through that, the government then tells us what price we must sell at.

Government does not solve problems, it creates them. And my problem with other American Chambers around the world, my problem with other AMCHAMs around this region, is they have forgotten this. They are willing to submit or silence their voice against government over-reach, all in the name of trying to help advocate for some pie-in-the-sky multi-lateral trade framework that's never going to happen. They are willing to put their communities of workers at the mercy of government regulation, all because they have forgotten this core belief.

But we don't have that problem here, do we? We know what it is to survive the great terror of big government, and we say "no" because we don't have the luxury of saying yes. But that doesn't mean we haven't forgotten, that doesn't mean we haven't forgotten something so vitally important, because the reality is we have forgotten how to believe.

You know, when I first became president of the American Chamber, of all the challenges we faced, it was not conflict, or economic ruin, or petty member disputes that worried me the most, it was your loss of belief.

And it was not that you had lost your belief in the promise of this country, or that you lost belief in our community, or even each other.

It was that you had lost belief in yourselves.

You became ashamed to tell people you made a living here, that you had a life here. For those of you who are from here, you felt like you had to hide the fact that you were from Myanmar, due to "my country's situation," quote, unquote.

Well, you don't have to hide anymore here, and regardless of the adversity we face as a community, I hope you feel this can be your safe haven because no matter what I face as your president, I will continue to believe.

I believe I have been sent here for a reason, I believe I was born into this world for one reason and one reason only, and that is the cause of America. I believe the cause of America is the cause of the world, and if the cause of America is the cause of the world, then the cause of Myanmar must be the cause of America.

And I don't care what anyone else believes, I believe!

And that is all that should matter to me, that is all that should matter to you, that you believe in yourselves, that you believe again.

You know I've been thinking a lot of my military service lately, about what I believed in when I was younger, how I became lost, and how I found myself again here in this country. Anyone here know where I fought when I was in the Marine Corps?

Afghanistan, I fought in Afghanistan as part of Operation Enduring Freedom.

Over 2,000 of my fellow Americans died in that country, over 400 of my fellow Marines died there, and one Marine died there on my watch, volunteering to fight in some war of egos, that same war of egos that's happening here right now in Myanmar, fighting the same fight they been fighting amongst themselves for over 70 years till today.

This country, painted red with the blood of young boys, women, and children—it is always the young and the innocent who are the casualties of war. The ones that survive suffer the same fate that happened to me, drifting away in some tireless abyss of forgottenness, barely a decision or two away from living in the street with all the other veterans.

Listen to my soul, my friends,

My ego, to not let someone else tell me a different opinion or to accept someone else's beliefs, led me to Afghanistan, where I was willing to kill my brother in humanity with malice in my heart.

Hatred, anger, ego nearly destroyed me; it's destroying this country now.

You listen to me. And take a lesson from the damned, take a lesson from all this:

If we don't come together, right now, and start believing in ourselves again, believing in the opportunity we have right now in this moment to change things, however small a chance that may be, then we too will be destroyed, our community collapsed into nothing, forgotten, just like the rest of this country.

I don't care if you like each other or not. I don't care if you compete against each other; you will respect each other when you are here in this community, under our Flag of American Commerce.

And maybe, I don't know, maybe, together, we'll learn how to believe again.

Thank you.

A VOICE IN THE ARENA

THE AWS COMMUNITY DAY SPEECH

Legacy begins with the next generation.

For all my speeches, achievements, and battles fought on behalf of my community, the true test of Myanmar's future would not be decided by me. It would be decided in the courage of its youth, their willingness to step into the arena when the world expected them to stay silent.

Yangon is the beating heart of Myanmar, the nation's largest city and commercial capital. Yet today, it is a city where conflict hides in the shadows, politics stays muted, and survival is waged in silence.

I remember Yangon in the late 2010s, when the city felt almost charmed. My home and my security business were rooted there in those peaceful years. The streets were calm and safe even after midnight, when I would walk through my old neighborhood without a second thought. Children played soccer barefoot in the alleys, neighbors traded greetings in the evening air, and the city carried an ease that rivaled anywhere in Asia. At the time, the idea of violent crime was nearly unthinkable. My security business thrived on industrial contracts, oil and gas, embassies, telecoms, because nobody thought of hiring guards for apartments or retail shops. There was simply no need. Yangon was a safe haven, and I carried quiet pride in helping keep it that way.

That city has vanished.

After the 2021 coup, these same streets became places where families were murdered in their homes, and entire buses of passengers were robbed in daylight. Families locked their doors before dusk, hid their sons from conscription, and prayed their children wouldn't be lost to drugs. For Myanmar's youth, the collapse was merciless: no jobs, no safety, no future. I watched their courage tested daily, then worn down, each one torn between abandoning their home or staying to endure.

It began quietly, almost imperceptibly, at the end of 2022. First came the robberies, at night, on empty streets, where whispers of knives and shouts in the dark spread faster than the news. Soon the stories piled up: a stabbing here, robbery there. Things once unthinkable became common. By the following year, the thefts had become petty and desperate: rampant fuel theft, copper wiring stolen across the city's infrastructure. The city was slowly eating itself, piece by piece, until what had once been familiar and comforting now carried only dread. To live in Yangon between 2022 and 2025 was to watch a loved one fall gravely ill, still recognizable but fading before your eyes.

I remember one story that struck me to the core. In 2022, a gentle retired professor named U Myint Wai, and his wife were murdered in their own apartment by intruders searching for valuables. They had survived the upheavals of the past, only to lose their lives in a home invasion robbery. A year later, an entire family of three, including a nine-year-old child, was butchered in their home by a local gang that had been scouting the neighborhood for days. In 2024, a woman was murdered during another home invasion, her life taken by four armed men who had broken into her house for trinkets.

Then came the buses. I will never forget one incident where two gangs struck simultaneously one day, boarding Yangon buses filled with commuters and terrorizing passengers with knives. Phones, wallets, and jewelry were stripped away in minutes. For many, it was the moment the unthinkable became ordinary, when even the daily commute could no longer be trusted. These bus robberies became so frequent that people no longer felt safe waiting at bus stops.

One morning, my staff called to tell me my Pilates class had been canceled. My instructor, the same woman I saw week after week, had been stabbed at a bus stop while waiting for her ride to the studio. That was how close the violence came. It was no longer a story about someone else, it was in our neighborhoods, our routines, our lives.

The collapse of law and order, not just in Yangon, but across the country, left communities to fend for themselves. Police were either absent, overwhelmed, or focused on political crackdowns instead of protecting neighborhoods. Thousands of officers had deserted after the coup, and those who remained rarely ventured out from their fortified stations.

My security company was often flooded with requests, investigating burglaries, tracing rampant fuel theft, uncovering counterfeiting rings that gutted legitimate businesses, and even murders of employees. Clients and their workers turned to us to pressure the police to open cases and act; otherwise, nothing would be done.

Nobody was policing, a problem that still exists today.

The robberies were only the beginning. Soon, a different scourge was spreading through the city: drugs.

For decades, Myanmar's narcotics flowed outward, exported across borders in a trade that enriched traffickers and armed groups but rarely touched everyday life in Yangon. Under past authoritarian governments, domestic consumption was tightly controlled. That changed after the coup. With no police on the streets, narcotics poured into the city unchecked. For the first time, large numbers of urban youth became not just bystanders to the trade, but its customers.

The options for escape were everywhere.

A gram of ketamine sold for around $23. A tablet of ecstasy could be purchased for just over $8. Even cocaine, once unthinkable in Yangon, could be bought for $170–$230 per gram, though much of it was laced with cheaper substances like ketamine or meth. Most alarming was the sudden affordability of methamphetamine. Before the coup, a single yaba tablet, meth mixed with caffeine, sold for about $1, already too expensive for many teenagers. By 2024, those same pills sold for as little as $0.15, while ICE, a stronger crystalline form of meth, sold for around $0.30 per tablet. Drugs were no longer rare luxuries; they had become cheaper than street food.

Of them all, Happy Water was the most insidious. What began years before the coup as a high-end indulgence in KTV lounges, where wealthy youth mixed methamphetamine, ecstasy, and ketamine into pitchers of water, soon evolved into a mass-market product. Traffickers began selling it in packets and tablets that could be dissolved into water. Each packet cost roughly $43 and was typically shared among four or more people, making it less expensive than alcohol and far easier to conceal.

The danger went beyond affordability. Happy Water had no consistency; each batch carried a different mix of chemicals, sometimes heavier in meth, sometimes spiked with diazepam, tramadol, or even caffeine. There was no quality control. A drink that seemed mild one night could be devastating the next. What began as a party drug for elites spilled onto the streets, where it was sold like bottled beer. For many young people, drugs were no longer just for recreation; they had become the only way to function in a city starved of hope.

THE LOST GENERATION OF MYANMAR YOUTH

Just when it seemed things could not get worse, 2024 brought a new kind of terror for Myanmar's youth: military conscription. The Tatmadaw-run government revived a long-dormant 2010 law and announced that men aged 18–35 and women 18–27 would be forced into the ranks. What began as a rumor quickly hardened into reality as community governors went door-to-door surveying households. Families knew their children were now targets. Panic spread overnight. Those who could fled on student or work visas or slipped across borders with the help of smugglers.

In practice, the military set quotas of 5,000 conscripts per month, but they were rarely met. Community-level governors, often bribed by desperate families, quietly shielded youth from being taken, creating friction between the military government and its own administrators. Still, the fear alone was enough to break a generation's psyche. Skilled professionals, entrepreneurs, and students who once believed in a future in Myanmar began leaving in waves. Those who stayed drifted from job to job, buying time until they could run for the Thai border, adding to the swelling ranks of undocumented Burmese migrants across Thailand.

For the youth who remained, the choices were bleak. Those who didn't choose drugs simply shut down, living with one foot in Myanmar and the other already out. What ties it all together is loss: of safety, of opportunity, of purpose. This is The Lost Generation of Myanmar Youth: a workforce the country can no longer rely on.

Even if peace came tomorrow, this generation now in their twenties to early thirties would still be missing, the very group meant to be the backbone of the economy. To rebuild, they would have to be persuaded to return, retrained, and culturally reoriented toward belonging, all while still needing to overcome the scars of addiction, trauma, and exile. The war robbed them of their streets, their classrooms, and the final years of their youth. Sanctions then erased what little economic hope remained. What was left was not just broken lives, but an entire generation adrift in a sea of oblivion.

In them, I saw a reflection of my own. I had been part of another lost generation, Marines who had returned from Afghanistan not in triumph, but in silence, carrying wounds no one could see and questions no one dared answer. I knew what it felt like to be discarded, to believe your country no longer wanted you, to look at the horizon and see only uncertainty. That same sense of abandonment gave me a deep empathy for Myanmar's youth, who were living through their own exile, only theirs unfolded in their very streets and classrooms.

My American business community tried to answer the youth's despair in every way we could. For more than a year, it often felt like searching for water in a desert, until at last, a prayer was answered. That answer was Amazon Web Services. They did not simply join our Chamber as another member; they entered as a Platinum Partner, the highest tier of commitment. Their decision was more than a membership; it was a declaration. It was the culmination of nearly half a year of effort to bring one of America's largest companies to raise its banner alongside ours, to place its logo upon The Flag of American Commerce in Myanmar. In doing so, it told our community, and the wider world, that American commerce was still here, still proud, and still ready to support.

When AWS was preparing to host its first annual Community Day event in Yangon on November 23, 2024, AMCHAM rolled out the proverbial red carpet. We threw our weight behind the event, making it one of our flagship partnerships for Myanmar's youth. Together we turned a conference into something larger, a beacon. On that day, hundreds of young people gathered, not to hide from the storm but to lift their eyes beyond it. They shared laptops and ideas, coded through the noise of a broken city, and carried themselves as if tomorrow still belonged to them.

In that room, for a fleeting day, I glimpsed a generation refusing to disappear. It was proof that belief here is not sentiment, it is survival. More than that, it was a glimpse of tomorrow's leaders already stepping into the arena, the arena of Myanmar's crisis, where their courage, not their circumstances, will decide the future.

So, when AWS asked me to deliver the keynote at Community Day, I didn't hesitate. This was not another AMCHAM forum for executives; it was a hall full of young people, unemployed graduates, struggling students, dreamers with little more than persistence keeping them afloat. I saw it as a chance to speak directly to them, not about commerce or policy, but about survival, purpose, and hope. I wanted to give them what I once needed when I was lost: the reminder that they still had a fight worth joining, a future worth building. That is why I turned to Theodore Roosevelt's "Citizenship in a Republic" speech, which famously included the "Man in the Arena" passage. For me, it was never just history, it was a lifeline, a rallying cry for anyone who feels beaten down by the world. If I could become the man in the arena for my community, perhaps they, too, could summon the courage to step into the arena for theirs.

The AWS Community Day was more than a conference; it was a shift in atmosphere, a moment that seemed to bend the arc of possibility. In a country where every headline spoke of collapse, here was a story of creation. To stand in that hall, to give a speech framed around President Roosevelt's "Man in the Arena," was to feel the hum of life return to a generation long dismissed as lost. Over 400 young people, coders, students, dreamers, had defied the risks of checkpoints and curfews to gather, not to protest or escape, but to learn. The air was alive with hackathons, cloud workshops, and the chatter of ambition. For me, it was proof that AMCHAM's partnerships could reach beyond executives and touch the everyday lives of Myanmar's youth.

That day also became the launchpad for something larger. AWS's re/Start program, a global initiative to equip ordinary people with cloud computing skills, found new life in Myanmar through our partnership. From the stage, I challenged AMCHAM members to go beyond applause and pledge internships, mentorships, and even job placements for graduates, ensuring training would not end with certificates alone. Over the following months, 40 young men and women completed the program, mastering cloud technologies and artificial intelligence, and earning globally recognized credentials. What made it transformative was not just the coursework, but the bridge into careers: AMCHAM companies stepped up to host interns, mentor them, and create jobs. Some graduates were placed in Yangon offices, while others worked remotely for firms abroad, demonstrating proof that Myanmar's youth could compete globally while remaining close to their families and communities.

These were not elite returnees with foreign degrees. They were ordinary Myanmar youth who might otherwise have been lost to conscription, migration, or addiction. Instead, they became part of something hopeful: a future grounded in skill and dignity. In a country where opportunity too often means leaving, AWS re/Start showed another path, one where the world comes to Myanmar's youth, and where belief in them is carried forward into reality. For families, it meant sons and daughters could contribute without abandoning their homes; for employers, it showed a glimpse of a workforce that could rise again from crisis.

The number may have been small, just 40 lives, but in Myanmar's fragile present, it was monumental. Each graduate became a living symbol of what could still be built amid the ruins. Their success gave other students a reason to keep studying, gave parents a reason to hold onto hope, and gave businesses a reason to believe in rebuilding human capital. For AMCHAM Myanmar, it marked the beginning of a new kind of partnership: not only advocating for policy and commerce but also for investing directly in the future of Myanmar's youth. For me, it was also a reminder that I was running out of time as president, with only six months left.

My hope was that this would be the start of a legacy, the spark of a torch carried forward long after me. To that end, I ensured AWS had a seat on the Board of Governors, represented by the youngest governor in our Chamber's history. By surpassing even my own record, she proved what I had always believed: that AWS was not only the future of AMCHAM Myanmar, but that she, and the generation she represented, were the future as well. In her, as in those 40 graduates,

I saw the promise that this torch would not be extinguished with me but would be passed on to inspire a city.

For all my speeches, achievements, and battles fought on behalf of my community, the true test of Myanmar's future would not be decided by me. It would be decided in the courage of its youth, their willingness to step into the arena when the world expected them to stay silent.

And so, in the middle of Yangon's unraveling, a voice rose, not mine, but theirs. Theirs was young, untested, but unafraid. That day, I knew their future would not be written by my words or my battles, but by theirs. For on that November afternoon, amid the silence and shadows of a broken city, it was their courage that rose above the noise, clear, untested, and unafraid.

It was not my voice that mattered anymore. It was theirs.

A voice in the arena.

THE AWS COMMUNITY DAY SPEECH

Ladies and gentlemen,

I first want to congratulate Amazon Web Services (AWS) for successfully planning this event today, and I am deeply honored that AMCHAM Myanmar is co-hosting. To that end, I challenge all AMCHAM members who sponsored today's event to take the AWS re/Start pledge, and offer internships in the coming months to the graduates of AWS re/Start's training program. You have an opportunity today to contribute to the future leaders of your company, the future leaders of this country. So, pledge your company's support of these internships today to make a lasting impact on Myanmar's youth.

On that note, I would also like to acknowledge the many Myanmar youth in attendance. I would like to commend you not just for showing up today, but for remaining committed to building your professional lives here in your homeland.

As a young man, I made the decision to leave my homeland in America for a better opportunity. I found that opportunity here in your homeland. Yet, my heart, my very soul will always yearn for my home-land, the family I barely have spent time with, the friends that have become distant memories, the country I so long to return to...this is a regret I still live with today.

Yet I believe that those of you today who stand here at the sunrise of your careers have demonstrated more courage and strength than I ever had at your young age. You have seen the temptations of life living abroad, but you chose to stay here to support your families, community, and country. You made an impossible choice, that you will not abandon your home.

Some will say there is pride in that, others may say even arrogance. But what I see is the moral courage and strength of the future leaders of this country, who are, sadly, too often forgotten about by this world. You have remained true to yourselves and to the promise of your home. Yet I urge all of you today, to keep in mind that if you were to leave your home due to the torments and challenges it faces today, it must be as a last resort. For when your home finally sees a brighter future, there needs to be a country of people willing to lead it, and that people must be from the collective youth I have seen here today.

To share the words of a famous American hero, Robert F. Kennedy, this country "demands the qualities of youth; not a time of life but a state of mind, a temper of the will, a quality of imagination, a predominance of courage over timidity, of the appetite for adventure over the love of ease."

While it is true that your generation of youth in Myanmar has had a hopeful past, you have a very unforgiving present, but I believe, with your commitment to yourselves, your families, and your communities, you will endure the tragedy of the present day in order to see a brighter future.

So do not fear the unknown. Do not let your minds wonder of dreams beyond the shores of your homeland, embrace the country you have been given, the good and the bad.

For you are the champions in the arena, the future of this country, the ones who will emerge from this crisis to lead this country's unknowing future.

And so, I will leave you with the words of another great American hero, Theodore Roosevelt, who once upon a time challenged his fellow countrymen to remain in the arena of struggle, the arena of tragedy, the arena of life, so that you may long carry yourselves proudly for living in a country that you call home. And home will always be where the heart is.

So, when someone else tells you otherwise, that you should not be proud of your home due to your country's situation, that you should not be proud to be Myanmar, that you should leave your country, community, and family behind, that you should leave your very heart behind. Remember these words:

That "It is not the critic who counts: not the man who points out how the strong man stumbles or where the doer of deeds could have done better. The credit belongs to the man who is actually in the arena, whose face is marred by dust and sweat and blood, who strives valiantly, who errs and comes up short again and again and again, because there is no effort without error or shortcoming, but who knows the great enthusiasms, the great devotions, who spends himself in a worthy cause; who, at the best, knows, in the end, the triumph of high achievement, and who, at the worst, if he fails, at least he fails while daring greatly, so that his place shall never be with those cold and timid souls who knew neither victory nor defeat."

Thank you.

A VOICE FOR PEACE

THE PEACE SPEECH

Leadership in crisis requires the
courage to forgive. Let go.

*Without peace, there is no path to rebuild this shattered
economy; without forgiveness, there is no hope; without
belief in each other, there is no future for Myanmar.*

For two years, I had led a chamber of commerce in exile. In January 2025, I returned to Washington, DC, not as a visitor, but as a witness to history at the inauguration of the 47th president of the United States. From January 14 to February 1, I moved through the capital not only as the president of my community, but also as the founder of the US–Burma Economic Forum, marking a new era in AMCHAM Myanmar advocacy. What had begun as an idea born of our Chamber's desperation now took its first steps into the arena of American politics.

The seed had been planted months earlier during my advocacy trip to Washington in July 2024. That summer, I asked myself:

What if we could build an institutional platform that would outlast my presidency and give AMCHAM Myanmar a permanent voice in Washington?

One of my first initiatives as president of AMCHAM Myanmar was straightforward: if our members wanted a voice, then they had to put in the work to create it. That was why I formed an advocacy committee, to put the ball back in their court. In theory, it was meant to gather input from across the Chamber's committees and, through them, the membership. I hoped this body would shape those inputs into a unified message for governments both abroad and at home. Yet theory and reality rarely align. Advocacy is work, hard work, and the hardest part is the writing. Few were willing to sit down and wrestle raw data, incidents, and even their own stories into a persuasive paper that said: here is the problem, here is the evidence, here is the solution.

Yet when I passed the advocacy ball to my members, it rolled right back to me. I had to write everything, every paper, every brief, every draft, every line. Every appeal that carried our community's name bore my pen. That burden kept falling to me, and over time the Chamber had grown too reliant on my voice. By early 2025, with less than five months left in my term, I asked myself:

How could I leave behind more than achievements? How could I leave a framework that my community could carry forward?

That question gave birth to the US–Burma Economic Forum. It

was never just about sharpening our advocacy abroad; it was about building something permanent. I was finished with our appeals being little more than emails to the US Embassy, vanishing into a bureaucratic void before they were ever read. What I wanted was a disciplined, professional mechanism to ensure our members' voices not only reached Washington but kept reaching it long after I was gone. To make sure it endured, I had to tie it directly to leadership itself, from the Board to committee co-chairs, and even to the AMCHAM staff. Advocacy would no longer be a matter of personal initiative or optional goodwill; it would be a permanent mandate of AMCHAM.

This had been my model for leadership all along: Don't just solve the immediate crisis, build the structure to withstand the next one. Don't just raise $100,000 in 100 days, establish a philanthropic institution within AMCHAM that could replicate itself. Don't just secure accreditation, forge an infrastructure that future boards could carry forward.

So, as I set off for Washington in January 2025, two things had to converge. First, the Forum's structure, policy paper, and message had to be ready, and once again, I did it myself, finishing and refining them by the close of 2024. Second, the gamble I had placed months earlier had to pay off, the gamble that Donald J. Trump would return as the 47th president of the United States. On January 20, 2025, that gamble paid off. President Trump was sworn in, and for me the inauguration was more than a ceremony; it was the starting line of a master plan.

I stayed in Washington for over two weeks, living out of the Holiday Inn National Mall. Every hotel in the city was packed for the inauguration, yet the National Mall had one advantage: it was within walking distance of the Capitol and the swearing-in ceremony itself. A massive hotel that shared a building with FEMA, it quickly became its own ecosystem. Most of the guests were the diehard 2015 crowd, the base. I was part of the second-iteration MAGA voters of 2024, the former Democrats, the former independents. Still, they were some of the kindest people I met all month. Each night, I'd walk back into the lobby in my tuxedo after an inauguration ball, only to be greeted like a minor celebrity.

"Do you know JD?!"

I always replied no, I didn't know the incoming vice president of the United States. That never mattered. They were just happy to be there, and so was I. Everyone wanted pictures, hugs, and to celebrate our candidate being sworn into the White House.

Ball season in Washington is its own battlefield. Four nights in a row of tuxedos, drinking, and endless hors d'oeuvres. Knowing what awaited me, I put myself on a kind of "petite Marine diet" in the weeks leading up to inauguration weekend, fasting, eating fish, and praying to God that my tuxedo pants wouldn't split open during a waltz. The routine became almost comical: wake up, workout, fast until evening, show up at the ball, grab a handful of cold cuts off the charcuterie board, have two drinks (which was more than enough to make me drunk), make the advocacy rounds, then head home. Every night ended the same way, back in the Holiday Inn lobby with the base, trading stories, taking pictures, and splitting a hot pocket like it was communion until exhaustion finally won out.

Then came the Arctic winds. For a California boy who lives in Southeast Asia, it wasn't just cold, it was like being stabbed in the face with a thousand frozen knives. People around me were devastated when the swearing-in was moved indoors, some nearly in tears, clutching their little tickets like they'd lost a loved one. I, on the other hand, felt pure relief. Six hours in a metal cage with porta-johns while my face turned into a popsicle was not my idea of patriotism.

Instead, I watched President Trump take the oath surrounded by the base, huddled together in a warm hotel lobby. These weren't strangers anymore. They were my people now, the frostbitten fellowship, bonded by group photos, drunken nights, and the miracle of central heating. All at the Holiday Inn, because apparently Chingy was right, it really does go down there, just not with champagne and models but with MAGA hats, hot pockets, and a broken lobby microwave.

The week that followed in Washington was not about prestige or photo ops. It was about planting a seed. I moved from think tanks to congressional offices, carrying one message into every room: sanctions had failed. They had not delivered peace or democracy; they had only punished the people of Myanmar and handed China a monopoly over our future. The outdated US–Burma policy conversation, long dominated by activists and academics who had perhaps spent a weekend in Myanmar, was now being confronted with a different reality:

Our voice.

A voice of business leaders who refused to give up on the country's future. What we brought forward was not a plea for profit, but a plea for our people. If Washington truly wanted to counter Beijing and help Myanmar's millions, it had to trade isolation for hope. For the first time, our community had a seat at the table, and we were no longer silent.

Amid the excitement of Washington, one quiet moment in my hotel room reframed my mission. I remember lying on my bed at the Holiday Inn, watching Senator Marco Rubio's confirmation hearing for Secretary of State on CSPAN. Rubio was asked about President Trump's approach to the war in Ukraine. His answer was blunt: Trump wanted just one thing.

The dying to stop. That was it. Period. End of sentence.

The line shook me. For all the fire I had poured into our advocacy, for all the hope I had placed in a new US administration, here was a truth I could not ignore. Peace would never begin in Washington or any other foreign capital. Even if Washington shifted course and every policy battle was won, what good would it do if the people of Myanmar were not ready for peace? It had to begin with the people of Myanmar.

That realization stayed with me. Myanmar is a country of scores; everyone has a grievance, everyone has a score to settle, and that stubbornness has made its civil war the longest running in modern history. No policy paper or law from abroad could change that human reality. The only influence within my reach was over everyday people, urging them to let go of hate, to choose compromise, to see peace not as weakness but as strength. Peace requires compromise; no one can have it entirely their own way, even when they believe they are right.

By then I knew I was entering the third act of my leadership. This act, and my final months as president, demanded something greater of me. The belief we had rekindled as a community could no longer be spent only on survival; it had to be lifted into something higher. My role was not to dictate peace, but to inspire it, to spark in others the courage to let go of hate, to choose compromise, and to imagine a future beyond vengeance. The question was no longer how to preserve AMCHAM, but how to help our people see that reconciliation itself was possible.

INTERNATIONAL WOMEN'S DAY

The right stage presented itself soon enough, our second annual International Women's Day on March 8, 2025.

This was only our second-ever International Women's Day event, something my executive director and I, two men, had first introduced the year before. It might have seemed unlikely, even ironic, that we would be the ones to make Women's Day part of AMCHAM's calendar. To some observers in the US, it was stranger still that I, a self-described MAGA conservative and unapologetic Trump supporter, would be the one to carry it forward. American media often caricature people like me as indifferent or hostile to such causes. That image never matched reality, certainly not mine, not Myanmar's, and not the world outside their bubble.

Looking back, I'll never forget that during our first Women's Day, one prominent female business leader in our community said the biggest problem wasn't men saying the wrong things, it was that men simply weren't there. She told us she had invited a fellow male business leader to attend. He brushed it off and said he'd just send his female staff. Her response was pointed:

"This is not a women-only event. This is an AMCHAM event. Where are the men?"

She was right, and it stung. Of our 11 board members, three were women, and all three showed up. Out of the seven men, only two came: me and one other. The room of 70-odd attendees had maybe ten men. For a Chamber where most of our active membership was male, the absence of men was glaring. It wasn't just the others, it was me as well. At that first Women's Day, I chose not to give any closing remarks, the only time I had ever done that at a major AMCHAM event. I stood back and ceded the stage entirely to our keynote speaker, thinking that was the respectful thing to do. In truth, I had treated the event as something "other," instead of giving it the same weight as any major AMCHAM gathering.

That was a failure of leadership on my part. Equal opportunity is not about sidelining one group to uplift another. It is about everyone feeling welcome and invested. Our women leaders were not asking for men's silence. They were asking for our support and our presence. I realized then that the issues women face, like the pursuit of peace itself, were not peripheral to our mission. They were central to who we were as a community. That realization flipped a switch. If International Women's Day was going to be a true AMCHAM tradition, it had to be treated as such. A day for all of us. Men and women alike. And if I expected my members to show up, I had to show up first, fully and without reservation.

By the time I returned from Washington in February 2025, my decision was made. Our second annual Women's Day would not be an afterthought. It would stand as one of AMCHAM's flagship events. Before leaving for the US, I told my executive director we needed to be organized and make it count. We formed a Women's Day Impact Committee, led primarily by women, with men included by design, and a clear mandate to build something worthy of our community. They delivered. What had been a one-hour program became a half-day of substantive discussions on leadership, opportunity, and impact. Even while I was still in America, the committee was building momentum, promoting the event, and securing sponsorships.

This was never just about scale. It was about direction. Before our first Women's Day in 2024, I insisted that women's health sit at the center of the agenda. That inaugural event included only a single presentation, but I knew it had to become the foundation we built upon. Women's health was not a side issue. It shaped families, workplaces, and daily life in ways no policy panel or business report ever could. For me, it was also personal.

That commitment traced back to the early years of building my company. Some of my longest-serving female staff began missing work or quietly enduring pain. When I asked why, I received vague answers. Fatigue. Stomach pains. It took pushing past cultural taboos to uncover the truth. Many were not receiving proper care, and some did not even know what care existed. I remember asking one employee when she had last seen a gynecologist. She did not know the word. She had never heard of a Pap smear. That moment floored me. These were women I cared about like family. They were suffering not from a lack of access, since my company provided healthcare, but from a lack of knowledge in a culture where women's health was never discussed openly.

Once I understood that, I acted. I personally brought my female staff to Bangkok, paid for their appointments, and made sure they received proper care. I saw firsthand what knowledge and openness could change. Women in Myanmar do not just need access to healthcare. They need access to information.

That lesson came full circle at our 2025 Women's Day. One panel highlighted projects funded through our Social Impact Donation Fund. These initiatives were led by women who had received grants from our "$100,000 in 100 Days" campaign and used them to improve health and education in their communities. They were breaking the same cultural barriers I had confronted years earlier, equipping women with practical knowledge and the confidence to care for themselves and their families.

That is why women's health became a cause I carried as president of AMCHAM Myanmar. Not because of politics and certainly not to appease a corporate diversity, equity, and inclusion (DEI) mandate. I had no interest in performative initiatives. I cared because of my mother, my sister, and women like Zar who helped me build my company.

All these threads, economic survival, community leadership, and women's health, were converging as March 8, 2025, approached. Less than three weeks after I returned from Washington, I once again stood before my community. Thanks to the Impact Committee's tireless work, our second annual International Women's Day was ready. Over 170 people registered, more than double the previous year. Our local hospital sent doctors and nurses to set up booths for on-the-spot health consultations. Families came with their daughters; colleagues brought their teams. The event buzzed with energy.

For me, this day carried a weight far beyond the panels and presentations. It was the stage I had chosen for one of the most important speeches of my presidency, *The Peace Speech*, one I hoped would live on in the memory of my community. I had begun writing it more than a month earlier, during long, quiet nights in Washington. At the Holiday Inn on the National Mall, as I wrestled with what peace could truly mean for Myanmar, I turned to one of the greatest pieces of American oratory on the subject: President John F. Kennedy's 1963 commencement address at American University, remembered now simply as the "Peace Speech."

Kennedy had spoken at the height of the Cold War, when two nuclear-armed superpowers stood locked in stalemate. His words were simple yet profound:

"I speak of peace because of the new face of war. Total war makes no sense in an age when great powers can maintain large and relatively invulnerable nuclear forces and refuse to surrender without resorting to those forces."

Myanmar, of course, had no nuclear weapons and no vast arsenals of annihilation. Yet the spirit of that line struck me. Kennedy was warning that even with the most powerful weapons on earth, total war was futile, no one could truly win. In Myanmar, the weapons were not nearly as advanced, yet the truth was the same. Stubbornness and ego had trapped the country in a cycle where no side could prevail, while all were willing to see it destroyed rather than compromise. Myanmar's forever war was not fought with nuclear weapons that could end the world, but with a mindset that guaranteed endless destruction just the same.

Still, it was not that passage alone that guided me. Of all Kennedy's words, the one I carried back to Yangon and etched into my own address was his immortal line, "not merely peace for our time, but peace for all time." That became the foundation of my speech. I built my address around that vision, peace not as an abstract diplomatic ideal, but as a living necessity. It had to be real, tangible, rooted in daily life. I also knew the right audience to begin with would be those most ready to imagine a different future.

When I took the podium on March 8, 2025 at the Novotel Max hotel in Yangon, I asked the audience to do the hardest thing: to let go of the generational grudges, the "scores" so many in Myanmar were determined to settle. I told them that peace requires compromise, that we cannot always have it entirely our way, even when we are certain we are right. From there, the speech widened in scope. I spoke of why I had founded the US–Burma Economic Forum just weeks earlier, not as a political instrument, but as a lifeline. At its heart, my message was painfully simple:

"I wanted the dying to stop. I wanted the bombings to stop. I wanted the sanctions to stop."

This was not about surrendering or about choosing sides. It was about survival. I wanted the children of this country, my workers' children, my community's children, to have a future filled with opportunity and hope. None of that would be possible without peace.

Unlike some of my earlier addresses, I did not rely on dramatic repetition or the familiar rhythms of speechmaking. I wasn't trying to rouse the room with fiery rhetoric or stir emotion for its own sake. What I wanted was clarity. What I wanted was honesty. Above all, what I wanted was peace.

Of all the speeches I wrote as president of AMCHAM Myanmar, my sentimental favorite will always be *The Awakening Speech*. Yet objectively, I know *The Peace Speech* was the best I ever wrote during my time leading the Chamber. In craft, content, and context, it came together in a way I had never achieved before. Built on timeless phrases from JFK's address, not copied but used as guideposts, it carried a resonance that reached beyond Myanmar's immediate crisis. With only minor adjustments, it could have been delivered anywhere in the world and still held meaning, because it spoke to universal human truths.

By March 2025, it was the eleventh major speech of my AMCHAM presidency, the product of nearly two years of crisis leadership and constant refinement. Writing and delivering those speeches without a professional speechwriter had sharpened me in a way nothing else could. I often tell young leaders: You don't become a strong public speaker overnight. You get there through consistency, by reading, writing, speaking, and above all, preparation. That is and will always be the winning formula for public speaking and speechcraft.

That same formula was the breakthrough for me as a leader and communicator. For over a decade I had written briefings, first as a Marine officer, later as a security and conflict expert. Briefings inform; speeches must inspire. To take something as heavy as Myanmar's peace process and turn it into a message people wanted to hear, that was an art form of its own. Yes, the speech was rooted in policy, the most policy-driven I had ever given. It called for peace as an economic imperative, aligned survival with reconciliation, and urged outsiders, from Washington to other foreign capitals, to rethink their reliance on sanctions. Perhaps sanctions and isolation without engagement only perpetuate the same civil war they claim to want to end. Yet *The Peace Speech* was never a dry brief aimed at diplomats and policymakers. It carried a singular vision of peace, the clearest reflection of what I wanted my leadership to stand for.

My hope is that those reading this book, especially those in Myanmar, will look at *The Peace Speech* as a guide that transcended that ballroom. It reframed everything my people had been working toward, the Chamber's mission, even my own leadership, through the single prism of peace and human dignity. I declared peace not as a diplomatic talking point but as a practical necessity.

Without peace, there is no path to rebuild this shattered economy; without forgiveness, there is no hope; without belief in each other, there is no future for Myanmar.

In declaring these truths, I repositioned AMCHAM Myanmar not as a bystander to conflict but as a bridge between economic survival and national healing. This was not surrender; it was a statement that peace must begin within our own hearts. It was not just a speech, it was a call to see beyond vengeance, to live differently, to heal our souls, and above all, to awaken what the world has always needed:

A voice for peace.

THE PEACE SPEECH

Ladies and gentlemen, excellencies, distinguished guests,

I want to begin by acknowledging and congratulating our sponsors, the Women's Day Impact Committee, and the AMCHAM staff for organizing this flagship event, the second of its kind in our community's history.

Last year, I spoke about the need for greater representation of female leadership within our community. I expressed my confidence that the future president of this Chamber could be one of the remarkable women in this audience. However, as I reflect on last year's event, I realize I misunderstood the deeper message. Women's Day is not just an event for women; it is an event for our entire community.

And yet, despite the significance of the occasion, the absence of men in both attendance and support were glaring. An event meant to celebrate women in leadership should have seen men standing alongside women, championing their achievements. As such, the men in this community failed our women last year. And so, I have made it a point in the past year to ensure every man on this Board, in this community, looks forward to attending this event just like any other AMCHAM event.

I have always treated every AMCHAM event as a chance to address my community on the broader issues we face or accomplishments we have achieved. Yet, last year I chose to limit my remarks because I also felt it was a day for women's voices only, this was the biggest failure of my presidency.

As my time as your president is drawing closer to the end, I have been thinking on the community I have tried to build, a shining city upon a hill, a beacon of light for those wayward wanderers to find safe haven in this eclipsing storm of darkness, or perhaps a place of truth; the admiration of our community should be in our creation of a haven that has become, as a famous poet [John Masefield] wrote: "a place where those who hate ignorance may strive to know, where those who perceive truth may strive to make others see."

I have, therefore, chosen this time and this place to discuss a truth on which we ourselves, both women and men, can strive for across our lives, from our families through our communities to the examples we set abroad, and that is the goal of peace.

But what kind of peace do I mean?

I am talking about a genuine peace, the kind of peace that makes life in our homes and our communities worth living, the kind that enables women and men to grow families together, for those families to hope and build a better life for their children, not merely peace for a particular gender, or ethnicity, or religion but peace for all women and men in Myanmar, not merely peace in our time in this country but peace for all time.

I speak of peace on this day of celebration because never-ending war makes no sense in Myanmar. That was true over 70 years ago and continues to be true today. In an age where genuine peace can be the product of the sum of many acts of kindness. For peace is a process that begins with us as humans: first in our individual hearts, then in the hearts of our families, then in the hearts of our communities, and then hopefully, by God's grace, maybe this country and even the world may one day find peace.

However, peace is not just a moral imperative, it is an economic necessity. The devastation this country has experienced over the past four years, marked by violence, bombings, and sanctions, erased a near decade's worth of economic progress. So even if peace were declared tomorrow, rebuilding Myanmar may very well take generations. And so, this country's continued path towards further violence and sanctions will bring an eventual economic collapse that will not just harm businesses, but ruin families and communities, the very fabric of Myanmar's future.

This is why I founded the US–Burma Economic Forum in Washington, DC. An initiative born out of our collective desperation with a simple yet urgent mission:

I want the dying to stop, I want the bombings to stop, I want the sanctions to stop.

This forum does not take sides: It takes action. It seeks solutions to end suffering, to end economic devastation, and to push for policies from America that will finally help Myanmar find peace to rebuild, rather than continue historical policies that only seek to punish.

The members of this American Chamber, of this community have worked tirelessly over the past four years to ensure economic hope survives for the people of Myanmar, whether it be by saving or creating jobs. The US–Burma Economic Forum was created to extend this work: to ensure our voices are heard in Washington, DC, so that US policy finally reflects not only the reality on the ground, but the reality of what the people of this country truly need: hope, hope.

This Forum is not about politics. It is about our people. It is about making sure that Myanmar's innocent millions are not left in the darkness of sanctions and despair that marked the decades prior to our community's formation. America needs to hear from those who know Myanmar best: You, the people. You, the people, who strengthened our unity as a community, turning doubt into resolve and reaffirming our belief not only in Myanmar's future, but ourselves.

And now is the time, my friends, to share this belief with the world.

While there will be others here and abroad that will cast doubt on our belief, who will work to block our mission due to their own distrust and insecurities, today I say this to them:

There will always be quarrels and conflicting interests between different groups, as there are within families, but we all are working towards this same goal of peace. For peace in Myanmar starts with not only peace between our communities, but ourselves.

Peace in Myanmar cannot be decreed from above but forged in the communities we build, where the women are safe and empowered, and the men are just and strong.

So let the cynics, if they wish, continue to doubt our call for peace; we will answer. For peace is not declared in a moment, it is built in the quiet strength of our daily actions, in the courage to listen, in the wisdom to embrace, and in the conviction that our shared future is worth saving. Let us choose peace, not as an ideal beyond reach, but as the foundation we lay as one people and one community.

Thank you.

INTERLUDE THREE

THE EARTHQUAKE

For the first time since 2021, people set aside the identities that had divided them. Ethnicity, religion, class, none of it mattered beside the work of saving lives. They did not care if the military threatened them with arrest. They did not care if pro-democracy groups threatened to brand them as collaborators. Myanmar's citizens led the relief effort for the nation's most tragic natural disaster, sending whatever they could spare to those who needed it. To help heal the country. If there was one ray of hope in the sea of despair and death that was March 28, 2025, it was this. This dream. The dream of what this country could be. The dream of Myanmar, not Burma, Myanmar. And the dream of one Myanmar people.

Earthquakes were not supposed to be part of my story in Myanmar. Not in Yangon. Not anywhere in the country. For more than a decade, I lived in this city without once thinking about tectonic plates. Civil war, yes. Cyclones, yes. Earthquakes? Those belonged to California, my home, my childhood, where I went to college and served in the Marines. Not here. Not in Myanmar.

Yet beginning in late 2024, the ground began to whisper a different story. On November 20, 2024, a 4.2-magnitude tremor near Yangon jolted me while I was working at my desk one night and alerted me to the possibility that this country was not immune. Living on the twelfth floor, I felt my building sway in the night. My staff downstairs barely noticed, but I did.

The next warning came on February 15, 2025: a 5.3-magnitude quake in Magway. The shock rippled all the way to Yangon. That was when one of my clients, a fellow American who had also lived in California at one point in his life, pulled me aside and asked:

"Do we need an earthquake procedure for our sites?"

Absolutely we did.

So, we wrote the procedures, trained the guards, and prepared for the unlikely. By March 28, 2025, the discussion had escalated into our request for an all-hands drill. That very morning, out of sheer chance, an email arrived: the client's CEO had approved it. Not just for the guards, but for their entire staff, scheduled for the coming Monday. Drill approved. Drill ready. We even joked about preparing for "the Big One."

By lunchtime, I had moved on with my day. Around 12:50 p.m., I was in the small gym inside my office-residence when I heard Zar, the same girl who had sat through so many of my speech rehearsals, screeching my name like a rooster. Her voice was panicked. Frantic. I instantly dropped the weight I was holding.

Then I felt it.

This was no drill. The joke was over. This was the reckoning. At first, it felt like walking down an airplane aisle in the middle of severe turbulence. Then the ground shifted into something stranger. The floor rolled. The glass walls around me groaned as if they might tear loose. The entire twelfth floor swayed so slowly it felt as though we were floating, like a surfboard sliding across invisible waves. For a brief, piercing second, I thought, this is it. This building might go.

I had grown up in Southern California; earthquakes were part of the landscape. I could sleep through anything under a 4.0. I remembered the Northridge earthquake in 1994. Yet this was different. Worse. Not only because of the magnitude, but because I wasn't in California anymore. I was in Myanmar, in a country not built for this, on the twelfth floor of a building not designed for this.

Instinct took over. I shoved my foot into the doorway, braced myself, and pulled Zar's arm in close. There was no table to crawl under, no open field to run to. We were twelve stories up. Running meant death. Some staff tried to bolt for the stairwell; others froze where they stood.

"Get down and cover!" I shouted, forcing them to react with the authority in my voice.

Then, just as suddenly as it began, the shaking eased. Still, I stayed in the doorway until the motion stopped.

By then, most of the building had been evacuated. Staff who made it to the ground floor later told me the streets outside had already descended into chaos, crowds crying, rushing, scattering in confusion. I wasn't among them. I remained with my security team, checking elevators and stairwells to make sure no one was trapped. I stayed behind on the top floor until every member of my staff was evacuated. We would be the last ones out.

Then, less than 15 minutes later, the aftershock struck. The ground convulsed again, nearly as strong as the first. Pavement rippled. From my twelfth-floor windows I could hear the screams rising from the streets below as people stumbled in terror.

Standing just inside beside my balcony, my eyes went instinctively towards Shwedagon Pagoda, just as a herd of birds erupted from the golden stupa, a dark, frantic mass swirling into the sky as if fleeing the earth itself. In that moment, none of us could grasp the scale of what had begun. This was no tremor. Later I would learn the earthquake had registered 7.7, the aftershock 6.7, a one-two punch against an already fragile nation. This was the earthquake that would be remembered as one of Myanmar's most tragic natural disasters. A reckoning that would test every instinct I had as a leader and redefine the closing months of my presidency.

I had watched this country endure tragedy after tragedy. First came the pandemic, hollowing out the streets and silencing daily life. Yangon's roads, once alive with honking traffic and street vendors calling out their wares, fell quiet, emptied by fear.

Then came the coup, and what fragile stability remained was shattered overnight. I stayed through it, as protests filled the streets, gunfire cracked through the air, and the city I had lived in for more than a decade dissolved into barricades, smoke, and blood. Conflict spread, and Myanmar's future began to bleed out slowly, relentlessly.

Through it all, I never once left for California, for home. For more than two and a half years, I stayed. My family asked, my friends asked, but I could not bring myself to leave. This country's struggles had become my own.

In September 2024, Typhoon Yagi struck. I was in Yangon when it hit, watching waterfalls of rain flood the streets and winds howl through the city. Myanmar suffered more deaths than any other nation in Yagi's path. Townships flooded overnight. Rivers burst their banks. Villages vanished beneath walls of water. Our members stepped forward. Donations were collected, and funds were passed directly to trusted local associations with partners already distributing relief supplies in the affected areas. For those who had survived pandemic, coup, and conflict, Yagi came like a thief in the night, drowning what little they had left.

Then came March 28, 2025, when the earth conspired with tragedy to break what little hope this nation still carried.

The earthquake struck Myanmar with a violence that defied imagination. Within minutes, thousands were gone. Entire neighborhoods crumbled into dust and ash. In Sagaing Region, the epicenter, nearly

80 percent of the urban center collapsed. Villages simply ceased to exist. In Mandalay, schools, markets, and homes were all reduced to rubble. The twelve-story Sky Villa condominium, once home to the city's highest rooftop bar, crumbled like a sandcastle, entombing those inside. Monasteries that had stood for centuries were reduced to mounds of red brick, their golden spires piercing upward like broken spears.

Volunteers and rescue workers said that within days the smell of death had become unbearable. Cigarettes became a kind of currency, stuffed into noses to block the stench as the dead were pulled from the ruins. With every gust of wind, the odor of the dead carried through the air. By the first week, more than 3,000 deaths were confirmed, with thousands more injured or missing. By April, the official toll edged toward 4,000, but that wasn't the truth. The truth is everyone just stopped counting. There were too many missing, too many trapped beneath the rubble, too many souls lost. Those who lived through the tragedy of Myanmar's earthquake know it claimed tens of thousands. Yet the world's media gave it no such weight, 15 minutes of coverage for the greatest humanitarian disaster in the country's modern history.

What went almost unnoticed outside Myanmar was how deadly the aftershocks were. Nearly 200 followed in those first few days. The largest, a 6.7, struck just 12 minutes after the first quake, collapsing what little remained of already-damaged structures. Survivors clawing their way out of the rubble were buried again in an instant. It was as if the earth itself was determined to keep Myanmar on its knees.

The earthquake also severed the country's critical supply route: the artery from Yangon, the main logistics hub, to Mandalay and onward into Sagaing. The epicenter in Sagaing lies just across the Irrawaddy River from Mandalay, connected by two bridges. One collapsed entirely; the other stood cracked and compromised. In desperation, volunteers risked small vehicles inching across the damaged bridge one by one. Others ferried supplies by boat or raft, crossing a river that had suddenly become the barrier between life and death.

That Mandalay–Sagaing corridor was the chokepoint. It did not matter how many international response teams arrived, how much aid was flown in, or how many pledges were made in far-off capitals. If supplies could not cross that river, the relief effort would continue to fail. In the end, it wasn't just buildings that collapsed.

The country was broken.

But, amid the paralysis of the usual disaster responders, heroes were rising from unexpected places. Myanmar's own citizens refused to wait. In the first hours after the earthquake, neighbors became first responders, digging with their bare hands, lifting broken concrete, pulling strangers out as if they were family. Families in Yangon pooled whatever they could, rice, bottled water, basic medicines, and loaded trucks bound for the north.

With the main Yangon–Mandalay highway broken, a trip that once took under eight hours stretched to 15 or more as convoys had to divert onto the now crumbling old highway. Still, they drove. Local businesses organized relief convoys, fueled not only by their own money but by donations from everyday people who wanted to help. Much of what we were doing as a business community was simply helping connect donors with whichever company's convoy was headed north next. If someone had something to send, they passed it to the next convoy.

If citizens were the heart of the response, two local member banks, our platinum AMCHAM members, became its backbone. They didn't just donate; they committed resources on a massive scale.

One bank pledged over 15B kyats for immediate relief and another 30B to build a permanent recovery center in Mandalay. When the center opened in June, it quickly became a lifeline. Every day, it provided free medical care to hundreds of patients, served hot meals from a community kitchen, and offered clean water, toilets, showers, and laundry facilities. Just as crucial, it created financial recovery services so families and small businesses could begin again. The bank also sent out thousands of bags of cement to repair monasteries and nunneries, rice for displaced families, and staples like instant noodles for villages on Mandalay's outskirts.

The other bank focused on the surge in medical needs right after the earthquake. Within the first week, it set up a 50-bed field hospital at Mandalay General, then added a 150-bed facility at another Mandalay hospital just two days later. Its teams repaired the nine-story general ward at Mandalay General, as well as the surgical and maternity wings at Sagaing General. At the same time, they deployed heavy equipment crews to clear debris and demolish unsafe structures.

This was the character of the first phase: citizens and local businesses carrying the country's hope across a broken map, 15-hour relief convoys, bare-handed rescues, and donations stitched together from whatever could be spared. In that struggle, something larger came into view.

For the first time since 2021, people set aside the identities that had divided them. Ethnicity, religion, class, none of it mattered beside the work of saving lives. They did not care if the military threatened them with arrest. They did not care if pro-democracy groups threatened to brand them as collaborators. Myanmar's citizens led the relief effort for the nation's most tragic natural disaster, sending whatever they could spare to those who needed it. To help heal the country. If there was one ray of hope in the sea of despair and death that was March 28, 2025, it was this. This dream. The dream of what this country could be. The dream of Myanmar, not Burma, Myanmar.

And the dream of one Myanmar people.

This is where my work truly began. AMCHAM stepped in alongside these citizens and local member banks, to reinforce what was already moving, to align resources with the routes that still worked, and to carry this fragile unity forward into the next phase of response.

By March 30, I had rallied partners in Washington and across Southeast Asia. Out of that effort came an unprecedented collaboration: the Tri-Relief Coalition, a partnership of AMCHAM Myanmar, the US Chamber of Commerce, and the US–ASEAN Business Council, created to coordinate international relief from the business community. The calls and emails flew overnight, and the response was immediate. Within weeks, pledges began arriving: medical supplies from a pharmaceutical company, food from suppliers in Thailand. We moved quickly, arranging sea shipments that delivered more than three tons of critical relief supplies to our distribution partner, one of our member banks.

THE REBUILD FUND

Relief supplies, however, were only half the battle. Rebuilding would be the greater challenge. Even as emergency aid moved, I laid the groundwork for a longer-term initiative: a fund dedicated to restoring what the earthquake had destroyed. I took an entity we already had, the SID Fund, once used for small community projects, and reshaped it into something larger, something lasting.

I called it the Rebuild Fund.

The mission was clear: to support two types of initiatives, water sanitation infrastructure and healthcare. This was not about abstract programming or lengthy reports; it was about bricks, pipes, wells, and clinics. On March 31, I announced the Rebuild Fund as a call to arms for anyone who cared about Myanmar's future.

By May, we were already funding our first project through our trusted local NGO network in a rural township of Mandalay Region. The goals were simple but vital: repair 15 water points, build 15 emergency latrines, and train 15 health workers on hygiene, assistance that reached more than 2,500 people. It was proof of concept. The Rebuild Fund was not charity in the abstract. It was a vehicle to channel resources into tangible recovery projects that international humanitarian organizations were far too slow to deliver.

By day I coordinated relief; by night I prepared for what I knew would be the bigger battle, changing the international policy environment that was choking off aid. One thought echoed in my mind: *Roads must not remain broken because of politics*. The military's policies made everything harder, but other barriers were strangling the effort: sanctions and our old buddy FATF, a.k.a. the banking blacklists.

This was not abstract policy, it was painfully real. A US donor tried to wire money for supplies, but no bank would process a Myanmar transfer. American companies struggled to send charity funds, automatically flagged as "high-risk." It was insanity. People were dying because of overcompliance and fear.

That's when I knew I had to take the fight directly to Washington. There was only so much I could do from Yangon. The earthquake had opened a brief window where even the hardest-line policymakers might reconsider their stance, at least on humanitarian grounds, and I intended to seize it.

I didn't fly straight to Washington. My mother begged me to stop in California first. She had been terrified, though she tried not to show it over the phone. When the news of the earthquake reached her and she finally knew I was alive, my sister told me she sighed and said, "I swear that boy has nine lives." Maybe that was the irony of living with five cats back in Myanmar, my feline divine messengers, bringing luck to a momma's boy too stubborn to stop fighting his way through a country of endless crises. I held my mom close, promised her I was fine, and then boarded another plane east.

By April 4, I stepped off the plane in Washington, DC, carrying the urgency of Myanmar's disaster like an extra piece of luggage I couldn't set down. The contrast was jarring. I had come from sirens, dust, and desperation into a city draped in cherry blossoms, the quiet bloom of springtime in the capital, where life moved untouched and unaware. There was no time to linger on that dissonance. From the Hill to the Treasury, I moved from office to office with one message I repeated like a drumbeat: If the United States was going to send more money, and eventually they did, $9M, don't pour it into the machinery of the big humanitarian organizations. They are too slow, too bureaucratic, too tangled in red tape to reach people in time. The real heroes in Myanmar were already on the ground, ordinary citizens and the private sector, moving relief within hours, not months.

Trust the people already saving lives.

At the Treasury, I pressed the point harder. Sanctions were a problem, yes, but the real chokehold was our old nemesis: the FATF blacklist. Even in the middle of a humanitarian crisis, banks kept pulling back. Transfers were blocked, donations stalled, compliance officers chose caution over compassion. Overcompliance wasn't an abstract policy debate, it was killing people. What I did not know then was that, just weeks earlier, meetings in Washington, DC, had already been working against this very message.

Our old friend, Sean Turnell, Professor Sanctions himself, had paid a visit in March 2025, just before the earthquake struck. (Remember him from the first interlude chapter and that infamous paper of his, the one that tried to slap sanctions on every private bank in Myanmar?)

Less than a month before my arrival, he met with the State Department and the Congressional Burma Caucus, the same caucus that was then pushing a bill through Congress to symbolically demand new sanctions. What was Sean's grand pitch in those meetings?

Sanction everything, starting with the banks.

In essence, he wanted Congress to paint a target squarely on the bank's back, so the Trump administration could flag them for punishment.

All of this came at a time when cash was among the scarcest resources in the earthquake-stricken areas. It was also the moment when Myanmar's private banks were acting as heroes, pouring billions of kyats into relief, funding clinics, rebuilding hospitals, and moving faster than the UN ever could. Even after the earthquake, Sean was still out there, insisting that, tragedy or not, the world must sanction Myanmar's "evil" banks. Sean's proposal was the disaster of all disasters, the number one way to cripple the very lifeline keeping people alive.

By then I could see clearly what had transpired in Washington, and I knew this was a fight I could not avoid. That recognition set the stage for the defining moment of my trip, April 9, when the Congressional Burma Caucus convened a special briefing on Capitol Hill to address the earthquake crisis. I was the lead speaker, asked to represent the American business community in Myanmar. I opened as I had in every other meeting: laying out the scale of the disaster, updating congressional offices on the conflict, and urging them to rethink how aid funds should be distributed.

I also knew I shouldn't carry this message alone. Beside me sat a young man who had since become a close friend, Win Ko Ko Aung. He had been a pro-democracy protester during the mass protests in February 2021 and was forced to flee the country after a warrant was issued for his arrest. That warrant was part of a large batch announced on live television during the Tatmadaw's March 2021 crackdown. The arrests targeted not only protest organizers, but also social media influencers and prominent individuals accused of amplifying anti-coup messaging. Win Ko Ko Aung was one of them.

Bringing him to the table was my idea. His story could reach Congress in a way mine never could. No statistic, no chart, no policy argument could match the force of his lived experience.

"WE NEED PEACE"

When Win began to speak, the bustling Capitol Hill briefing room fell into a hush. This skinny, soft-spoken 32-year-old transformed the briefing into a living, human story. He began with memories of growing up under a government controlled by the military and hemmed in by sanctions, a childhood of candlelit studies during blackouts, hospitals without medicine, and families scraping by while the generals endured untouched. Isolation had failed to break the generals, he explained, but it had succeeded in breaking ordinary people like his own family.

Then, with a faint smile, he recounted how he escaped Myanmar after the coup.

"I found this crazy American Marine online. His name is Adam Castillo, and somehow, amid all the chaos, we connected through LinkedIn," he said, glancing over at me.

It was a gentle roast of the main speaker, and I tipped my proverbial hat with a grin. A ripple of laughter spread through the room, and even a few congressional staffers couldn't hold back a chuckle. In that instant, amid talk of death tolls and sanctions, there was a spark of human connection bridging Myanmar and America, a moment of levity piercing the heartbreak.

His tone shifted immediately. He described the night he fled for his life, following the instructions of a stranger from California he had never met. He told them how he escaped, how he was granted refuge in the United States, and how he began again, starting with one minimum wage job to keep the lights on, then stacking two side gigs on top just to survive. His days began at McDonald's, working the fryer until his clothes smelled of grease, and ended hauling packages for Amazon or behind the wheel of an Uber late into the night. It was exhaustion, it was survival, but it was also the first step toward building a new life and, eventually, a career in New York City.

He spoke with pride of earning his green card and securing a career in the nonprofit sector. Yet even with safety and success, he admitted he still carries the weight of those he left behind. By the time he spoke of the earthquake's devastation, the room had fallen silent; you could have heard a pin drop. He closed with a plea as simple as it was unflinching:

"We need peace, not more sanctions and isolation."

His voice was steady, rising with the kind of conviction that can only come from lived pain. Those words hung in the air, echoing off the walls of that congressional room. Across the table, a staffer who had been shuffling papers sat frozen, brow furrowed. In that silence, Win Ko Ko Aung's courage shifted something fundamental. He had put a human face, his face, on a debate too often stripped of humanity. No one in that room would leave untouched by it.

When the briefing adjourned, a knot of attendees gathered to thank us. Win was still trembling with adrenaline as congressional staffers and NGO representatives leaned in with handshakes and encouragement.

Among them was a Burmese woman from the activist diaspora. (For privacy, I'll call her Miss K.) She had long been active in exile circles, outspoken in her pro-democracy stance. She approached Win with a broad smile. Win, showing the kind of respect younger Burmese instinctively give to elders, bowed his head slightly and thanked her in return. From where I stood, the exchange felt encouraging, perhaps even a flicker of hope, that in this moment of crisis, solidarity could bridge divides. For once, it seemed everyone was on the same side, trying to get help to Myanmar's suffering people.

That sense of solidarity was shattered within 24 hours. The same woman who had smiled at Win launched a vicious Facebook attack. In blatant violation of the briefing's confidentiality, she singled him out by name, twisting his plea for peace into an accusation of sympathy for the military. The implication was unmistakable. Win was branded by a mob of Facebook activists. The lie caught fire. Her post ricocheted through diaspora circles, drawing venomous comments: "Traitor." "He's sold himself to the military." "Such people deserve a bullet." Death threats poured into Win's inbox. Just days after baring his soul to Congress about nearly being arrested by the Tatmadaw, he now faced calls for his head from supposed allies.

It was madness, and it was cruel.

I learned of the Facebook post almost immediately when a trusted Burmese friend in DC phoned me in a panic: "Win Ko Ko is being shamed online. It's bad, you need to see this." Win called soon after, his voice carrying the weight of disbelief and sorrow. Miss K, the same elder who had only hours earlier greeted him with warmth, had branded him a sympathizer of the Tatmadaw. She knew his history: the near arrest, the flight into exile, the life he had lost. Yet she took his plea for peace and turned it into a public indictment. For Win, it was not just an accusation; it was a profound betrayal. The elder he had trusted now stood as his accuser, and that reversal cut deep. Shame, sadness, and anger surged together, leaving him stunned. In the hyper-polarized Burmese diaspora, such a charge was no mere insult; it was a scarlet letter.

Miss K's attack was more than a personal slight; It was a ritual of the activist diaspora, a performance of loyalty that demanded victims. I had seen the pattern before: rival exiles denouncing each other, factions competing to prove who bled most for the cause, loyalty measured by slogans shouted louder than the rest. For years it had festered as a sickness. Now Win Ko Ko Aung stood at its sharpest edge. Instead of being embraced as a courageous new voice, he was cast out as an imposter. The community he longed to serve turned against him, not for betraying them, but for daring to speak a truth too complicated for their theater of slogans.

One of the briefing's organizers, an American citizen who herself had fled another war-torn country, said something to me afterward that I will never forget:

"Adam, where I'm from, elders take care of the youth, especially refugees who stand alone. Why are these Burmese elders tearing him down?"

Her question pierced the heart of it. What should have been a circle of care had curdled into something darker. In Washington, the Burmese activist diaspora had become infamous for what many called *the Purity Olympics*, a relentless competition of infighting, righteousness, and factional smears. Exiles fought not to lift each other higher but to prove who was most uncompromising, who was the "truest" revolutionary. Win was only the latest casualty of that performance, a young man crushed beneath the weight of a contest he never asked to enter.

We tried backchannels first. Mutual friends urged Miss K to remove the post, but she refused, basking in praise for having "exposed" him. Each new reply cut deeper into Win. At last, enough was enough. With a few close allies, he drafted a cease-and-desist letter, measured yet unyielding, citing her breach of a congressional briefing's confidentiality, defamation, and the danger she had created. Either she retracts or faces consequences. To her credit, or perhaps her fear, she backed down. By the next day the post vanished, replaced by a clipped apology that pinned everything on a "language barrier." She implied that since the briefing was in English, and she was a native Burmese speaker, she had simply misunderstood Win's words.

The apology was as perfunctory as expected, an exercise in saving face rather than contrition. Yet, in the digital age, nothing truly disappears; her words had already been screenshotted and circulated. That was the cruelty of it: A young man who had lost his country, his career, and nearly his life for democracy was now scarred by whispers from his own supposed community. That was the bitter irony of it: those who shouted loudest for liberty had no tolerance for free speech, exposing the hypocrisy at the core of their cause. This self-righteous diaspora of "freedom fighters." Who, in the end, looked less like champions of democracy and more like zealots, preaching freedom with one breath while purging anyone who dared to think differently.

Yet, instead of breaking Win Ko Ko Aung, the ordeal steeled him. He refused to be silent, returning to New York with even more resolve, throwing himself back into human rights advocacy. Nothing could erase what had happened in that congressional room on April 9. His testimony cut through the fog, forcing Washington to confront the human cost of its policies. It was not a policy win, but it was a different kind of victory: truth over silence. A refugee from Myanmar had walked into Congress and shifted the moral compass of the most powerful country on earth.

In the end, the US government did approve $9M in earthquake funding, though predictably, every cent was funneled to the usual humanitarian giants, bypassing the local civic and business networks we had fought to include. On paper, the system held; our push for reform failed, but I do not count those weeks as a failure. Before, local private-sector channels were never even considered in Washington. After that, the idea was no longer foreign. That alone was progress. I would also note that the private banks were left off that congressional bill sponsored by the Burma Caucus when it went into committee. That alone was worth the trip.

Out of tragedy, however, rose something greater: a new voice, the voice of my community, the voice of a leader, the voice of Win Ko Ko Aung. His words carried a fragile truth, and that truth became a seed. A seed of understanding. A seed of a future that might yet grow beyond vengeance and purity tests into something more enduring.

By the time I returned to Myanmar, I had barely a month left in my presidency. Yet the earthquake had given me something more enduring than any speech or ceremony: it revealed what leadership in crisis truly demands. A leader must prepare for the trials of the crucible yet also stand ready for those that strike without warning. Sometimes you face the storm with a plan; sometimes with nothing but grit, instinct, and resolve.

The question is whether you can hold your people together at all costs.

That was the question Myanmar's earthquake answered, and the lesson it seared into me. Leadership is not avoiding disaster but answering it: standing in the doorway when the walls shake, carrying the burden when the ground gives way. In that crucible, legacies are forged.

THE CONGRESSIONAL TESTIMONY OF WIN KO KO AUNG, APRIL 9, 2025

Honorable members of Congress,

My name is Win Ko Ko Aung. I was born in Burma, also known as Myanmar, and grew up in the 1990s under military rule. Today, I stand before you not only as a refugee who found safety in America, but as a voice for the innocent people of Burma, especially those whose lives have been shattered not only by tyranny, but by isolation, by sanctions that punished the poor more than the powerful, and most recently, by a devastating earthquake that struck an already broken country. The ground shook, but the pain had long been there.

As a child, I lived through a time when the Burmese military controlled everything, and when the outside world, hoping to weaken them, imposed broad economic sanctions. These sanctions cut off foreign assistance, restricted access to financial markets, blocked international investment, and isolated our country. Instead of breaking the regime, sanctions broke our economy.

I remember the darkness, literally and metaphorically. Our power supply was so unreliable that I studied by candlelight if we even had candles. Our textbooks were outdated, our desks broken, and our classrooms short of teachers. Hospitals had no medicine, and vaccines were scarce. While sanctions didn't bomb our clinics, they did make it harder to import the machines and supplies we needed to save lives.

Foreign investment never came. There were no jobs. There was no hope. After decades of isolation, the Burmese military did not collapse. They built patronage networks and enriched themselves, while families like mine had to survive with less. But it wasn't the military that prospered the most, it was China. China, who have armed the military for generations, only to arm their enemies as well. They did all this to choke and control Burma, to exploit my country's resources. When I was a child, I lived in the darkness of sanctions, where the military ruled at the mercy of Beijing. The world didn't see this then. We were too isolated, but my hope is the world can see this happening now.

I didn't learn about the outside world until I found the American Center in Yangon. An extension of the US Embassy and America, you taught me English, and you opened my eyes to freedom, leadership, and critical thinking. I eventually became a youth leader, author of the bestselling book A 21st Century Burmese Guy, and helped mentor others in technology and confidence-building.

In 2018, I visited the United States through the Young Southeast Asian Leaders Initiative, your program. It changed my life. But that hope was shattered in 2021, when the military staged another coup and began crushing the protests for democracy across the country. I was one of the peaceful protestors, but not only did I have to run for my life when the troops came to the street to kill us, the military government then issued a warrant for my arrest on national television. The charge was what our Penal Code classifies as a 505(A). I faced detention, torture, and most certainly years of imprisonment.

During this time, there were rumors circulating among the protest networks, of a bold American man, a former US Marine, who had somehow stayed behind in Yangon. They said he was speeding around the city in a 4x4 black Ford Ranger, helping foreign families, mostly women and children, evacuate, and also evacuating trapped locals to safety who were behind protest lines. This was at a time when all mobile data was cut off and SIM cards were basically useless; Yangon was a communication blackout zone. Outside your home, you were on your own.

I had no idea how to escape. But through sheer luck, and maybe fate, I found this crazy American Marine online. His name is Adam Castillo, and somehow, amid all the chaos, we connected through LinkedIn.

What began as a few messages quickly became a lifeline. Adam had a security company and deep local knowledge. He gave me instructions on how to move, how to stay hidden, and how to get across the border safely. I followed every word.

And that's how I got out, with the advice of an American who didn't have to care but did. I crossed into Thailand, and four months later, the United States welcomed me as a refugee. I arrived in California in August 2021. I started from scratch, working as a barista, then a cashier. I applied for my green card in 2022 and received it in 2023. Today, I live in New York and work for the Human Rights Foundation, defending civil liberties in places like Burma.

I am grateful to this country, not only for saving my life, but for giving me purpose. But I must also testify about what I experienced growing up in Burma, and what I see happening again.

Sanctions, as they exist today, are not working. They are hurting the people, not the regime.

In the 1990s, sanctions made my childhood a struggle. In present day, they are pushing Burmese businesses and Burmese workers abroad like myself to use the black market. Not only because of sanctions, but because the FATF's blacklist designation of Burma, grouping us with North Korea and Iran, has caused nearly all US and international banks to sever ties with Burmese account holders. If I want to send money to my mother in Burma, I must go through an agent who then uses the black market, and who controls and profits from the black market? Criminal networks and the military regime.

And now, after the recent earthquake, the impact is even more devastating. Humanitarian organizations, NGOs, and relief groups are unable to get funds into the country; there is not enough cash in people's hands in the hardest-hit areas. International banks are blocking or delaying wire transfers due to FATF-mandated compliance checks. Relief is being held up, not by politics, not by the military, but by the international bank's arbitrary decisions that Myanmar-related transactions are simply "not worth the risk." Even legitimate local NGOs and relief groups now rely on hundi, currency swaps, or personal courier networks, deepening the country's dependence on the very black market we're supposed to be dismantling.

Sanctions have isolated legitimate business and my fellow entrepreneurs back in Burma. Even more alarming, sanctions have inadvertently strengthened the same military regime they aim to weaken. When Western oil companies like TotalEnergies and Chevron left Burma, this didn't punish the generals, it helped them, it made them richer. They handed more shares of revenue to the military-controlled state-owned enterprise: MOGE.

All of this at the expense of the people, while the regime survives, propped up by China. More sanctions won't change that. In fact, they will only continue to empower China's control over my country.

Burma doesn't need more isolation. It needs US engagement, investment, and smart diplomacy that empowers all armed actors in the conflict, which will undermine not only the military's control, but China's control over them and the country.

I share this story not to ask for pity, but to honor the truth. America helped me become who I am. And today, I promise to use my voice to help others, to fight for peace, because peace is what we need in Myanmar today, now more than ever with the rebuilding that must happen after the earthquake. We need peace, not more sanctions and isolation.

Thank you for the opportunity to speak. Thank you for the freedom I now live under. And thank you for listening, not just to a refugee's story, but to a country's forgotten future.

Thank you.

A VOICE ETERNAL

THE FAREWELL ADDRESS

A leader leaves. A people believe. A city eternal.

Maybe I am crazy to do this on my farewell night, but fighting against the times is not for the sane. Real change never comes from being comfortable, it comes from leaders willing to stand up for what's right when the world says no.

I stood at the edge of the stage, the weight of five and a half years of leadership pressing on my shoulders like armor. Outside, the monsoon winds rattled the windows of the Melia Hotel in Yangon, their steady percussion a reminder that nothing in Myanmar ever stood still for long. It was May 30, 2025, and in a few minutes, I would deliver *The Farewell Address* at our eighth Annual General Meeting, the culmination of a journey that had tested every ounce of faith and courage I possessed. My heart was full, my mind steady, my eyes clear with purpose. This was it.

My final act as president of the American Chamber of Commerce in Myanmar.

As others took the stage to mark my years of service, offering gifts and warm words, my thoughts drifted elsewhere. Laughter rippled across the ballroom, but in my mind, I was back on the other side of the city, standing once more on my balcony overlooking Yangon. At dawn, the city stretched out in silence, its streets waiting for the day's noise, while Shwedagon Pagoda pierced the horizon, its golden spires catching the first light of morning. That view had become my compass. A reminder of permanence when everything else in the country felt fragile.

How many mornings had I stood there, sweat cooling after an early workout or bleary-eyed after an all-night writing session for one of my company's conflict analysis reports? Staring toward that same horizon and wondering what all these years in Myanmar would one day mean.

I remembered the promise I made to myself at the very beginning of my presidency, a promise that our community could be more than a business association. It could be a beacon in the darkness, a refuge of resilience and belief in a country battered by crisis. In my dreams I called it a shining city upon a hill, borrowing the words of President Ronald Reagan, who believed that America's greatness rested not in power alone but in its ability to inspire hope. That vision was no longer a distant ideal. It stood before me in this very room, faces bright with belief, a community forged in hardship, glowing with the inner light we had kindled together.

Yet the path to this moment was anything but straight.

A year before my final event, one unresolved duty still hung over my presidency: the Chamber's constitution. After our seventh Annual General Meeting in 2024, the Board reached a unanimous conclusion. Our structure was flawed, and it was vulnerable. Months of internal conflict and a lawsuit had exposed weaknesses we could no longer ignore. We could not hand the next leadership the same fragile foundation that had nearly undone us. So, we engaged a law firm to formally review and amend the constitution.

AMCHAM's constitution had been adopted in 2018, in a different Myanmar and a different era for our Chamber. It was largely copied and pasted from AMCHAM Thailand's constitution and written for ordinary times. After 2021, it became clear that the constitution was not enacted for times of turbulence. It guarded against entrenchment, but it did not protect continuity in crisis. Most importantly, it failed to place the membership, our true source of legitimacy, clearly and consistently at the center of authority when it mattered most.

What began as a legal review became something more. It became a decision about what AMCHAM Myanmar would stand on after I was gone. If the Chamber was going to endure, its foundation had to reflect our reality, and it had to anchor power where it belongs:

With the members.

By the time we reached the constitutional vote on May 30, 2025, one truth had been echoing in my head for months, and I said it plainly to the room:

"The greatest threat to our survival as a chamber is two things: a lack of leadership continuity and membership apathy."

Continuity mattered because the pipeline of quality leaders was tightening. Foreign talent was thinning out. Multinationals were localizing. Future leaders on the Board would take longer to develop. Without stability, AMCHAM risked becoming a revolving door, with leaders arriving just as quickly as they departed.

Apathy was a disease because a chamber can survive crisis, even violence, but it cannot survive indifference. Empty committee seats, silent members, people not renewing memberships or simply not showing up, these are not small issues. They are early signs of surrender. Once enough people start asking, *What's the point?,* belief slips, and everything else follows.

Those two threats, continuity and apathy, became the backbone of the amendments we brought forward. Not as a Band-Aid, but as a safeguard for a future we could not yet see. The amendments were designed around a single principle: returning authority to where it belongs.

The members.

The first amendment addressed continuity. While strict term limits are a point of pride across AMCHAMs globally, Myanmar's reality was different. Our community was shrinking. Experienced leaders were leaving. Without adjustment, the Chamber risked starving itself of institutional memory at the very moment it was needed most. The change was modest; a limited extension of consecutive board service from two terms to three. Accountability would be preserved, while time would be gained to identify, mentor, and develop future leaders. Stability, not entrenchment.

The second amendment clarified sovereignty in moments of crisis. The scars of the EGM and the constitutional breakdown were still fresh, exposing how easily the procedure could be weaponized for a purpose. If a crisis struck again, authority could not rest with the Board or the president alone. It had to rest with the members, be exercised temporarily, be transparent, and be bound by majority will. What some later called a power grab was, in truth, an act of trust. It placed final authority exactly where it had always belonged. The membership.

The third amendment looked outward. For too long, our advocacy had been diffused and easily ignored. To ensure our voice endured beyond any single presidency, we embedded the US–Burma Economic Forum into the chamber's constitution, making advocacy not optional, but structural. It gave the membership a permanent channel to speak directly into Washington, free from inertia and internal bottlenecks.

These amendments were not about mechanics or governance theory. They were about resilience. About ensuring continuity without complacency, authority without ego, and a voice that could not be silenced by distance, fatigue, or fear. This was the last battle I had to fight for my community. By bringing the amendments to a vote, we affirmed the oldest truth of liberty:

Power to the people.

If the amendments were my final act as president, then ensuring the vote happened was the fight that made everything else matter. None of the speeches or philosophy would mean anything if the membership was denied the chance to decide. Resistance emerged from two directions at once, outside the Chamber and within it. The motives differed, but the aim was the same: to keep that decision out of the members' hands.

Externally, our former governor, now suing the Chamber, attempted to paralyze our event. Absurdly, his sole demand from the outset of his dispute was for AMCHAM to hold an election for a new Board. But when elections were formally scheduled for the AGM on May 30th, he pivoted. He attempted to delay and obstruct our election efforts long enough to keep the lawsuit alive. In April, his lawyers filed an injunction seeking to block the election. Hearings stretched into late May, leaving the Chamber in limbo as the AGM date approached. Only a week before the event did the court finally rule.

The injunction was denied. The vote would go forward.

What caught me off guard was the resistance from within. Less than two weeks before the AGM, two incoming board nominees, both people I had personally endorsed, asked that the constitutional vote be deferred. Their concern was not principle, but discomfort. They feared inheriting a lawsuit. In my opinion, they wanted to retreat from the constitutional changes in order to pursue an easier settlement once they were in power, even if that meant negotiating with the very man suing to block their election to the Board. In asking us to cancel the vote, they were not seeking prudence.

They were asking to avoid the burden of leadership itself.

Despite the hollowness of their appeal, they circulated a letter to the full Board in an attempt to manufacture doubt and sway opinion. Yet they had been largely absent for most of my presidency, only to reappear at the eleventh hour, less than two weeks before the vote to try to sow doubt in our vision. Swaying opinion takes time and, more importantly, trust. By the following Monday, I sent my reply. It was courteous and unambiguous. I made clear that the AGM agenda was valid and that the proposed constitutional amendments had been properly noticed. More importantly, I reminded them of a simple fact: authority in AMCHAM rests with the members, not the president and not the Board. If they believed the amendments would harm AMCHAM's defense of a lawsuit, then they were free to vote no. If they were unwilling to serve on the Board under those conditions, they were free to step aside. Plenty of alternates stood ready. And by the next morning, the debate was over.

The vote would proceed. The show goes on.

MAY 30, 2025

After these ordeals, a close friend asked why I did not simply take my roses, deliver a graceful farewell, and leave on a high note. The answer was simple, because it was the right thing to do. For the members. For the community. For those who would come next. This fight was never about me. It was about protecting the most fundamental right: the right to vote. That was a responsibility I could not walk away from.

That conviction carried me into the ballroom on the night of May 30, 2025. The stakes could not have been higher. Nearly 200 people sat before me. Many were eager. The few critics who had spent the previous weeks trying to stop the vote were among them. I could see them in the crowd, the ones who preferred delay, deferral, or dismantling.

This was the moment when everything converged. The lawsuit. The letters. The shaming. The battles inside and outside the Chamber.

I had to make the membership understand that this vote, something as simple as amending a chamber constitution, was in fact a stand for something far larger. I told my people plainly:

"Look at us. For years, we've been written off, shamed, forgotten in someone else's war. For all the hope we have for this country's future, we know what most people say of us: that we're crazy, that we'll probably all be long gone from this world before Myanmar finds its way back to peace. And yet: Here we are. Still standing. Still fighting for what's right, for our people's futures.

Maybe I am crazy to do this on my farewell night, but fighting against the times is not for the sane. Real change never comes from being comfortable, it comes from leaders willing to stand up for what's right when the world says no.

So here I am tonight. Where are you, my people? You're here, you're here in this room, and you're ready to vote!

Remember this moment. Remember this night. When each of you refused to walk away. When you decided your voice mattered, and moreover: In a country so starved to be free, what could be more fundamental than this? Exercising your right to vote."

When I opened the floor for questions, a remarkable thing happened. None came. Not a single hand was raised. In that silence, I sensed a collective understanding. The debates were over. Everyone knew where they stood. The membership was ready to decide.

"All in favor of adopting the constitutional amendments?" I called out.

Dozens of hands shot up instantly. I recognized them all. Entrepreneurs who had built companies here. Business leaders who believed in our mission. Corporate executives who had stayed in Myanmar against the advice of their headquarters because they believed in the long game. Row after row of raised arms, a visible expression of belief.

"And opposed?" I asked.

A smaller cluster of hands, eight in total, lifted into the air. A member of the AMCHAM staff walked to the stage and handed me a small slip of paper containing the official tally. I unfolded it slowly, my hands steady even as my pulse raced. Lifting the microphone, I read the result aloud.

"Forty-two in favor, eight against."

Eighty-four percent in support, comfortably above the three-fourths threshold required. The amendments had passed. The constitution was adopted and signed into history.

And just like that, a new Board elected, a constitution amended, a shining city upon a hill.

When I look back on my tenure leading AMCHAM Myanmar, I am struck by how much our community achieved against impossible odds. The transformation of the Chamber was not abstract. It was measured in concrete victories that became our shared legacy.

We grew our corporate partnerships from 20 to 44, including an unprecedented expansion of Platinum Partners from four to 14.

We launched the Social Impact Donation Fund and raised $100,000 in under 100 days.

We created the Rebuild Fund to finance recovery efforts after the earthquake in March.

We co-sponsored the Tri-Relief Coalition with the US Chamber of Commerce and the US-ASEAN Business Council, delivering more than three tons of critical aid into the hardest-hit regions.

We founded the US–Burma Economic Forum in Washington, giving our members a permanent and lasting voice in the halls of power.

We earned US Chamber of Commerce accreditation, not in a time of prosperity, but in the depths of crisis.

These accomplishments belonged to every member who stood beside me and refused to let the Chamber's light go out. Together, we achieved more in those years than anyone thought possible.

As I gave *The Farewell Address* that night, I did so with pride and with peace in my heart. We had built a foundation that would outlast my presidency. I knew I could step away with the Chamber stronger than I had found it. Leaving was bittersweet, but it was the right time. The mission had been fulfilled.

The American Chamber of Commerce in Myanmar would survive, even as I moved on with my life.

FAITH IN GOD, BELIEF IN MY PEOPLE

When I reflect on what sustained me through every challenge, it always returns to my own belief, my own faith. Faith in the cause. Faith in my community. Faith in God. From the very beginning, I never concealed the place of faith in my life. In moments of doubt, I prayed for guidance. In moments of triumph, I gave thanks to God. That is why I chose to begin *The Farewell Address* with a blessing:

"May God give you, for every storm, a rainbow. For every tear, a smile. For every care, a promise. And a blessing in each trial. For every problem life sends, a faithful friend to share. For every sigh, a sweet song. And an answer for each prayer."

That blessing was my way of passing on what carried me through the hardest nights, a quiet act of gratitude and hope. I wanted to leave the community with a gift of grace. Leadership in those years demanded more than words or prayer. It demanded sacrifice. Yet any sacrifice I made was repaid many times over by the courage of our members. Together, we survived a pandemic, a coup, an unrelenting war, a typhoon, and an earthquake. In the darkest moments, when silence and apathy threatened to take hold, they showed up. They kept meeting. They kept building. They kept working.

My proudest moments were never the achievements or awards. It was when our community stood together and said, "We believe," and meant it. That resilience is the legacy I hold most dear. It was the moment in time that I called "The Awakening." Yet, for all my grandiosity in calling it that, at heart, it was:

The moment my people found their voice again.

And that, ultimately, is what this book has tried to capture. In every chapter, it was never just about the speeches themselves. It was about the battles behind them and the people who brought the words to life. Some chapters mirror the speeches line for line. Others pull back the curtain. In the end, the speeches were only guideposts. The story was always the point. It is the story of a spirit that burns brightest wherever it is tested.

The American spirit.

Burning bright abroad in a distant land. A spirit carried by a leader who failed, fell, and refused to stay down. My hope is that this book has served, in some small way, as a mirror for you, the reader. A mirror to reflect on your own voice, your own community, and your own leadership journey.

As I write the final lines to this chapter, I am no longer president of AMCHAM Myanmar. I am simply a member. The monsoon winds still blow, and Myanmar's challenges remain real. Yet, the light we kindled together continues to burn.

And so, as I close out the story of AMCHAM Myanmar, I turn to you now, my people, the very ones to whom this book is dedicated. These final words are yours.

So long as belief endures, the light of our community will never be extinguished.

So long as belief remains, The Flag of American Commerce will fly eternal.

Our shining city upon a hill will stand the test of time, radiant with hope, unity, and belief.

The voice we found is no longer mine alone.

It is everywhere now.

It lives in each of you.

In the companies you have built.

In the communities you have built around you.

In every quiet act of resilience that declares one word:

Believe.

THE FAREWELL ADDRESS

Ladies and gentlemen, distinguished members of AMCHAM Myanmar,

Over the past few months, many of you have asked me how I feel about leaving. And the truth is: "parting is such sweet sorrow." [Borrowed from Shakespeare's Romeo and Juliet.] The sweet part? My own personal freedom to pursue new dreams, new battles. The sorrow? The goodbyes of course and the closing of a chapter I will never forget.

You know I lived in this city for over 11 years, and from my terrace balcony in Sanchaung, I've spent many mornings staring out at the sunrise over Shwedagon Pagoda. Lately, I have been reflecting on what these past years have meant. And the image that keeps coming back to me, time and again, is one of faith.

Over the years, many of you have commended me for sharing my faith in God so openly. I have always sought to foster a community where everyone feels free to express their faith in their own way. Whether you believe in God as I do, follow another faith, or choose no faith at all, it is through the expression of belief that we reveal our love to this world.

And so, as I begin this farewell, let me offer you a departing blessing:

May God give you, for every storm, a rainbow. For every tear, a smile. For every care, a promise. And a blessing in each trial. For every problem life sends, a faithful friend to share. For every sigh, a sweet song. And an answer for each prayer.

You and I have been together for a very long time. But I know, in my heart, I have always needed you more than you needed me. And so, today, I stand before you to give the closing address for the twelfth and final time as your president of this incredible Chamber. Serving this community over five and a half years, as a governor, vice president, and president, has been the honor of a lifetime.

When I first took this presidency, I dreamed that our community could be something more than just a chamber of commerce. That it could be a shining city upon a hill:

A shining city upon a hill.

That phrase was popularized by President Ronald Reagan, who spoke of it frequently to describe the America he imagined.

Growing up, even when I was still a Democrat, President Reagan's vision of America through his unwavering optimism, his ability to inspire a nation, profoundly shaped my own belief in the promise of America.

Ronald Reagan spoke of the shining city all his political life, and from the very beginning, I had that same vision. That our community could be a tall and proud city, built on unity, blessed by God, and open to all with the will and the heart to get here. And today, that vision shines, not as a distant dream, but as a city we built together.

But our journey together has not been easy; I was first elected to this Board of Governors in January 2020. Back then, it felt as if our Chamber, like Myanmar itself, was only just beginning to reach its potential. The future seemed limitless, our ambitions were bold, as if economic prosperity was just within our grasp.

And yet, my time on this Board was not defined by prosperity.

It was defined by one word: survival.

We survived a pandemic that shut down the economy. We survived a coup that shattered stability. We survived a conflict that continues to destroy the future of this country.

We survived a typhoon that tried to drown us. We survived an earthquake that tried to break us.

And, we survived an international community that only embraced us with sanctions and doubt.

And yet, through all of that, The flag of American commerce endured. In every crisis, we didn't just survive, we answered.

Desperation became destiny. Crisis became calling.

And in that forgottenness, we answered a call that no one else would: to raise $100,000 in less than 100 days.

That $100,000 became more than a fundraising goal. It became a declaration. It fueled the launch of our Social Impact Donation Fund, but it didn't stop there.

That fund, the SID Fund, became something more. It became a permanent mechanism to mobilize our collective strength in the face of crisis. And when crisis struck again on March 28th, when a devastating earthquake fractured this nation to its core, our Chamber was ready.

From that tragedy, we gave birth to the Rebuild Fund, an evolution of our original vision, now poised to finance long-term recovery initiatives for years to come.

And behind all these efforts stood the strongest corporate alliance in our Chamber's history: 14 Platinum Partners, united in purpose, bound by charity.

And in that same spirit, together we earned something that had long eluded us since the earliest days of our creation:

Accreditation from the US Chamber of Commerce, not during times of ease, but in a time of exile. When the world looked away, when no one wanted to stand beside us, our friends in Washington, DC, reached out to us, not as a reward, but to recognize a simple truth:

An AMCHAM Myanmar today. An AMCHAM Myanmar tomorrow. An AMCHAM Myanmar forever.

And then, we built something new. The US–Burma Economic Forum.

A voice in Washington, DC. A force to challenge the policies that would rather erase this country than help it. A symbol that we will not go gentle into that good night.

But our struggle was never just about enduring sanctions or surviving tragedy. It has, and remains, a struggle for peace.

True peace will never be handed down from leaders or written into law. It must come from the hearts of the people.

So, to our local members, to the citizens of this country, I speak to you directly now:

Let go. Let go of the hate that has taken root in your hearts.

Let go of the anger that has burdened your families for generations.

Peace begins not when others change, but when you choose forgiveness.

Not because your enemies deserve it, but because you do.

Only then can you imagine a Myanmar not built on vengeance, but on love.

Imagine a Myanmar where the burdens of the past give way to the promise of tomorrow.

Imagine a future where people of every faith and every ethnicity grow up not as enemies, but as neighbors.

Imagine a Myanmar where opportunity is no longer the privilege of the few, but the promise of the many.

Imagine a future where your children awaken not to division, but to the dream of one Myanmar people finally realized.

You know, for years, I was told I was wasting my time. That it wasn't my place to speak of peace in Myanmar. That this country's crisis was too big, too broken, for any of us to change.

I was told to accept the inevitable. To move on. To let go.

I have been threatened. Shamed. Sued. Ridiculed. And not just by outsiders, but by some who once stood right here with me in this Chamber.

But if I'm being honest, there was a time when most of you lost yourselves.

When silence felt safer. When hiding in the shadows of this country's tragedy seemed wiser.

But then, something happened. We found our voices again.

We stopped accepting that economic collapse was inevitable.

We stopped apologizing for doing business here.

We stopped apologizing for having lives here.

We stopped letting the world tell us that our work didn't matter.

And when the world said we should give up, when the world said we should shut up, we said no. No.

Our strength has always been in our unity. And it was in this very community that an awakening happened.

A rediscovery of our confidence and our love for this once golden land that we still called home.

Of all the accomplishments we achieved together over these years, my proudest moment came with the resurgence of our community pride, a moment in time that I called: The Awakening.

When this community turned back the critics, the naysayers, the stone throwers, and said: We believe.

We believe in our community. We believe in each other. We believe in ourselves.

And we believe in the transformative power of free enterprise: to uplift the lives of every individual in this country.

So, in times of great doubt, remember it was belief that brought us together. And it is belief that will carry us forward.

And as we enter the unknown future of our great community, I challenge each of you to be the living proof that even here, even now, a light still shines.

Through four years of darkness, we did more than survive.

We chose hope over fear. We chose courage over silence. We chose to believe again.

And together, we built something that will outlast all of us:

A shining city upon a hill.

EPILOGUE

A CHILD OF GOD

"Blessed are the peacemakers, for they shall be called the children of God."
—MATTHEW 5:9 (KJV)

"Adam, they're just shooting at us!"

The scream cut through the cab of my truck as gunfire cracked across the skies of North Okkalapa. We had no idea where the shots were coming from or who they were meant for, only the deafening confusion of a city breaking apart around us. A soldier had forced us back at gunpoint, spinning us into the unknown. The confusion thickened into a screen of smoke, my staff shouting in panic as I pressed the gas pedal hard, steering us through streets that once held daily life but now held only fear. In that instant, the peaceful protests of February 2021 were gone. The tide had turned, pulling us into something darker, and I was about to be cast adrift in a sea of blood.

This was the beginning, the first rupture, the day that made Yangon bleed.

What led to that moment had been building quietly for weeks. For a month after the coup of February 1, 2021, the pro-democracy protests carried a strange kind of order. Every morning, crowds poured into Yangon's streets, chanting that echoed for blocks, and every night, balconies erupted with the clatter of pots and pans, driving out the darkness. There was courage in that rhythm, but beneath it I felt the ground shifting. The military seemed willing, almost deliberately, to let the demonstrators have their days in the sun. Yet by late February, intimidation had hardened into preparation. A handful of killings had already surfaced, protesters beaten or shot in what could still be dismissed as isolated incidents of excessive force. On the surface, the protests looked almost festive, even joyous. That veneer didn't fool me. I knew tranquility in Myanmar never lasted long, and one of my clients, a hardened security manager, born and raised here, never trusted the military a day in his life. He reminded me of it daily.

"Adam, it's time we start moving women and children out of the country while we still have a window."

From that moment, we began preparing evacuations before anyone else would admit they were necessary. We helped our clients evacuate what the security world calls "non-essential personnel," in practical terms, mostly the families of foreign national workers. The airport was officially closed under the COVID-19 lockdown. There were no tickets to buy, no departures board to check. The only way out was through chartered aircraft or the occasional embassy relief flight, mostly organized by the United States, a few European governments, and regional players like Singapore or the Philippines. Those flights took time to arrange, and time was the one thing no one had.

When companies wanted their people out immediately, they had to charter an entire plane. Once families were counted, mostly women and children, it was rarely just a handful of passengers. Some clients had sprawling expatriate workforces, and a single request could mean evacuating 40 or 50 people at once.

That scale was compounded by years of neglect. Security had long been treated as a joke. Instead of housing their staff in secure neighborhoods or pre-designated serviced apartments, companies handed out large stipends and let them live wherever they pleased. Many expats, especially those with families and pets, chose villas with big yards and pools on the city's edge, townships far from the airport, far from the center, that were later placed under martial law.

Yangon city is officially divided into 34 townships, but they are not all the same. Only a handful at the center, Bahan, Kamaryut, Hlaing, Dagon, and Sanchaung, offered what expatriates needed: serviced apartments, reliable access to the airport, and some sense of security. A step beyond that core, the city sprawls into suburban, locally dense neighborhoods that feel a world apart. Mayangone Township, where the airport is located, is partly safe along the main road, but once you pass the airport itself you are already in suburban territory. Across the river it is another world. Places like Hlaing Tharyar township, with its golf course and country-club-style expatriate housing, are located in dense worker districts connected to the city only by bridges. Those bridges quickly turned into choke points once the protests began. For expatriates scattered across these outer townships, distance was not just measured in miles. It meant being far from safety, far from the airport, and often cut off completely when barricades went up or the security forces sealed the roads.

To compound these challenges, after the coup the military cut off the internet. For months, the only access was through fixed lines in hotels or commercial offices, connections most families in their outer township villas never had. Mobile data was blacked out entirely, leaving phones useless. Trapped in far-flung neighborhoods, many families couldn't even check a map to see what lay ahead. Without their drivers or Google Maps, they were blind to the city. That became one of our greatest challenges: driving into townships without knowing whether we would run headlong into barricades, protests, or troops.

The mission, however, remained the same, extract expatriate families from scattered homes and consolidate them into a secure hotel zone. Those late February days were a race against the clock. We moved families into safe hotels, arranged travel documents, secured landing permits from the Thai government, drove people to clinics for their COVID-19 tests, and finally escorted them to the airport once their aircraft was cleared to fly to Bangkok. Every step carried the knowledge that the airport could close completely, or the streets could erupt without warning.

Yet even then, part of me clung to the hope that all of it would prove unnecessary.

That hope was shattered on March 3, 2021, in North Okkalapa Township. Just a week earlier we had completed the precautionary evacuations of non-essential staff and families. With those departures behind us, I allowed myself the faint hope that perhaps the worst could still be avoided.

I was wrong.

North Okkalapa is one of those outer townships past the airport, suburban on the map but restless in reality. By mid-morning that day, thousands of protesters had gathered there, their chants rising through the streets in defiance of the warnings and the rumors of a looming crackdown.

I was in the office when three of my staff, one of them my Head of Finance, Zar, the same colleague who had helped shape so many of the speeches in this book, came to me visibly shaken. Their families were calling, urging them to come home before it was too late. They asked if I would drive them, stopping for groceries and supplies along the way. I agreed without hesitation. It sounded routine, food, a ride home, ordinary acts in a city about to break apart.

At the supermarket, my staff darted through the aisles, filling carts with rice, oil, and anything that might last. Next door, I ducked into a barbershop for a quick trim. It felt absurd, sitting under fluorescent light with a drape around my shoulders while soldiers massed only miles away.

By the time I loaded my staff and their groceries back into the truck, my phone rang. A client from overseas spoke in an urgent tone. He needed an evacuation from his local office in Yangon. "Nothing serious," he insisted, just a few employees too afraid to get home on their own. What I thought was a small favor became anything but.

The silence broke as soon as we reached North Okkalapa. Gunfire cracked in the distance, sharp and relentless. Tear gas drifted across the road. People were running. As we rounded a corner, the scene came into view: lines of security forces blocking the street, rifles leveled, opening fire into a crowd of unarmed protesters. Chaos consumed everything, shouts, screams, the staccato bursts of gunfire.

Then a soldier stepped out, rifle raised, aiming straight at my truck. For a split second I thought it was over, that the windshield would shatter and we would be left on the side of the road. His eyes locked with mine, and he seemed to register my face, foreign and out of place. At the last instant, he jabbed the barrel toward a side street and barked at us to get out.

I slammed the gear into reverse and tore away, my staff screaming as bullets cracked around us. The sounds of gunfire and the cries of bystanders chased us down the road as I floored the accelerator, desperate to escape the killing ground.

"Adam, they're just shooting at us!" Zar screamed. My hands clenched white on the steering wheel as I swerved around debris and makeshift roadblocks, heart pounding, fighting to put distance between us and the gunfire.

Minutes later, though it felt like an hour, we reached a quieter area. I turned toward a hotel by the lake near my home, a place that had become a kind of safe haven. It was an expatriate enclave, people lying low, close to the stillness of the water and far from the streets where the city was unraveling.

Walking into the lobby felt surreal. I sat my staff at a table near the bar and told them to order food. Then I stepped out onto the lakeside patio, where the general manager was drinking wine with a group of expatriates who were laughing, detached from the storm gathering around us. I didn't have time to explain. Yangon was under curfew, from eight o'clock in the evening until five in the morning, and it wasn't safe to keep crossing the city with soldiers on the streets. "If I'm not back by seven o'clock," I told him, "put them in a room, feed them whatever they want, and put it on my account." He nodded without hesitation and went back to his drinks.

I went back inside to my staff to say goodbye. Zar grabbed my arm and begged me not to go. The others looked at me with dread in their eyes.

"This is the job," I told them with a forced smile. "Now call your family. I'll be right back."

In truth, I had no idea if I would be back or what awaited me. I couldn't turn back now. I left them at the hotel, their faces a mix of relief and fear, and drove back into the city as dusk closed in. When I reached the client's address, I realized what he hadn't explained. His employees weren't simply afraid to go home.

They were trapped.

The street in front of their office had been sealed by barricades. Sandbags were stacked chest-high, bamboo poles lashed into crude spikes, wooden structures made from broken furniture overturned into the road. Tires burned in the middle of the street, black smoke curling upward, stinging the eyes and choking the lungs. Protesters crouched behind them in yellow construction helmets and masks, while clutching metal shields.

Everyone knew by then that the security forces were not holding back. Those barricades were the only thing slowing their advance. Crude as they were, they carried a weight far greater than their materials. They marked the point where peaceful protest was hardening into something else: the embryo of resistance in Myanmar, ordinary people realizing that ingenuity and courage were the only shields left between them and the bullets.

I pulled my truck up just short of the barricade and stepped out. Our team that day was two vehicles, my truck in front, and a second driven by one of my team members as a follow-on vehicle. If something happened to me, he would still be there to get people out.

I motioned for him to take the lead at the barricade. He spoke to one of the protesters in Burmese, explaining who we were and why we were there. I stood back and let him do the talking. A few nervous young men in construction helmets and flimsy goggles peeked over the debris, eyeing us warily. After a tense pause, a man who looked like their de facto leader motioned us closer. My teammate explained that we were only there to pick up office workers trapped in the building behind them. The leader studied us, then glanced at me, clearly foreign, not military. Finally, he gave a nod.

The protesters cleared a narrow gap, just wide enough for me and my teammate to walk through. I moved calmly past the line of crouching protesters, my colleague following close behind. The scene was unforgettable: young men and women in helmets, clutching bottles of water and balloons to douse tear gas, gripping makeshift shields cut from aluminum sheets and plywood. Their faces were drawn tight with fear but also with resolve. To remain there knowing what waited for them, rifles and machine guns against hard hats, safety goggles, and water balloons, took a courage I still struggle to describe.

As we entered the client's compound, I expected their staff to be waiting at the gate, ready to flee. The front of the gate and even the office building entrance were deserted. I ran inside, shouting up the stairwell, but nothing answered. The building loomed dark and silent. Room by room I kicked doors open until I found them in a back office:

two young men and a woman crouched under desks with the lights off. The woman trembled so violently she could barely stand.

"Let's go, now!"

I snapped, frustrated that they hadn't followed simple instructions to wait outside. She clutched her purse as if it were a life vest, frozen in place. I pulled her up by the arm and half-dragged her out of the building, the two men trailing close behind. When we reached the barricade again, the protesters were still holding their ground, eyes fixed down the street where the soldiers would soon come. The woman's hysteria grew as she realized what we were walking back into. I hauled her forward through the line of protesters, their faces twisting in astonishment at the sight of me dragging her toward my truck.

Once I finally secured her inside, I caught sight of the same leader who had granted us passage. I gave him a nod. He returned it without a word. In that silent exchange, everything was understood. He knew what was coming, that they would likely be beaten, maybe killed, but he still gave strangers safe passage. His eyes held no hesitation, only resolve. I mouthed "thank you" as sincerely as I've ever said anything, then climbed into my truck. We sped off, my teammate right behind me, just as security forces, military and police, moved in from around the corner to crush the barricade we had slipped through by what felt like divine grace.

By now evening was closing in, and the entire township felt like a war zone. We hit barricade after barricade, some thrown up by protesters, others by ordinary residents trying to slow the security forces' advance. I smashed through more than one obstacle too large to swerve around, the truck's bull-bar slamming into bamboo and debris with bone-jarring thuds. At one point we detoured down a side lane only to find it dug up and filled with bricks. Every route seemed cut off, forcing us to zigzag in confusion. Fires burned in the distance, and the acrid stench of rubber and tear gas hung low in the air. Inside my truck, the three evacuees were silent except for the woman's muffled sobs beside me, her face streaked with tears, her eyes blank with disbelief at what was happening.

At last, we reached her condominium. It wasn't far away, but to get there felt like escaping a labyrinth from hell. The tall building loomed above us, usually bustling with life, but tonight its windows were dark. With the daylight fading, the only safe entry was through the underground garage. I pulled in and stopped at the elevators. She was still shaking as she exited out of my truck. At the elevator doors she turned to me, her voice small and broken.

"You come take me tomorrow?"

It took me a second to understand. She was asking if I would pick her up for work in the morning, as if this had just been a bad detour and she might still return to her desk. Something inside me snapped.

"Fuck no!" I barked, maybe too harshly. "You don't go back, ever! If your boss tries to make you, call me first."

She nodded, fresh tears spilling, and finally seemed to understand. In that moment I realized how sudden and disorienting this nightmare was. Only hours earlier we all thought there might be a normal tomorrow. Now people had to be told that normal was over.

I would later learn why she and the two others had been in the office in the first place. Their boss had sent them on an errand tasked by the company CFO: to collect the company checkbooks.

Checkbooks.

She risked her life for some damn checkbooks. At that moment the banks were closed, and checks weren't even being accepted. Yet they were nearly killed chasing paperwork. This was the deeper failure of the business community. We were not ready for this, and it wasn't for lack of trying on my part.

In peacetime, money talks and security is the first thing discarded. Evacuation plans were nonexistent. Expatriates were scattered in unsafe housing. Most glaringly, in too many companies, crisis decisions were left to leaders with no experience in high-risk security environments.

The worst offender was always the CFO, the Chief Financial Officer, the guy who thinks you can budget-cut your way out of a massacre. In normal times, essential. In a crisis, useless, paralyzed by procedures when the only thing that matters is speed. Crisis doesn't give you time to get three suppliers. Crisis doesn't give you time to do a cost analysis.

Sending employees into a killing zone for checkbooks wasn't just poor judgment. It was madness. That woman didn't need the orders of a CFO. She needed someone who understood survival. That's why she listened to me, and why that company became one of my clients for years.

After dropping the other two men at their homes, curfew was closing in and I had to clear the streets. Still, I needed to check on my own staff at the hotel. They were safe, thank God, though frantic until I walked back through the lobby doors. By then we had worked out a plan. Two of them would spend the night with friends, safer than risking the roads. Zar's brother met us with a motorbike, taking her back into North Okkalapa through off-road routes. Every main road into the township was already sealed by the military. I left her in his care and told her to call me the moment she was home.

I then returned home and began calling clients. Almost immediately, my phone lit up with a call. It was Zar. She had made it home finally. Her voice shook as she described what she saw: blood pooling in the streets. Bodies lying there like broken dolls. Windows shattered by stray bullets.

"Adam," she whispered, "it was like zombies...like a horror movie. Blood was everywhere."

Her voice trailed off, and for once, I had no orders to give. I hung up, walked into my bathroom, and sat on the floor of the shower, letting the hot water run over me as I cried for what seemed like an hour. It may have been the last time I cried since this crisis began.

After that day, I didn't have any more tears to shed.

That was the beginning. The first day of the killings. We later learned that at least 22 people died in North Okkalapa township within just a few hours, though in the unknown of the midnight internet shutdown, we couldn't verify anything after eleven at night.

For my company's part, this was just one of many evacuation jobs. Some were locals desperate to escape hotspots; others were foreigners and their families wanting to leave the country. We evacuated over 100 foreign nationals that month, nearly all of them women and children. That number does not include the locals we pulled out of dangerous situations, like those trapped on March 3rd, or the many more we quietly advised on how to escape the country, including our dear friend Win Ko Ko Aung.

As the weeks went on, the violence spread beyond that fateful day. By month's end, hundreds more would be dead, primarily in Yangon but also in urban centers across the country. The names and places remain seared into memory: the bridge massacre in Hlaing Tharyar Township on March 14th, when an attempt to block security forces from sealing off the bridge into the city turned into a killing field, at least 33 were killed. Then came the countrywide slaughter on Armed Forces Day, March 27th, when security forces turned their guns on civilians in multiple cities across the country. Women. Children. No one was spared.

This was the hell of March 2021.

Yet, for us, it began on that day. The day normal life ended, and survival became the only language left.

I write these words not to glorify my own survival, nor to dress my leadership into some packaged tale of heroism. I write them because I know what it is to hate, to feel the pull of revenge, to want the world to burn. I write them because I know there are critics, both among those who will read these pages and those who have followed me for years, who will accuse me of sympathizing with the Tatmadaw. Of not condemning them enough in this book. Of daring to call for national reconciliation with the very institution that brought this country to its knees. To them, I say this:

You weren't there on March 3, 2021. I was.

I watched soldiers fire on unarmed crowds. I saw blood on the streets where students and workers had stood minutes before. I tasted the acrid mix of burning rubber and fear. I watched smoke and tear gas climb over the same neighborhood I called my home. After that day, hatred boiled in my veins; there were nights when revenge was the only dream I knew. Yet I have seen, firsthand, where that road ends.

By the time I write this epilogue, this civil war has been burning for almost 80 years.

Myanmar is defined by its endless civil war. A war perpetuated by those who need to seek revenge. This has only led to more blood, a bloody loop that devours the guilty and the innocent alike. An endless loop that has never produced peace. Is the Tatmadaw a great evil in this country? Yes, undeniably yes. Yet they are a product of the one true evil, with them being just one of the many players who feed its fire.

War.

War is a hydra: Cut off one head and two more grow in its place. That is Myanmar, a war of endless complexities, where every attempt to destroy one enemy spawns new grievances, new complexities, new wounds. It will not vanish simply because we hate it passionately enough. Peace will never come from pretending otherwise.

I chose a different path. Not from weakness or naïveté, but from faith, in God, and in Christ's teaching that hatred only begets hatred.

"Blessed are the peacemakers, for they shall be called the children of God."
—MATTHEW 5:9 (KJV)

I choose love now and forever, to "love thy enemy," to carry the willingness to forgive, to break this cycle before it destroys Myanmar, and before it destroys the world. If we continue to feed our own personal need for revenge, we will lose ourselves to our own fury. That is why I choose peace, even with those who have wronged me, even with those that have been condemned as evil.

Blessed are the peacemakers.

As I look beyond Myanmar's borders, across the ocean to my own homeland, I cannot help but see the same lessons reflected. The futility of revenge and the hope of forgiveness that I learned in Myanmar are lessons the United States itself desperately needs. For just as Myanmar has been trapped in an endless war, America has too often been defined by endless wars of choice abroad.

We emerged from the Cold War as the world's sole superpower. Yet instead of embracing peace, we went searching for new enemies, new battles to wage, and new interventions to justify. By the early 1990s, America stood at a crossroads. Pride and fear, however, pushed us down the well-worn path of conflict. And one must ask: Did these wars, all this interventionism, truly make America, or the world, any safer?

After the Cold War, America fell under the influence of two competing doctrines that promised dominance but delivered decay. Neoconservatives believed military force could remake the world, dragging the nation into endless wars with no clear end and devastating human cost. Neoliberals pursued the same ambition through economics instead of arms, hollowing out American industry, outsourcing jobs, and enforcing compliance abroad through trade leverage, sanctions, and financial pressure. One ruled through bombs, the other through balance sheets, but both were driven by the same hubris: the belief that American power could impose order on the world without consequence.

Both were proven disastrously wrong.

The neoconservative project reached its peak under the Bush family and Dick Cheney, who turned post–Cold War triumphalism, and later the grief of September 11, into a doctrine of perpetual war. The invasion of Iraq in 2003, launched on false claims of weapons of mass destruction, shattered the region, empowered extremist groups, and locked the United States into an open-ended occupation disguised as nation building. The cost was staggering: thousands of young Americans killed or permanently scarred, trillions of dollars wasted, civil liberties eroded at home, and a democracy weakened by fear. Decades later, the consequences of that choice still define America's foreign policy failures, and the generational toll they imposed.

That turning point drew me into political debate in college. My entry into this world was never about titles or career ladders. It was about taking on the neocons and their endless wars. I saw the cost of their arrogance with my own eyes, friends sent to fight wars that could not be won, lives shattered, families broken, trillions of dollars wasted. I went myself to Afghanistan, a fight I never truly believed in. If politics meant anything, it had to mean breaking this cycle of deception and destruction. My fight began there, with a rejection of the neoconservative lie that America's greatness rests on perpetual war.

The Republican Party I grew up around was never one I wanted to join. For years, I believed that as a Mexican-American I would never be truly accepted in the GOP. I was wrong about the prejudice being racial, yet not wrong about the prejudice itself. The old Republican Party was less about race than it was about class. It was run by financial and political elites who had no place for people like me. If you weren't one of them, you were expendable, voters included.

The year 2016 changed everything.

President Trump turned the Republican Party upside down and drove the elites out. This was the same globalist class that had cheered outsourcing of American jobs, applauded forever wars in Iraq and Afghanistan, and rewarded Wall Street bailouts while millions of Americans lost their homes and would never own one again. They had never stood with the American working class.

When Trump disrupted their comfortable arrangement, they fled, many, like the Cheneys, straight into the arms of the Democratic Party, the last bastion of establishment elites, both neoconservative and neoliberal alike. The roles were familiar. Neoconservatives bled America through endless wars abroad, while neoliberals hollowed her out at home through economic policy.

That's what still infuriates me when I think about working-class liberals back at home in California. By 2016, the country knew it was on the wrong track. People admired President Obama; they loved him and his wife as personalities, as role models. Yet deep down, they knew he hadn't delivered the change he promised. For the first time in generations, Americans believed the future would be worse for their children, and the neoliberal elites were comfortable with it.

When America's factories closed, it wasn't just jobs that vanished. It was dignity, stability, and entire ways of life. Communities built on skilled manufacturing hollowed out, families fractured, and despair took root through addiction and hopelessness, even as elites called it "progress" and insisted globalization was inevitable. Neoliberalism outsourced American strength while enriching financial elites, then finished the job with a financial collapse that erased ordinary savings without holding a single senior banker accountable. What followed was an economy rebuilt for asset holders, not workers, where speculation replaced production, ownership slipped out of reach, and entire generations, better educated than ever, were left without a real stake in the future.

Americans believed the country was on the wrong track, the American Dream slipping further away with each generation. Among the working class especially, hope gave way to anxiety about jobs, housing, and whether their children would ever live better than they had. Out of that despair rose a demand for sovereignty, dignity, and a government that put its own citizens first. That was the spark that lit the fire of the America First movement.

America First was never about race, religion, or gender. Economic nationalism doesn't care who you are; it cares that you are a citizen who deserves a better deal. It rests on three promises: stop mass illegal immigration, put America's interests first abroad, and restore economic sovereignty. Contrast that with the neoliberal mantra of maximizing shareholder value, a creed that trained elites to treat patriotism as a liability and the American worker as expendable. That mindset produced corporations led by executives with no allegiance to this country, boards stacked with non-Americans, and policymakers who sneer at the very people they are meant to serve.

That is why people turned to America First, a populist movement whose central mission is to dismantle the administrative state long dominated by neoconservatives and neoliberals, what we now call "the Deep State." A system where unelected bureaucrats slow-walk laws, twist executive orders, and subvert the policies chosen by the American people. An unchecked bureaucracy run by elites who believe they know better than the voters themselves.

America First is not just vital for America, but for the world. Critics call it extreme, but the truth is simpler. Economic nationalism declares that the purpose of government is not to maximize stock portfolios, but to restore the value of citizenship. That is why President Trump renegotiated NAFTA during his first term, the cornerstone of America's deindustrialization and China's rise. It is also why tariffs became the central tool for reclaiming economic sovereignty in his second term. The message landed. Country after country lined up for deals, from Korea to Japan to even China, because whatever the tariffs, they know access to the American consumer remains the most powerful economic growth engine on earth.

This was one of the reasons the American people chose a different path in the November 2024 elections. They elected a president who vowed to end the era of predatory trade deals, endless wars, and broken promises. In doing so, voters said enough. America chose to give peace a chance. It was no accident that the 47th president ran as an anti-war candidate, a clear break from the interventionist consensus of the past. The result marked a populist rejection of the old order, a repudiation of elites and professional warmongers who had delivered failure abroad and decline at home. At long last, Americans across the political spectrum awakened to the same conclusion I had long held: the party of war had to become the party of peace.

That awakening did not come from theory or slogans. It came from cost. It came from the working class whose children were sent to Afghanistan and Iraq, whose sons and daughters returned wounded, broken, or did not return at all. Their families paid the price for wars they never asked for and never benefited from. While elites moved on to the next conflict, their voices were ignored, wages stagnated, debts rose, and stability slipped further out of reach. What Americans rejected in 2024 was not only war, but a system that demanded endless sacrifice from the same people while offering nothing in return.

America First is not isolationism. It is realism. We cannot impose our culture or our democracy on others. Our military should be feared by our enemies, but it should not be stretched thin occupying foreign countries; nor used to solve the world's problems on the backs of our sons and daughters. America is not an idea. It is a country with borders, citizens, and a history that cannot be exported. America First believes in peace through strength. A strength that protects our people and our interests yet demands sacrifice from those who serve. That strength must also be guided by leaders with the judgment to act decisively and the wisdom to avoid unnecessary war.

American strength should not be measured by how many wars we can fight, but by how many futures we can save. Not a Pax Americana enforced by policies of war, but a new generation of American peacemakers. A generation committed to solving problems through engagement, not intervention. Through fair trade, not exploitation. Through peace, not war.

Blessed are the peacemakers.

THE PRICE OF LEADERSHIP

Living through war, first as a Marine in Afghanistan and later as a witness to Myanmar's civil war, opened my eyes to a deeper truth: Hatred only breeds more hatred, and violence only breeds more violence. If I, having fought in one war and seen another tear through my adopted home, could let go of hatred and choose peace, then I believe America can choose a different path as well. From my own life, I have learned that it takes more courage to fight for peace than to fight a war.

I found myself once again in Washington, this time carrying a peacemaker's philosophy into the corridors of power. On a hot, humid afternoon in mid-July 2025, I walked into the White House for a meeting on Myanmar. I was not carrying secret deals or lobbying for an armed group. I was not angling for a job or seeking personal gain. I came with one purpose: to present new ideas.

The new Trump administration had set out a clear foreign policy of non-intervention. America would not plunge into another endless war or pour trillions into foreign "nation-building." No more sanctions as punishment, no more picking favorites. My main goal was to present the administration with an opportunity to help bring peace to a country ravaged by civil war, to encourage engagement with all armed actors in the conflict toward compromise and, ultimately, a peace deal.

One idea I raised to that end, involved Myanmar's heavy rare earths. Not as a master plan or silver bullet, but as one angle worth considering. Rare earths may sound exotic, yet they are simply 17 metals pulled from the ground that make the modern world work. Without them, there are no smartphones, no electric cars, no fighter jets, and no nuclear power. The "heavy" rare earths are the rarest and most valuable, the metals that power advanced technology and weapons systems.

China controls nearly all global supply, while America produces almost none. Myanmar, for all its turmoil, happens to hold significant deposits. If America continues buying these materials from China, it remains vulnerable. If it looks for ways to diversify, even in places like Myanmar, it begins to protect itself. It was not a grand solution. It was one idea among many, offered in the spirit of exploration, nothing more.

The meeting itself was straightforward, an hour of serious conversation with people who carried the weight of America First on their shoulders. They were gracious, attentive, and willing to listen to new ideas. When it ended, we exchanged warm handshakes, and I stepped out of the White House with a sense of peace. For me, it wasn't about secret deals or career ambitions; it was about keeping a promise. I had told my community in Myanmar that their struggles, their businesses smothered by regulation, their voices drowned out in crisis, would one day be heard at the highest level.

And on that day, that promise was fulfilled.

A week later, that peace was broken. I was in California visiting family when a Reuters reporter called. He knew the date and time of my White House meeting, who was in the room, even a rumor that I was a frontrunner to be named US Special Envoy to Myanmar, details that could only have come from a leak inside the administration.

I was stunned.

No such offer had ever been made. I was not seeking one either. Rather than getting defensive, I took a breath and gave him my time. For more than an hour, I walked him through the conflict, explained the reality of rare earth mining in Myanmar, described China's leverage over armed actors, and laid out the plight of a country trapped in turmoil. When the article appeared later that week, it told the truth: ideas were discussed, rare earths were mentioned, nothing was decided. Even so, that simple, accurate report became a fire storm I never saw coming.

Within hours, Washington's activist-policy machine roared to life. Think tanks that normally took six months to cobble together a report were suddenly spitting out "instant analysis" at machine-gun speed. I had never seen the US–Burma policy world move so quickly or predictably. The verdict was unanimous: outrage. Simply mentioning Myanmar's rare earths was branded "impossible," "dangerous," even "immoral." One think tank rushed out a piece titled, with no subtlety at all, "The Dangerous Allure of Myanmar's Rare Earths." Overnight, the simple act of putting a new idea on the table was treated not as policy debate, but as heresy.

That frenzy had little to do with minerals and everything to do with enforcing orthodoxy. The activists and policy hands attacking me were products of that world, trained to guard its boundaries and punish dissent. The Washington I walked into that July afternoon under President Trump was different. It was a new day, shaped by America First, where the door had cracked open for voices outside the orthodoxy.

When I argued that Myanmar mattered to America not only as a morality play but as a strategic interest, I broke that orthodoxy, and the machine snapped to attention. My so-called "radical" proposals were, in fact, practical ones, asking how the United States could engage Myanmar without war or isolation, loosen China's grip on critical minerals, and align peace with American interests.

To the activist-policy machine, new ideas themselves were the enemy. For decades their answer to Myanmar never changed: sanctions, isolation, then more of both. The result was predictable. Myanmar slid deeper into China's orbit, poorer, weaker, and more fragmented. By any honest measure, the policy failed. Failure should have invited humility and rethinking. Instead, it made the establishment defensive. Too many careers, reputations, and funding channels depended on the claim that there was only one "acceptable" approach. Challenge that premise, and they would not debate. They would attack.

The attacks began as whispers in Washington's echo chambers. "He's angling for a Special Envoy job." "He's cutting backroom deals." None of it was true. Soon the whispers hardened into slander. I was suddenly branded a lobbyist for the Tatmadaw.

It was the night of August 23, 2025. BBC News Burmese presented translated comments made by an associate professor at an otherwise obscure university in the United Kingdom. He dismissed my July meeting at the White House and discussions around "rare earth minerals in northern Myanmar" as "meaningless" proposals. The Burmese narration then escalated the allegation, reframing the meeting as an attempt to pressure the US government to lift sanctions on individuals and companies tied to the Tatmadaw. The Myanmar journalist then posed a question in Burmese:

"So, do we know exactly who those business intermediary lobbyists are, and who they are working for?"

The answer followed immediately in English.

"An American citizen named Adam Castillo."

That was it. No documents. No evidence. No explanation of how I was supposedly hired by the Tatmadaw to lobby for sanctions relief, an act that would not only be illegal but would also require registration as a lobbyist, which I am not. The allegations were as false as they were defamatory. Yet that did not stop the BBC from uploading the video to its social media channels and pushing it across Facebook in Myanmar, which for all practical purposes is the internet and the primary source of news in the country.

And just like that, I was branded as a lobbyist for the Tatmadaw.

I found out the way bad news usually arrives in Myanmar, late on a Friday night after work, via a message from my head analyst in Yangon. "There's an interview online," he said. Watching it, I felt more confused than angry. An English academic I had never met was introduced with all the confidence of authority, carefully delivering my name in a posh, almost colonial-era accent. To my eye, he looked like a weasel and spoke like a goose.

By Monday morning, I pushed back. I hand-delivered a cease-and-desist letter to the BBC's Yangon office. Within a week, they admitted to me that "the original version fell short of our editorial standards." Of course it did. It was amateur hour at the BBC. They uploaded a pre-recorded, edited video containing false allegations with my photographs without ever reaching out to me for comment. That is journalism 101.

To their credit, the BBC took the video down, re-edited it, and re-uploaded it, this time removing my name and image entirely. What they did not do was issue a public retraction or apology to the audience they had misled. Instead, they attempted to quietly erase the error, as if it had never happened.

That was when I lawyered up. Of course, the BBC did everything it could to sandbag the legal process, delaying the handover of the official broadcast video for months. The intent was obvious: drag it out, drive up my legal costs, and hope I would walk away because it was no longer worth the expense. I didn't. I was not even asking for money. All I wanted was a genuine public apology acknowledging that their broadcast defamed my reputation in Myanmar, which it did. Yet that, apparently, was too much to ask of the BBC, given their fondness for themselves.

So, if the BBC wanted to continue standing by its editorial judgment and its refusal to publicly admit error, then I was adamant they should explain it to a judge.

Ironically, the BBC World Service, including its Myanmar operation, was deeply entangled with activist reporters drawn from the same academic and advocacy networks, many operating within overlapping Washington group chats that collapse journalism, activism, and policy advocacy into a single loop.

In time, it became clear that the backlash against me was not accidental. It was coordinated. Activist groups in Washington moved quickly to shut down what they saw as a threat: my access, my ideas, and the possibility that a different approach to Myanmar might reach the highest levels of government. Rather than confront the failure of decades of entrenched policy, they chose a familiar tactic: manufacture a villain. They made me the villain, because making me the issue was easier than answering the harder question:

Why has your way failed for so long?

That reflex, the instinct to shut down every new idea, was never limited to Myanmar policy. It was woven into the culture of Washington itself. Neoconservatives rejected non-intervention and dragged America into wars that could not be won. Neoliberals dismissed economic nationalism and hollowed out the industrial base. And on Myanmar, both left and right spent a generation saying the same thing:

"No. You cannot think differently."

The result was a policy vacuum. A country left to decay, its past, present, and future quietly handed to China. That was the world before me in 2023, when I made the decision to carry my community's voice to Washington. I had one mission as their leader: to give a voice to the voiceless and carry that voice to the highest threshold of power.

By July 2025, that mission was fulfilled. I brought my people's voice to the White House, farther than it had ever traveled and farther than anyone believed possible. For a moment, the door opened. New ideas, our ideas, entered the room. A voice long dismissed finally broke through the orthodoxy.

My journey through Washington was never about securing political appointments or reshaping American foreign policy. It was about setting an example for my community, showing my people that leadership requires absorbing controversy, attacks, and manufactured outrage in order to carry an entire people forward.

Did I become the US Special Envoy to Myanmar? No.

Not because I was not "MAGA enough," and not because activist attacks succeeded, but because Myanmar never had its day in court in the Oval Office. The issue never reached the room where real decisions are made, let alone the President's desk. New wars took priority. Trade negotiations demanded attention. The longest government shutdown in American history swallowed the news cycle and paralyzed the capital. The bandwidth disappeared, and with it, Myanmar's moment, but that's Washington. And so, Myanmar returned to the place it has occupied for decades:

Important enough to moralize about, never important enough to prioritize.

Unless you arrive in Washington with vast sums of money, a long-term lobbying operation, or a crisis that directly threatens America's national security or economic stability, advocacy takes on a very different meaning. If these years taught me anything, it is that real advocacy is about offering policymakers one more idea to consider, one more perspective to weigh, one more voice they can no longer ignore. For anyone hoping to launch their own advocacy campaign, let that be the aim. Move the needle or hold the line. That alone is victory.

And yet, the merits of my efforts in Washington were never the point of this leadership story. The point was to prove that leadership begins with a single act of belief, that your people's voice can rise farther than you ever imagined.

And that is where my Washington story ends. At least for now.

MY OWN RIPPLE OF HOPE

In a strange way, the end of my Washington story created its own *ripple of hope* in my life. It raised my profile back home far more than I ever expected. As the dust settled, one question kept following me: "Will you run for office?" Friends, colleagues, even strangers urged me to consider it. "We need leaders like you in Washington," they said. I was flattered.

Like leadership, I have always thought of a life as a play told in acts, distinct stages where one may get one, two, or, if fortunate, three chances to redefine themselves and their story. Act One was my youth and early adulthood: a Mexican-American kid from California who joined the Marine Corps, went to war, and learned the cost of leadership the hard way. Act Two was my journey to Myanmar, where I spent over a decade building a business and a community, enduring another war, multiple natural disasters, and leading others through crisis. Now I stand at the edge of a possible Act Three:

A life of American public service.

Public office had always been a quiet dream tucked in the back of my mind, and if Act Three ever comes, I know what it must mean. Public service cannot be about titles or prestige. It must be about answering a calling to confront the hard truths this country has avoided for too long.

My generation stands able to answer that call, forged in trial and raised in the shadow of consequence. We came of age in the wreckage of the dot-com crash. We carried rifles and buried friends after 9/11. We entered the workforce only to be hit by the Great Recession. In the prime of our working lives, we endured a global pandemic that shuttered economies, destroyed livelihoods, and tore families apart. Each time, we endured. Each time, we rose again.

Now greater challenges confront us, and they demand the same resolve. We are called to summon the courage to solve problems we did not create, so our children, and their children, are not condemned to inherit a broken nation.

Perhaps that is why I feel called toward an Act Three of American leadership. At its core, that leadership must protect the promise of America, a promise never rooted in marble halls or monuments of stone, but in the sacrifices of ordinary people. That is America at her best. Not an empire built on power, but a community bound by peace and courage.

If we have the will to sacrifice, and to lead, we can still be that shining city on a hill, a beacon not of dominance or wealth, but of freedom, faith, and possibility. That is the America I believe in. That is the America I will fight for.

That is the city we can still become.

I no longer lead a community in Myanmar, but the story of who I am, and who I must become, carries on. How I lead in the future, whether in American public service or in any other arena, was forged and proven in the fires of Myanmar. One truth I know about my future is this: I will continue to lead, true to the principles that have guided me thus far.

Others may tell their own version of my story, good or bad. That is irrelevant. My fight for my community was never about being loved or being popular. I had a plan, a vision, and expectations, not only of myself, but of everyone I was leading. My mission was simple: save my people and give them an example that could outlast me. To accomplish that, my priority could never be the individual. It had to be the survival of the community.

That is why I demanded sacrifice from my fellow leaders, and I demanded it without apology. If you were not willing to give yourself fully to this community and to the future of our people, then you had no business serving on the Board of the American Chamber of Commerce in Myanmar while I was leading it.

I spent weeks in Washington, DC, fighting for our voice to be heard; trips I funded out of my own pocket. When I was in the United States, I should have been spending every possible moment with my family in California. Instead, I sacrificed that time to fight for my community. That was the price.

If I could give that much, then I expected others to give as well.

They had to feel the weight of sacrifice. They had to feel they had earned the success we achieved together.

I spoke when others stayed silent. I pulled people forward when they resisted. I challenged them when they did not want to be challenged. I put us under spotlights others feared to face. I did all of it relentlessly, some would say ruthlessly, because I knew that one day my Board, my staff, and my members would have to lead without me.

Leadership has a price, and survival has a price.

I arrived in Myanmar with nothing more than conviction and debt. I stayed long enough to watch the country burn, bleed, and fracture around me. I stood on the streets of Yangon in March 2021, knee-deep in a sea of blood.

This was the path God had placed me on. Whatever He asked of me, whatever it demanded, I carried it forward willingly.

And yet, somewhere along the way, I learned to accept that leadership does not come with universal understanding, popularity, or forgiveness. Some decisions will divide people. Others will disappoint them. A few will fracture friendships. That, too, was part of my own personal cost. Yet, that was the price of leadership I was willing to pay, and in Myanmar, it was also the price of survival.

Leadership is service, you serve a mission greater than yourself, and you serve the people who believe in that mission.

Leadership is sacrifice, you give until it hurts, and then you give a little more.

Leadership is moral clarity, you keep your eyes on what's right and refuse to waver, even when it is hard or unpopular.

As I write these final lines, I do so with the weight of my journey behind me and the uncertainty of whether an Act Three lies ahead. I don't know if my future will involve public office. That decision is not mine alone; it belongs to my family, to the times we live in, and ultimately to God. Whatever path I take, I will hold fast to the creed that has carried me this far. I will strive to be a peacemaker when it is easier to wage war. I will lead by serving, not by chasing titles. I will take up the shield of faith when the arrows fly and wield the truth

God has given me, not for myself, but for the country I love and the cause of peace.

If there is one final lesson I have learned in my nearly 40 years on this earth, it is that life tests you in ways you never imagined, and those trials reveal why you are here. My story began as the son of the working class, a kid from California who was not expected to rise very high. I became a Marine and went off to war. I built a business in a foreign land. I led a community through crisis. I have seen innocents die and the guilty prosper, yet I have seen greatness rise from ordinary people. I fought for the voiceless and shouted truth into the deaf ears of power.

Suffering may mark us, but sacrifice defines us. What endures is not a legacy of power or wealth, but the testimony of a life lived with faith and purpose. In my final moments in this world, I hope I will be welcomed at the gates of heaven not for what I built on earth, but for who I became.

A child of God.

ACKNOWLEDGEMENTS

I am deeply grateful to my family, whose patience, sacrifice, and unwavering support made this work possible. You carried far more of the weight than you should have had to, and I never lost sight of that.

My thanks to my legal counsel, Eric Rayman and Miller Korzenik Rayman LLP, for their careful review of this manuscript and for helping ensure that it was written clearly, honestly, and responsibly. Your rigor and judgment mattered.

I thank Carlin Stiehl for the author photograph, and for capturing the perfect photo of both my personality, charm, and even arrogance.

My thanks to Lisa Caskey, my editor, for her careful attention, judgment, and steadiness throughout this process.

To Kristiana Kuqi, thank you for your continued belief in my mission and in the work we set out to accomplish together, especially in moments when belief mattered most.

I honor the memory of the late, great Gwen Robinson. Her imprint on my thinking, writing, and analysis is permanent, and I carry her influence with me on every page.

And finally, for Zar, my best friend, confidant, and right hand. None of these speeches, and none of this journey, would have been possible without you.

ABOUT THE AUTHOR

ADAM CASTILLO is the Founder and Owner of AGS Myanmar, the country's premier security risk management firm. He is an expert in leadership in crisis, security, and conflict, with more than 12 years of on-the-ground experience in Myanmar spanning civil war, sanctions, and humanitarian crises. Since March 2021, he has personally authored or edited more than 1,760 AGS Myanmar analytical reports, including five 100+-page year-end assessments, totaling roughly 8,300 pages and nearly three million words of original conflict and business analysis on Myanmar.

A former United States Marine Corps (USMC) commissioned officer and veteran of Operation Enduring Freedom (Afghanistan), Adam is also the founder and current chair of Republican Overseas Myanmar, an organization established in 2024 to promote America First policies in Myanmar and across the region. Since 2018, he has served on the Overseas Security Advisory Council (OSAC) Steering Committee for the US Embassy in Rangoon.

From 2020 to 2025, Adam served on the Board of Governors of the American Chamber of Commerce in Myanmar (AMCHAM), including as Vice President (2021–2023) and President (2023–2025), guiding the organization through a pandemic, coup, civil war, natural disasters, and international isolation.

Adam received the Rising Star of the Year Award at the *2020 APAC Chamber of Commerce Awards* (presented in 2021), was named one of *White Page International's 100 Inspirational Leaders of Asia in 2022,* and was included in *Asia One Media's Top 40 Most Influential Young Leaders in Asia in 2023.*

He earned his undergraduate degree from the University of California, Riverside, and holds two graduate degrees from Norwich University: a master of arts in International Relations (Terrorism & Conflict) and a master of business administration (2016).

He has five cats, one being his lovely soulmate Simba, otherwise known as the queen of AGS Myanmar. Born in California, USA, he is currently based in Yangon, Myanmar.